A LETTER TO MY WIFE

A LETTER
TO MY WIFE

John B. Koffend

Saturday Review Press · New York

Published simultaneously in Canada by
Doubleday Canada Ltd., Toronto.

Library of Congress Catalog Card Number: 74–154273

ISBN 0–8415–0127–0

Saturday Review Press
230 Park Avenue
New York, New York 10017

PRINTED IN THE UNITED STATES OF AMERICA

Design by Tere LoPrete

AGREEMENT made this 1st day of November, 1969 between ANN KOFFEND, residing in Westchester County, New York, hereinafter referred to as "Wife" and JOHN B. KOFFEND, residing at Wedgewood Apartment, White Plains, N.Y. hereinafter referred to as "Husband."

WITNESSETH:

WHEREAS, the parties were married at Sun Valley, Idaho, on March 6, 1950 and there are three children who are the issue of said marriage,

WHEREAS, irreconcilable differences have arisen between the parties, as a result of which they are now living separate and apart, and the parties intend to live separate and apart; and

WHEREAS, the parties desire to enter into an agreement under which they may continue to live separate and apart, and to avoid litigation respecting provisions to be made for the support and maintenance of the Wife and said infant children, and for the custody of said children,

NOW, THEREFORE, in consideration of the

) v (

mutual covenants herein contained, the parties agree as follows:

1. That from and after the date hereof, the Husband and Wife shall continue to live separate and apart from each other at any place they may respectively choose, and neither party shall at any time sue or suffer the other to be sued in any action for separation for so living separate and apart, nor shall either party compel the other to live with him or her, nor shall either party molest or trouble the other.

2. (A) The Husband shall pay to the Wife for the support and maintenance of each of the children the sum of $2,000 per year until each such child shall attain the age of 21 years or finishes college, whichever is later.

(B) The Husband shall pay to the Wife annually for the support and maintenance of the Wife in monthly instalments a sum equal to the difference between the total amount of said support and maintenance payable for all of the children in such calendar year and a sum equal to 50% of the gross taxable income of the Husband for such calendar year.

Said monthly amount shall be computed on the basis of the salary rate of the Husband on the first day of the calendar year plus the annual amount of estimated additional income, excluding capital gains and losses, reportable by the Husband for Federal income tax purposes for such calendar year. Adjustments for the total annual payment determined to be due the Wife pursuant to the Husband's Federal income tax return for such calendar year shall be made by the Husband or the Wife within 30 days of the filing date of such return of the Husband.

(C) The amount of support and maintenance payable to the Wife as aforesaid shall not be less in any calendar year than the difference between the amount of support and maintenance payable for all of the children in such calendar year and the sum of $12,000.

(D) In addition to the foregoing the Husband shall be responsible for the payment of 50% of the room, board, education and incidental college expenses, including transportation, in connection with any college education of the children and the Wife shall be responsible for the remaining 50%.

(E) The Husband shall provide hospitalization and major medical payments insurance coverage for the Wife during her life and the premiums therefor shall be paid to the Wife as additional alimony on or before the premiums are due.

(F) In addition to the foregoing the Husband shall provide hospitalization and major medical insurance coverage for the three children of the parties during their respective minorities in the event the Husband terminates his present employment, and the Husband shall pay the premiums therefor as a part of their support and maintenance.

(G) The Husband shall assign the ownership of life insurance policies listed on Schedule A attached hereto in favor of the Wife and the cost of the premiums shall be paid to the Wife as additional alimony on or before the premiums are due.

(H) The obligation of the Husband to pay support and maintenance of the Wife and additional alimony to the Wife shall cease in the event the parties are divorced and the Wife remarries, but the Husband shall remain liable to the Wife for arrears of payments.

(I) All payments under paragraph (A) shall be made in equal monthly sums of $166.66 on the first day of each month for each child, and all estimated monthly payments under paragraph (B) shall be made on the first day of each month.

3. In addition to the foregoing amounts, the Husband agrees to pay to the Wife the following lump sum amounts:

(A) In the event the Husband terminates his present employment or for any other reason becomes entitled to withdraw any profit sharing, pension or retirement benefit, the Wife shall receive 50% of the total benefit to the credit of the Husband, or such lesser amount as may be then available to the Husband, and the balance of said profit sharing, pension or retirement benefit shall be bequeathed by the Husband to the children of the parties hereto by his Last Will and Testament.

(B) The Husband will assign the automobile presently registered in his name to the Wife; and the Volkswagen shall be the property of the Husband who shall be solely responsible for the instalment obligations in connection with the purchase thereof.

4. The Wife shall have the sole and exclusive care, custody and control of the children except that the Husband shall have unlimited visiting rights on reasonable notice to the Wife.

5. The parties hereto are now the owners of a residence in Westchester County, New York, as tenants by the entirety. The Husband will join in the execution of a Bargain and Sale Deed in order to convey such property to the Wife simultaneously with the execution of this agreement, and hereby releases any claim or interest which the Husband may have in any furniture, furnishings and other tangible personal property on the premises.

6. The Husband agrees to name the children of

the parties as the beneficiaries of one-half of the proceeds of any life insurance policies listed on Schedule B attached hereto. The Husband agrees to pay all premiums on said policies as they fall due and to maintain the policies in full force and effect.

7. As security for the payments to be made by the Husband to the Wife under Articles 2 and 3 the Husband will, on the Wife's request, execute, acknowledge and deliver to the Wife an unconditional assignment in form for recording and acceptable to the Wife wherein the Husband sells, assigns and transfers to the Wife a 50% portion of all his right, title and interest in and to any property to which the Husband is entitled or may be hereafter entitled by way of inheritance.

8. Both parties warrant and represent that neither has made or will make any purchase or contract, or enter into any other transaction in the name or on the credit of the other, and they agree to indemnify and hold each other harmless from any and all liability, cause, obligation, or expense involved in or in connection with any purchase or contract of sale or any services of whatsoever nature or description entered into by him or her respectively.

9. The Wife and Husband hereby release, relinquish, and discharge each other, and his or her heirs, representatives, and assigns, from all manner of actions, causes of action, suits, debts, controversies, claims and demands whatsoever in law or in equity, which he or she has or may hereafter have against the other, for or on account of any matter or thing to the date hereof, excluding from the operation of this release, however, any claim of any kind, nature or description which may arise under or pursuant to this agreement, or any claim for final judgment or decree of absolute

divorce and/or separation in his or her favor, if any such final judgment or decree be obtained by him or her, provided that such final judgment or decree shall not contain any provision in conflict with this agreement.

10. Each party hereby waives any rights in the estate of the other including, without limitation, those rights which he or she may now or hereafter have, to elect to take against the Last Will and Testament of the other, pursuant to Section 5-1.1 of the Estates, Powers and Trusts Law of the State of New York, or any law amendatory thereof or supplementary thereto, or any other similar law of another jurisdiction wherein the decedent shall have died a resident. The consideration for each party's waiver and release is the other party's reciprocal waiver and release.

11. Each party shall be free at any time hereafter to institute suit for absolute divorce against the other. The execution of this agreement shall not be deemed a waiver or forgiveness of any conduct on either party's part constituting grounds for divorce. However, the Wife shall not in any such divorce suit, or in any action for separation, seek or accept any order, judgment, or decree providing for alimony, counsel fees, or other provisions for her benefit, other than as provided herein.

12. If, at any time hereafter, either party becomes a resident of any state or country other than New York and commences an action for an absolute divorce against the other party for just and legal grounds recognized in such state or country, and shall effect service of process in such action upon the other party in accordance with the legal requirements of the jurisdiction in which such action may be commenced, the other party undertakes to interpose a general appearance by an attorney duly authorized to practice in

such state or country. However, the party so appearing shall be wholly free to contest and defend such action on any ground or grounds he or she may be advised.

13. It is agreed by and between the parties hereto in the event that any controversy arises between the parties with respect to the terms or conditions of the agreement or with respect to the duties or obligations of any of the parties thereto, said controversy shall be submitted to the Supreme Court of the State of New York, County of Westchester, for determination pursuant to the New York Simplified Procedure for Court Determination of Disputes as provided for by CPLR 3031, et seq.

14. The parties hereto declare that each has had independent legal advice by counsel of his or her own selection; that the Wife admits that she has had adequate opportunity to, and has satisfied herself as to the financial and other resources of the Husband; that each fully understands the facts and has been fully informed of all legal rights and liabilities; that after such advice and knowledge, each believes the agreement to be fair, just and reasonable; and that each signs the agreement freely and voluntarily.

15. All matters affecting the interpretation of this agreement and the validity thereof shall be governed by the laws of the State of New York.

16. The Husband, upon the execution of this agreement, will pay the fees for legal services rendered to the Wife in connection with the negotiations for and the preparation of this Separation Agreement in the sum of $250.

17. This agreement shall be binding upon and inure to the benefit of the parties hereto and their respective heirs, executors, administrators, and assigns, except as other-

wise provided in paragraph 2 (H), herein, with respect to the payments for support.

IN WITNESS WHEREOF, the parties hereto have hereunto set their hands and seals this 1st day of November, 1969.

STATE OF NEW YORK   )
) ss.:
COUNTY OF WESTCHESTER)

On this 1st day of November, 1969, before me personally came ANN KOFFEND, to me known and known to me to be the individual described in and who executed the foregoing Agreement and she duly acknowledged to me that she executed the same.

STATE OF NEW YORK   )
) ss.:
COUNTY OF WESTCHESTER)

On this 1st day of November, 1969, before me personally came JOHN B. KOFFEND, to me known and known to me to be the individual described in and who executed the foregoing Agreement and he duly acknowledged to me that he executed the same.

Asunto: REGISTRO

El C. _____ LICENCIADOANTONIO LOPEZ BUSTAMANTE _____ SECRETARIO DEL H. AYUNTAMIENTO DEL MUNICIPIO JUAREZ, ESTADO DE CHIHUAHUA.

C E R T I F I C A :

Que bajo el número _____ 13100 _____ y a folios _____ 3276 _____ del libro que para el efecto se lleva en esta Presidencia Municipal, se encuentra registrado (a) _____ LA SRA. _____

_____ quien dijo ser de Nacionalidad _____ NORTE AMERI

CANA _____ de _____ 48 _____ años de edad, de ocupación _____

_____ AMA DE CASA _____ y para el efecto de cumplir con lo ordenado por el

Artículo 24 de la Ley del Divorcio, a solicitud de parte interesada, se expide el presente en una foja utilizada para los usos legales que a la misma convengan en Ciudad Juárez. Chihuahua, a los _____ 21

días del mes de _____ NOVIEMBRE _____ de mil novecientos sesena y _____ NUEVE _____

SUFRAGIO EFECTIVO; NO REELECCION

LIC. ANTONIO LOPEZ BUSTAMANTE

CUBIERTO EL IMPUESTO CORRESPONDIENTE

SEGUN CERTIFICADO No. _____ 72967

COMPARECIENTE _____

LIC. XAVIER ROSAS C.

The undersigned Rodolfo Silva, clerk of the First Civil Court for the Bravos District, Chihuahua, Mexico, *certifies*: That in the record of the suit for necessary divorce instituted by Mrs. *Ann Koffend* against her husband Mr. *John B. Koffend*, several writs are recorded herein which to the letter say: ___ *DECREE*:_ "City of Juarez, Chihuahua., December 1st., 1969.—WHEREAS to resolve definitively this suit for necessary divorce instituted by Mrs. Ann Koffend against her husband Mr. John B. Koffend (File Number 13262/969); and, *RESULTING*. That by written complaint dated in this city on November 21 of the current year, Mrs. Ann Koffend submitting expressly to the jurisdiction of this Court, instituted action for necessary divorce against her husband Mr. John B. Koffend, giving as ground incompatibility of characters, stating: That the marriage was performed on March 6, 1950, in the United States of America, as it was proved by the testimony that was rendered; there are three minor children of said marriage whose situation has been resolved as per Agreement; and that the parties executed and signed a separation agreement on November 1st, of the current year in the County of Westchester, State of New York, United States of America, which among other things states: That the husband shall pay to the wife, for the support and maintenance of each of the children, $2,000.00 per year, until such child shall attain the age of 21 years of [sic] finishes college, whichever is later, according to paragraph "2". (A)". The husband shall pay to the wife annually for her support and maintenance, in monthly installments, a sum equeal [sic] to the defference [sic] between the total amount of support and maintenance payable for all of the children in such calendar year and a sum equal to 45% of the gross taxable income of the husband for such calendar year, all according to paragraph "2". Custody of the children shall be with the wife, with the right of visitation to the husband, according to paragraph "4" of the agreement, which was asked to be approved in all its terms, incorporated by reference to this resolution and to continue to survive._ The complaint was admitted and the defendant was ordered summoned and as the plaintiff Mrs. Ann Koffend personally appeared before the undersigned Judge accompanied by her Counsellor Xavier Rosas Cevallos to present her complaint was notified that the same was admitted and she ratified it in all its parts including her express submission to the jurisdiction of this Court, exhibitting [sic] a Certificate Number 13100 issued by the Municipal Board in which appears that she personally inscribed her name in the Municipal Registry of Residents of this City; and by writ presented today, Counsellor Miguel Gomez Guerra as Special Attorney for the defendant Mr. John B. Koffend submitting him expressly to the jurisdiction of this Court, answered the complaint confessing the same in all its parts asking to render the corresponding judgment in view of the fact that all the legal requirements have been complied including the payment for the publication of same, as per Receipt Number 9435; and, CONSIDERING._ This is a competent Court to render a decision in this action according to Articles 22 and 24 of the Divorce Law as the plaintiff obtained a Certificate of Inscription at the Municipal Registry of Residents of this City; according to Article 23 of the same Law, both parties submitted expressly to the jurisdiction of this Court and in accordance with Article 29 of the said Law, the existence of the marriage and the children was proved. As ground for divorce plaintiff stated incompatibility of characters, ground set forth in Section XIX of Article 3 of the Divorce Law and confessing the complaint in all its parts was fully proved according to Article 373 of the Code of Civil Procedures. Having stated that of the marriage there are three minor children whose situation has been resolved as per agreement, according to Article 11 of the Divorce Law and taking into consideration the opinion given by the District Attorney said minors shall continue in the situation agreed._ For all the above stated facts of the Divorce Law, it is decreed:_ FIRST._ The marriage of Mrs. Ann Koffend and Mr. John B. Koffend, performed on March 6, 1950, is hereby declared dissolved together with all its legal consequences, leaving both parties free to contract new marriage._ SECOND._ The separation agreement executed and signed by the parties on November 1st, 1969 in the Coutny [sic] of Westchester, State of New York, United States of America, is hereby approbed [sic] in all its terms, incorporated by reference to this resolution and shall continue to survive._ THIRD._ The minor children of said marriage shall continue under the custody of the mother, with the right of visitation to the husband, according to paragraph "4" of the agreement._ FOURTH._ The husband shall pay to the wife, for the support and maintenance of each of the children, $2,000.00 per year, until such child shall attain the age of 21 years of [sic] finishes college, whichever, is later, according to paragraph "2". (A)"._ FIFTH._ The husband shall pay to the wife annually for her support and maintenance, in monthly installments, a sum equal to the difference between the total amount of support and maintenance payable for all of the children in such calendar year and a sum equal to 50% [sic] of the gross taxable income of the husband for such calendar year, all according to paragraph "2" of the agreement.– SIXTH.– This judicial decree must be registered, published and the certified copies requested by the interested parties must be issued to them and in due time must be filed. This was decreed and signed by the Honorable Judge of the First Civil Court for the Bravos District.– I witness.– L. Holguin C.– R. Silva."– Rubrics. – – – – – ORDER:– "City of Juarez, Chihuahua., December 1st, 1969.– Recorded the writs of this date and in view of the fact that the parties to this action Mrs. Ann Koffend and Mr. John B. Koffend, had no objection to the foregoing resolution declaring the legal dissolution of their marriage contract said judgment has been declared final according to the Law, Thus was decreed and signed by the Honorable Judge of the First Civil Court for the Bravos District.– I witness.– L. Holguin C.– R. Silva."– Rubrics. – – – – – – – – – – IT IS A TRUE COPY LEGALLY TAKEN FROM ITS ORIGINAL, CORRECTED AND COMPARED IN ONE LEGAL SHEET, ISSUED, AUTHORIZED AND SIGNED IN THE CITY OF JUAREZ, CHIHUAHUA, MEXICO, ON THE FIRST DAY OF DECEMBER NINETEEN HUNDRED AND SIXTY NINE,– I ATTEST.– THE CLERK.– R. SILVA Rubric.– THE SEAL OF THE COURT. –

Approved by:

       Hon. Atty. Lorenzo Holguin Cisneros.– Rubric.–
       Judge of the First Civil Court.–

Psychological Evaluation
NAME: John Koffend
AGE: 52
DATE TESTED: July 17, 1970
TESTS ADMINISTERED:
   Bender-Gestalt Test
   Wechsler Adult Intelligence Scale (WAIS)
   Rorschach Test
   Thematic Apperception Test (TAT)
   Sentence Completion Test (SCT)

Mr. Koffend was pleasant and cooperative throughout the testing session. He appeared interested in all tasks and was quite spontaneous with the examiner.

He is presently functioning at the overall very superior level of intelligence, with a WAIS full-scale IQ of 132, a verbal score of 130, and a performance score of 131. Only a minimal degree of impaired over-all efficiency is suggested by subtest scatter ranging from the average to very superior levels.

Quantitatively and qualitatively, all verbal skills are very superior. These include factual information, rote memory-attention span, abstract reasoning, and arithmetic problem solving.

While graphomotor speed is superior, perceptual motor skills are quite variable. His copies of block designs were very superior, but performance was only average on a subtest involving the fitting of pieces into familiar configurations. This relatively low score was caused primarily by some confusion and a break in critical judgment—i.e., his expressed satisfaction with a slightly incorrectly assembled item.

Social skills are superior to very superior in both structured and unstructured situations. He has little difficulty understanding the motives and actions of others, but there is a slight tendency to unreflectiveness in the area of social conventions. Attention to environmental detail is high in the very superior range, indicating an extremely acute response to his surroundings.

With the exception of an isolated instance of confusion, this is in general a highly powerful intellectual performance.

Rorschach responses reveal that reality testing is somewhat variable when Mr. Koffend must rely solely upon his own resources. Percepts occasionally deviate from the form of blot areas, but not to a degree indicative of grossly pathological thought processes. There is a heavy reliance upon obsessive-compulsive defenses, including intellectualization, affective isolation, and reaction-formation. At the same time, the use of projection is apparent, seen especially in his percepts of faces and in his attribution of emotion to the neutral blot areas. A tendency to marked passivity permeates the entire record and has definite defensive implications. A slight somatic preoccupation is also suggested.

At present Mr. Koffend is rather depressed, a reaction consciously attributed in SCT responses to loneliness, felt rejection, and the loss of needed figures. Further, he feels friendless and, indeed, without any warm human relationships. He states: *More than anything else he needed* "reciprocal human connections"; *a person who falls in love* "is able to connect with others." And his statement that *A lot of people* "live empty lives" is elaborated in more personal terms on TAT Card 14 in a story redolent of dreariness and isolation. He describes "An apartment dweller, a man. . . . He's come home late, so before turning on the lights . . . he walks to the window . . . and looks at the starry sky and city lights. After which he'll turn the lights on, have a glass of apple juice, brush his teeth, and go to bed."

This situation appears a prime motive for seeking treatment at this time—e.g., on TAT Card 3BM he focuses upon a "lonely" woman "deficient in real human connections. . . . If her family is well-to-do enough she'll wind up in psychotherapy, so the story will have a happy ending." Optimism, however, seems tempered slightly by a vague cynical, satirical sense; and the "happy-ending" motif, rather typical of his stories, also points to denial and perhaps magical hopes.

Consistently, depression is deepened by Mr. Koffend's great dependency, well illustrated by his story to TAT Card 18BM in which a passive drunken man, who has "not been obstreperous or made trouble," is being helped from a bar and put in a taxi, and "if necessary they will instruct the driver where to go." In line with this he has always felt controlled and weak with his mother, stating that *My mother* "is a domineering person" and *When he was with his mother*, he felt "less than his age." Further, a felt lack of affection and a sense of emotional removal are clear in other statements: *When I think back, I am ashamed that* "I have no recognizable warm feelings toward my mother"; *When my mother came home, I* "was not there."

The crux of the relationship, with its guilt-laden dependence-autonomy struggle is seen on TAT Card 6BM: "The woman is the man's mother; both are very unhappy. She is probably an overweening mother and forces discipline by feeling, looking, and acting hurt, not by spanking—he's too big for that. He's feeling guilty but he really hasn't done anything; feels it but he really doesn't understand why he should. Two possible endings: the mother's domination will continue . . . or he may find the strength to break away and live his own life."

There is much evidence that, feeling affectionally deprived and dominated by his mother, he turned to his father for a degree of maternal love, with a concomitant dependent bond formed with the older man. For example, his story to TAT Card 7BM concerns a father and son who are "very close. . . . A happy end: he's gone to the right place and will get the help he needs from someone who loves and understands him." And on TAT Card 8BM a son "reveres" his father "and so will follow in his footsteps."

These stories are on one level profound wishes, particularly the latter. Mr. Koffend feels that he cannot measure up to his father, a man recalled as incessantly working and engaging in such standard masculine pursuits as baseball (SCT). Further, there was an aloofness in this relationship, the older man not being fully approachable: *Whenever he was with his father, he felt* "a slight reserve." In compensation for this parental coldness there is much wishing for an idyllic family life and, with this aim in view, desires to remarry.

Depression is also deepened by internalized anger which is additionally projected and denied. The latter is sharply illustrated by such statements as *He felt he could murder a man who*—"I wouldn't murder anyone" and *A man would be justified in beating a woman who*—"no, never justified." His only significant admission of anger is contained in the statement, *I could lose my temper if* "criticized by a peer." But in his daily life few people are deeply regarded as peers; they are largely perceived as authority figures with powerful retaliatory capacities and with whom he must behave in a passive, compliant manner.

Strife and competition are givens in all human encounters. He introduces anger into relationships, then denies it with a driven intensity. Examples of this permeate Rorschach responses: "two gorillas . . . touching in a friendly way. A game" (Card II); "two little elves in an amiable conversation" (Card X); "a squinty face—not unfriendly" (Card III). Aside from desires to alleviate anxiety connected to aggressive impulses, he denies anger in order not to alienate needed others; when denial fails he tends to avoid others and to withdraw.

Mr. Koffend overtly expresses anger in only one further SCT response, and the context is extremely important. He states: *He boiled up when* "they forced him." The remark is elaborated and tied to the maternal figure in his story to TAT Card 1 which involves "A little boy whose mother has commanded him to take violin lessons against his will. He's looking distastefully at the instrument. . . . After he finishes his lessons he's not a good violinist, will never play the instrument again." Here he is forced to perform against his will (with some implication of self-defeating oppositional behavior). He cannot oppose his mother directly as he cannot gain independence from her since it is equated with great aggression—e.g., one means by which he might gain autonomy in his story to TAT Card 6BM is through her death.

Guilt-provoking anger and resentment are extended from parental values to society in general. He states: *He felt he had done wrong when he* "bucked the system"; *I felt most dissatisfied when* "the system did not appreciate me." Clearly he feels that relinquishing his own wishes and freedom has brought him little, if any, reward. In sum, he feels insignificant, with minimal integrity, and with no impact upon others—a persistent source of anger. He states: *I was most annoyed when* "no one listened." This, too, appears rooted in the maternal relationship. For example, on Rorschach Card VII, a stimulus which elicits associations to the mother and to women in general, he perceives two women "arguing with each other, no one winning—no one listening, either."

Mr. Koffend's felt lack of assertiveness and sense of castration bear directly on such SCT responses as *His greatest worry was* "his psychic impotence." Indeed, his style is consistently intellectualized in dealing with sexual matters—e.g., *When I meet a woman, I* "examine her configuration." Such statements strongly suggest both obsessive defenses in the sexual area as well as the compensation for sexual inadequacy and castration via intellectual channels. Needless to say, his problem with impotence is not fully "psychic." He clearly states that *He was most anxious about* "his performance in bed." Further, there are many Rorschach images in which "imperfections" are stressed. On Card X, for example, he perceives "A coathanger for a roundshouldered person. But there's no way to hang it—no hook." Here he is already physically bent, needing but lacking a "missing piece" to lend him an erect posture.

And while he consciously states that heterosexual contact is "good" and his own desire "normal," an inhibition of sexual performance is quite apparent in his story to TAT Card 13MF. Here he describes "A sad scene—no violence indicated. . . . Could be a sexual affair that he is unable to consummate for moral reasons. The girl is willing, but the Protestant-Puritan ethic will not let him because he really loves her. She's a little disappointed at that. They will not get married."

Thus sexual potency is equated with aggression and finally violence which is strongly denied; sexual and aggressive impulses appear fused, with concomitant guilt and "shame." Oedipal implications appear inescapable, as well as the inference that, deeply, he searches in marriage for maternal dependency gratification rather than for a mature, sexual relationship. There are also suggestions that impotence, or at least periodic loss of erection, is allied to fears of aggression and subsequent passive defenses against it. For example, on Rorschach Card X he describes "The face of a rabbit with ears sticking up"—a both passive and assertive image, heavily weighted toward the former.

Consistently, psychosexual confusion and underlying homoerotic impulses are apparent. On Rorschach Card III he cannot decide whether to attribute male or female gender characteristics to ambiguous figures, and passive floral imagery abounds—an apparent polar opposite to his father. In more heavily identifying with his mother he apparently perceived her as consistently the more powerful parent—symbolically castrating both himself *and* his father. Her control, perhaps in part resulting in a resentful paternal aloofness and covert competition toward the son, has left Mr. Koffend with fears of male attack. But the strength of his castration fears seems in direct proportion to his driven need to deny all negative or aggressive feelings toward men. He attempts to diminish the frightening power of other males in an almost hysterical counterphobic manner. For example, on Rorschach Card IV, a blot which stimulates paternal and male imagery, he describes "A view from the floor of a heavy-set humanoid creature with very large feet. It doesn't look particularly menacing—in fact rather furry, like a woodchuck." Here he attempts to convert a domineering menace into a small cuddly dependency object.

Thus he must avoid power struggles with males, inevitable via his projections of anger as well as being rooted in feelings of weakness and vulnerability. As he turned the encounter of the gorillas on Rorschach Card II into a "game," he apparently attempts to neutralize even real aggressive attacks against him in much the same defensive manner. For example, his story to TAT Card 12M is set in "a fraternity house. One of the brothers popped off to sleep and a fraternity brother is going to play a good-natured trick on him. . . . The sleeping guy, when he wakes, won't be cross. It goes on all the time in fraternity houses." In reality he may well feel himself to be the butt of perpetual teasing and practical jokes, particularly among men. But while he attempts to be "good-natured," he feels unabatedly humiliated, which angers him further and seriously diminishes an already extremely frayed self-esteem.

Now Mr. Koffend feels deeply inferior and quite anxious interpersonally, and appears to be losing confidence in his intellectual capacities—his major source of potency and self-esteem. Withdrawal fantasies of a Gauguin-like flight to the "tropics" are prominent, as is other test imagery of "exotic" and "tropical" phenomena—all dealing with desires for warmth and peace. This suggests some possible flirtation with suicidal ideas, although test evidence in this direction is not impressive.

Diagnostic impression: Passive-aggressive personality, with paranoid, depressive, and withdrawal features. Obsessive-compulsive features are marked, and schizoid traits are apparent.

To: The Staff
From: Henry Grunwald
Date: November 12, 1970

As most of you already know, the most spectacular departure since Gauguin left for Tahiti is about to be staged by John Koffend, who has decided to bestow the benefit of his presence upon Pago Pago.

Those of us who remain behind must console ourselves as best we can. Fortunately, an excellent opportunity presents itself in the TIME anniversaries of no fewer than eight of our colleagues. Douglas Auchincloss, Ruth Brine, Dorothy Haystead and Vincent Puglisi have all been with us for 25 years, with nary a thought of Pago Pago, while Gene Coyle, Arnold Drapkin, Erwin Edelman and Harriet Heck have triumphantly reached the 20 year mark.

To honor them all, and to wish John Godspeed, let us gather in the Eighth Floor auditorium next Tuesday, November 17, 5.00 p.m. until closing. Drinks, buffet and dancing.

H.A.G.

Preface

In June 1970 I was living alone—for the first time in my life—in a one-room apartment in White Plains, New York, thirty miles north of Manhattan. I was not there by choice, and I was desperately lonely. The apartment was furnished with a double bed, a few chairs, a card table, a Herman Miller dresser; all second-hand, all given to me by my former wife. Since I entertained no visitors, I made no effort to decorate the apartment or to keep it clean. Painters had applied a fresh coat of white paint to the walls before I moved in nine months before. When I moved out in November I had put nothing on them, not even finger prints. I hated that apartment in rather the same way that the prisoner hates his cell or the hospital patient his room. It was a place to sleep, to eat Carnation Instant breakfasts and Swanson TV dinners; nothing more.

Each day, Monday through Friday, I commuted to and from New York City, usually on the Penn Central Railroad, occasionally (as a self-indulgence) by car and sometimes, after a particularly late night in town, by cab. At the time, I had been working for Time Inc. for fifteen years, the last twelve in the company's headquarters at Fiftieth Street and Sixth Avenue, across from Radio City Music Hall. My name has vanished from the magazine's masthead—a list of employees, mostly editorial, that appears in very small type opposite what is known as the Publisher's Letter. It was there a long time—too long a time: from January 1955, when I joined the magazine's Los Angeles bureau as a correspondent, until December 1970, when, some weeks after my actual departure, someone thought to delete it. My title was associate editor, one that will mean little to someone unacquainted with *Time*'s editorial pecking order. I was, in fact, a writer for the magazine. It was a duty that, in *Time*'s practice of journalism, involves very little travel. The writer sits in his office, digesting files sent from one or more of the magazine's correspondents in the U.S. and abroad, reading pertinent material—books, monographs, encyclopedia entries, other *Time* stories—sent down to him from the magazine's library and, at last, turning to his typewriter and composing the articles which, if he is lucky, will appear in the next issue much as he wrote them.

Above him, on the masthead, stand superior titles in the *Time* hierarchy, together with the names of those who have achieved them: in ascending order, senior editors, assistant managing editors and managing editor. The names beneath these titles have not changed much since I left the magazine. Henry Anatole Grunwald is still managing editor, an urbane, rotund man in his late forties who began his career on *Time* as an office boy. Edward L. Jamieson and Richard M. Seamon are still assistant managing editors. All but one of the ten senior editors I said good-bye to, and many of whom I worked directly under as a writer, are still there. These superiors have the authority, frequently exercised, to overrule the writer by asking him to revise his story or to rewrite it entirely.

No writer I knew learned to accept such commands with composure. The *Time* writer's lot is not easy. At least one day a week—commonly known as the writer's day—he will face his typewriter at, say, ten in the morning and will not leave it except for meals until midnight or later. In some weeks there are two such writer's days; in some weeks, three. After such a massive expenditure of time and effort, it is no fun to be summoned before the senior editor or the managing editor and asked to do the story again in a different way.

You will meet some of these names in the letter to my wife. Managing Editor Grunwald appears as HAG (pronounced Hag) because that was how he was known to many of his staff. You will also encounter the names of colleagues elsewhere on the masthead. I have not identified them except by name. They were my lunch and dinner and evening companions, and my friends; that is all you need to know about them. In other cases, for discretionary reasons, I have changed names and circumstances as well as the contexts in which they appear. I have no wish to embarrass or offend persons whom I esteemed then and esteem now.

It was in June 1970 that I decided to leave *Time*—although six months were to pass before my departure—and to begin a new life, or try to, somewhere else. My choice of Pago Pago was made at the same time, for no good reason. Some five years before, in a period of restlessness, I had written letters to newspaper publishers throughout the islands of the South Seas with a view to buying into their operations and moving there. Islands have long tugged at my spirit; the South Pacific, about which I knew nothing, spelled adventure. This correspondence came to nothing. But the place names—Suva, Papeete, Apia, Port Moresby, Noumea, Pago Pago—clung to some recess of my memory, and one of them leaped out at me on that June night: Pago Pago (which I then pronounced Paygo Paygo, just as most casual visitors to American Samoa still do*).

My reasons for seeking a new life were just as ordinary. The old one had suffered a series of radical shocks, some of

---

* In Samoan, the letter "g" has the strength of "ng" as in singing. The "g" is more sensed than sounded. The "a" is flat: Pahngo Pahngo.

my own engineering. My marriage had been deteriorating for several years and was clearly headed for divorce. The final impetus, I regret to say, came from me. I had met a young married woman, mother of three, whom I shall call Jocelyn Bannon. Her marriage, like mine, was no longer working well, but for different reasons. Her husband Guy was a successful and ambitious physicist who had let his professional career overwhelm his family life. Over many months of clandestine meetings I fell in love with Jocelyn—or thought I did, which is the same thing—and she with me. One night, by pre-arrangement, we informed our respective spouses that we wanted to be married. My wife accepted this decision. Within a week we were living apart. Within a month she divorced me in Mexico.

Guy elected to fight for his marriage. And in the face of his determination, Jocelyn wavered. Even before my wife flew down to Mexico, Jocelyn had announced to me her decision to stay with Guy. I did not resent her decision then, nor do I now. I cherish the months we had together. I cherish her still.

But the loss of my wife and my children and of her, combined with a life of enforced solitude, plunged me into a depression in which nothing seemed to have much point. I tried ways of relieving the depression, a few positive, many negative. I drank more. With a brilliant young friend, Steve Englund, then working towards a doctoral degree at Princeton, I laid out a 5,000-word prospectus for a book on sociology which, we hoped, would do for that science what Robert Ardrey had done for anthropology. When G.P. Putnam's Sons signed us to a contract, I set to work at once. I used my job at *Time* as an anodyne, with some success: before I left the magazine I was under active consideration for promotion to senior editor, the next step up the masthead. I found another woman, Barbara Smith (which is not her true name), a terribly attractive woman, who played a vital if peripheral part in satisfying my need to be needed. There was never any thought of marriage, but I wonder still how I could have got through those months without her.

And, because I was lonely and missed my wife, I began a letter to Ann. I wrote it at odd moments, in the apartment, in bars, on commuter trains. By that time I had discovered Franzl's, a gemütlich German restaurant not five minutes' drive from my apartment, whose proprietor, Franzl Vogl, was my equal at chess and at quaffing beer. Franzl's and its steady patrons were my family. In its warm and undemanding ambiance, at a table, on paper borrowed from Franzl, with a dozen seidels of Michelob under my belt, I wrote many of the passages in the letter to my wife.

It appears here just as I wrote it, except for changes necessary to disguise identities that might suffer from public exposure. All my wife's friends and mine will easily pierce their flimsy disguise. It is a difficult question. I confess I don't know how to answer it. Perhaps the fact of publication is my answer. I know this much. After fifty-three years, I no longer believe in secrets. The letter was written from my heart, at the feeling level. I don't believe in the head any more either. In fifty-three years it has dispensed to me nothing but bad advice.

There remains only this to say. I showed the manuscript to a friend, who, after reading it, said: "The sad part is, you still love her, don't you? You don't really want to go." I will never be sure, but I think he was right.

John B. Koffend
Fagatogo, American Samoa
July, 1971

A LETTER TO MY WIFE

Dear Ann—

It's going to take me a long time—months—to write this letter; the reasons why will become clear as you read along. It begins one June night in my apartment, which has become a prison. There are five Valiums in me and I'm waiting for them to work. David Frost is on TV, but I'm not paying attention. It's quite early—9:30—because tomorrow will be a long day and I want to get an early start. Given the scanty furnishings of this room, the apartment is a mess: last Sunday's *Times* all over the floor, several weeks of nail parings on your rug, socks and shoes everywhere, ashtrays overflowing, the bed unmade, the linen unchanged for two weeks. I despise being here, and find it almost impossible to apply myself, in it, to the book. Your mother's slipper chair—is that what you once called it?—is slowly dying, bleeding its stuffing from a dozen wounds. Tonight I passed up the chance to go to a press screening of *Myra Breckenridge* and a party in Raquel Welch's honor at *Time* afterward. It was to have started late—after 10:30—and then of course I wouldn't have got back to White Plains, by Dial-a-Cab, much before one. I took Valium last night too, again quite early; there was nothing to do, I couldn't face the book, was overcome with guilt (as now) because of it, and so conked myself out and climbed into bed by ten. Slept till 7:30. It's been a long time since either Valium or a load of Franzl's beer hasn't put me to sleep. Outside of the office, Franzl's is my only important human connection. As I told you, Gil Gordon identified the plaque on my face as ringworm, which is not caused by a worm but a fungus. He prescribed a salve that, applied nightly since, is clearing it up in good order. I also took a chest x-ray, which Gil pronounced clear as a bell. I just can't believe him. I'm smoking two packs every day now; more than that now that I'm a try-out senior editor, an assignment that, despite my earnest effort to play it cool, still makes me anxious, because it's a judgmental situation. My guess, after two weeks, is that I can probably make it, in six months or so, but I don't really want it. I'm with the younger generation now—everything seems irrelevant: the book on the new sociology, another possible book sale in the offing (that old Jonathan Doe novel), a real chance for promotion when I'm long past the promotion age. All of it should cheer me, and none of it does. No woman connections, except the casual ones at the office. It isn't that I'm afraid to get into a sex situation because of my psychic impotence, it's just that it doesn't seem worth it since, when that moment comes, my head will not let Grosser do his business. I know enough about it, from Masters & Johnson, to understand that individual therapy wouldn't work. It's quite an obstacle. As I tried to tell you that night I called, you and I entering their clinic together, both in a cooperative mood, might have put me (*and* you) back into the sex business. As these people say again and again, there is no such thing as an uninvolved partner in a sexually distressed marriage. I'm sure you think I have no right to be bitter, since it was I who made the first move toward divorce. But was it really? One could argue just as plausibly that it was not the first move but the last; the culmination of many years of not being together. To get back into the sex business is not of course the whole of therapy, nor do Masters & Johnson say that it is. They say only that with sex restored, the other problems generally seem less crucial. Without it, no marriage has much of a chance. I'm still sorry you rejected so vigorously my suggestion that we consider trying to recover that ground in their St. Louis clinic. It's much different with a man, Ann; you should read the book and discover for yourself.

The fact that the Jocelyn thing fell through, surprisingly enough, doesn't bother me much. I may never be a wise man, but this whole experience has given me *some* wisdom. It's an effort, but I try now to take stock of my virtues rather than my flaws. No doubt it was my doing and not yours, but during much of our marriage it was the other way around. As I've said many times, I would never win any serenity or security contests, and I wouldn't care to enter any even today. You think I criticized you overmuch, and I won't defend myself against the charge. But I, too, felt the same. The significance may not have occurred to you, but it did to me. After I left, you subscribed to *Life*, not *Time*. *Time* is the magazine I work and write for. You don't even see it any more. After all the years, I can still take satisfaction and pride in a story I've done well and that remains mine in print; the Rollo May takeout, for instance, which through special circumstances got into print almost unscathed, just as I'd written it. I remember one of your old things for Bob Young—you know, when you were drawing the illustrations for his lectures on psychiatry at med school in Lincoln—I remember one that, unless I'm mistaken, showed one of your little creatures dreadfully sad and rejected because, after exhibiting her creation to a circle of friends, they didn't respond with enough appreciation. I don't buy that point of Bob's any more. People *need* to be needed; the best human relation, I think now, is a mutual and reciprocal exchange of needs. I don't know whether you and I ever had that, but looking back now, after the separation, I wonder whether we did. I do miss you, but I can't honestly tell you what it is I miss—maybe just the ruts and habits of living together. One gets used to them, and the marriage wasn't all bad. Don't you ever miss me? You've never said so. You just rushed down to Juarez angry and hurt, in what was in part, I'm sure (and I think you know it too), an "I'll show you" mood.

I've taken another Valium, the others haven't worked. Tomorrow, unless it's terribly chilly, I'm going to wear shorts to work—which, by *Time*'s stuffy unwritten code of suitable office costumery, is considered about as indecent as no pants at all. Perhaps a silly bit of bravado (I recognize that) but part of a concerted effort on my part to break out of the mold. It has occurred to me that I've lived all my life for other people, not for their sake, like a saint, but on their say-so. Be nice to your mother. Don't slap your wife. Responsible fatherhood. Succeed at the job. Pick up your socks. Don't offend anybody. Don't make waves. Conform. What do they expect? Do it. What is one's social role? Play it. I'm tired of all that. I'm fifty-two, one of Thoreau's quietly desperate, what Wilhelm Reich called a "living machine." It's all so pointless. To live just to die. I can't believe the trip shouldn't be more fun than it has been so far for me. And maybe for you. But it's always struck me that you get more from life because you put more of yourself into it, though the goals you set don't interest me now. Someone once said that if you're not radical when you're young you should get your heart examined, and that if you're radical when you're old you should have your head examined. I was no young radical —quite the opposite—but I'm learning to be an old one. My ambition for the Establishment's goals in life no longer interest me much. I wouldn't refuse money, but I don't really want it. I want to enjoy, enjoy, as Harry Golden said, and there aren't all that many years left to learn how. But I'm dying to learn.

I'm in a suicidal mood but I know I'll never do it—and this letter is not leading up to that. Still I find the thought of it almost irresistibly tempting. It's a Saturday afternoon, after a disastrous week. I certainly scored no Brownie points as an editor. I'm not an editor, and I guess not a writer either. I can't bring myself to face the book. I slept till 11:30 and have been mooning around the apartment since, trying to stop smoking and failing, watching any old thing on TV, nothing to do and nowhere to go. I appreciate what a heavy content of self-pity there is in all this.

A mad installment. It's 2:45 A.M. and I'm in the apartment after two long difficult work days, sleepless and full of booze, mostly beer. My mind busily rehearsing what to cram into the consultation appointment I have made with a head candler (no one you know) five days from now. Here's a bit of candor: I don't really miss your society, but I miss you. I can't quite figure that out, so I can't expect you to, either. Nursing a grudge against you because you haven't written and don't write. Thoughts trending in this direction: if I take a job as a dishwasher at $80 a week, and give you $40, I fulfill to the letter my legal obligations to you. So why should I kill myself earning a single penny more? Your mother would be compelled under such circumstances to come to your aid, and Lord knows she has the wherewithal to do it. With all those millions your sister married, she doesn't need a dime. You should get all your old lady's bread after she dies, and you *would* get it all if I made such a move. She'd rewrite her will in your favor. Don't count on my conscience smiting me; in every direction I look now, surveying the present, I see a bleak and very dead end. Psychically impotent, solitary, busting my fucking ass at *Time*—for what? Let's say I've got $40,000 in the profit sharing—you can have it all. Let's say we crack my Uncle George's trust and I, personally, realize fifty grand from that—you can have it all. I don't want money. Fourteen years ago, to *you*, I suggested we buy a twenty-acre strip of land clear across Eleuthera, which we could have picked up then for a song—$25,000. It was a clear bid from me—a plea—to haul out and try something else—anything else. Well, that proposition went the way of all my propositions. There's no way to revise the past, I know, but at the tender age of fifty-two I want to scrub the past and make a fresh start. I don't want to climb back into the same old ruts any more than you do. You're doing fine without me—or so you say. If that *is* the case—and I don't entirely believe it—part of the reason is that I scrupulously pop those biweekly checks that take you to East Hampton, etc. and one of which, sent to you three months ago, has yet to be cashed. You were always a holdout. In fact, you stubbornly resisted pooling your separate checking account from March 1950, when we were married, until it ran out. Ask yourself why. I know you well enough, Ann, to realize what a fine smolder this page in particular has put you in. If we were face-to-face and I were saying these things, you would simply storm out of the room, your lips pursed, flatly refusing to talk any further to that totally unreasonable and irrational man—your husband. The one human connection to which, through no fault of yours, you *must* be unalterably opposed. I look back now and understand that the marriage, even though it survived in form for nineteen years, never had a chance. Why didn't it? Partly me, but also partly you. You think I missed all your good points, and you have many. But you also missed most of mine. For me to call from the office, as I more than once did, and suggest dinner at that restaurant in Bedford (forget the name), and be turned down, is sad enough. What's even more desolating, at least to me, is that *even before calling* I knew I would be turned down. Such a tiny price to pay to accept such an impulsive invitation, but it was more than you could give. It's no excuse at all that you didn't want to go. You *did* want to go, but you couldn't say yes. An invitation like that simply cannot be declined, and if you think about it you will understand why.

You never wearied of condemning my drinking and never missed an opportunity to drive that nail home. Don't hold your breath until I die of acute alcoholism. I'll bet it never *ever* occurred to you to consider any other approach but censure. Like, for instance, accepting an invitation to dinner at Nino's and saying, "Okay, let's make a night of it; let's both get smashed." You and your one or two drinks every night— every night. Me and my three martinis every *third* night, and nothing at all between. I am not and never will be a lush, but you will never accept that simple fact.

I'll go to work tomorrow after no sleep and three martinis, a glass of wine and a cognac (on the house) at dinner tonight; after which I went back to the office, edited three stories, and took a Dial-a-Cab to White Plains, lubricating the trip with three cans of beer. Two more since—but that's from 12:30, when I got here, to now (3:45). I'm sure that consumption appalls you. But I'll naturally have nothing at all tomorrow, and I'll get through the day. I don't deny a certain defensiveness on the subject, but my God! I once drank twenty scotches at a country club dance in Neenah, Wisconsin, and managed to drive the car home. Today, I rarely drink anything but beer; and have *never* had a bottle of liquor in the apartment. Does that sound like a man with a serious drinking problem? Now that I'm a try-out senior editor, the bottles blossom every Friday night, as if by magic (I don't order them, the secretary does), and there's always a lot left over. I could, if I chose, smuggle them home—most of the last fifth of gin, vermouth and scotch. But do I? No. Not once. Why in the world that punishing attitude from you? You'll react to all this as naked hostility, and maybe so. But what was my crime? That I walked like a fairy, as you once said, with three martinis under my belt? That I beat the children? You? That I burned down a house, like a friend of mine did? That I couldn't get up in the morning and go to work? What was my crime?

How you must warm to all this. You rate some of it—maybe not all of it. Was I always that critical of you? I remember, still with astonishment, something you said when I called one time after our divorce—that it was a pleasure to get through Christmas without being criticized for doing everything wrong. Do you genuinely mean that I spoiled every single Christmas for nineteen years by being a mean bastard? Read Rollo May sometime. The opposite of love, he says, is not hate, but apathy. You and I were never apathetic, now were we? Hate is a very strong emotion, that can bind two people as tightly as love. In fact, as you know all too well, it is a part of love. If, towards the end, you felt neither, then of course the union was over; unions are not nourished by apathy. But if you felt a vestige of *either,* it was not over. Injured pride can carry a person quite a long way, but always in the wrong direction. Injured pride, or something like it, bore me in a dumb direction, and your response—injured pride—sent *you* flying down to Mexico. Now, I haven't the faintest idea whether I'm right or wrong in all this, but I do think I know something now that this mutual stupidity has taught me: I'm never going to do any better than when I had you. And neither are you. 4:30 now.

Another day. Rough week at the office, as usual, and nothing to show for it but lungs like cinder pits. Ed Jamieson, sitting in as managing editor for HAG, didn't like the "People" section, which is one of mine—but one can't *manu-*

facture items. It's the three-day July Fourth weekend, which means three days of solitude. Went over to the Kunhardts' to borrow $25 from Phil and found them packing to leave for Maine. Phil gave me a copy of his book inscribed "To my dear friend John." My eyes teared then when I read it; there must be a certain catharsis in crying. I know I do rather enjoy it or I wouldn't do it. Never in public though; just in this one-room cell, over *any* story on TV—*Gunsmoke* particularly, which is a morality play.

I mustn't let too much ride on the consultation I'm going to Monday. They're not magicians, but one is tempted to cast them in the role of instant problem solvers. He comes highly recommended, by a girl whose taste in people is very like mine. She is a graduate of his—just did it, in fact, and still feeling a bit uneasy. She's been going with a rich architect who can't make up his mind to marry her and probably won't. Now she's broken off in a way—therapy no doubt responsible.

Phil's book *is* good. I couldn't bear to think of reading it yesterday, but today, after a good night's sleep thanks to Valium and the whole July Fourth afternoon taunting me with its presence, and after having ennobled myself by doing my exercises, I drove out to Franzl's to read it over beer. The cover is in poor taste: it's plastered with pre-publication blurbs, suggesting that Random House is not as sure of the book's success as it was when Bennett Cerf paid Phil all that money for it. But as I began reading I also began to cry. I think partly because I know Phil and most of the people he names, partly because it is unabashedly sentimental, partly because I need very little excuse these days to cry, and partly for the same reasons that can make you cry at a beautiful sunset, or after a story in which everything comes out right, the way we never stop believing things will. Well, you can't cry in public, even silently, so I left. The day has turned fine.

Just back from Franzl's, which is only five minutes drive from the apartment, the way was lined with picnic groups and people in folding chairs. Now I'm back in the apartment, with the air conditioner blowing, and have broken one of my rules: I've laid in a supply of G-bottles of beer.

Both reviews Phil showed me—one from *Harper's*, the other written but not yet published in *Time*—were by strangers. Neither knows Phil and their response was remarkably alike: they envied the childhood Phil had, and the strength of his attachment to his father. This is the way families are supposed to be, and seldom are. It's a dream, of course; Phil has idealized like mad. He skips all the dark colors. It's the way he remembers everything, not the way it really was. But that's the observation of a cynic, I suppose, reading a book written by a believer; since I have a bad track record in the being-right department, maybe he's right after all. If those first two reviews are any omen, the book could conceivably tap a rich vein. I suspect it will. I really do believe there is such a thing as a chosen person, and Phil is one of them.

This weekend has been endless. I can't believe it's still only Saturday afternoon, with a whole day to get through tomorrow. Naturally, I failed at my no-smoking campaign, which was intended to justify all this moping around doing nothing.

I have the feeling the children don't really want to go on the fishing trip, and will discuss this with you when I call—as I will shortly—to arrange the logistics. They hinted something of the sort when I last talked to them. My guess is that they're finding plenty to do in and around East Hampton. Allen might want to go just for the chance to tool the VW cross-country; but if he's a little patient, he'll have ample opportunity to drive it—a cryptic remark that I'll explain later on. You ought to get rid of the Ford soon anyway. If you're serious about moving out west for keeps, get a VW bus. You never would when we were married, but it makes a lot of sense.

I'd ask how Grundy likes East Hampton except that I'm not really that all hung up on dogs. Funny, but I don't miss *her* much either. I love her all right, but when that last awful accident happened to her—well, I don't quite know what I want to say, except that the emergency took over, I realized she had to be rushed to the vet or die, I understood clearly that death was a strong likelihood, and I did what had to be done without too much emotional involvement. Baldy's death was different. His eyes, when you and I last saw him at the vet's, were *so* imploring, and so trusting too; as if he were saying, Boy, this has really been rough, but now that you're here it's all right—I can stand it. The baby raccoon hit me hard too, though he never knew us, because we'd invested so much in trying to pull him through. I know just where he's buried on what was once my property, and I haven't ever forgotten him.

My plans for the evening would curdle you. Though I've done all my exercises, I'm going to do them all over again, sponge up some more beer, and sack out early. None of it may make any sense, and all of it may sound very self-indulgent, but what does make sense? Even Phil's scheme doesn't make any sense. His life is a Xerox copy of his past; he's duplicating yesterday. He's a nice guy and I love him and maybe a heart attack was genetically coded into his life, but he sure helped it along. In his book he emphasizes the importance of family ritual; it was that way in his youth, and so it is now. Can you imagine a Kunhardt summer without Maine? Or the Kunhardts not sending every one of their children away to school? Or Phil even breaking out of the pattern? I used to be able to do that. I tugged at the apron strings until they snapped. I ran away from home. I joined the merchant marine and sailed all over the Caribbean— hell, what didn't I do before the horizon closed in again: wife, kids, job, grass, cars, house—all those roots that hold a man in place, all those societal ceremonies that embrace him as possessively as a church.

My mind keeps playing with the thought, like a tongue with a sore tooth, that for a wide variety of reasons I was never more than a figurehead in our marriage, itself a ritual. You were the one who worried when you didn't get knocked up at once, and began keeping temperature charts. What were you worrying *about*? We had three children and, given an earlier start, might have had more—whatever that proves. I'm not at all sure that the Kunhardt approach is the right one. There's much to be said for the baboon approach: keep the kids out of heavy traffic and the aspirin bottle, but other- wise let them alone. I didn't always live up to this creed, but it was in my mind (or, more accurately, not in my mind). We've talked about this, but I repeat anyway: it's hardly by chance that Frank turned out to be the most self-sufficient of the Koffend children. It was lucky for him, really, to be a menopause baby. He was raised, figuratively, by grand- parents: mother in her late fifties, Dad pushing seventy. Frank had to develop his own resources, and he did.

Finished another set of exercises, while watching the emetic Honor America proceedings in Washington. Some blond young thing with an uneducated diction ("truhmen- jious" for "tremendous") swinging—or, better, swung—on her thesis that a Mississippi catfish-fryer is happy to be an American (her example, not mine); equated Orlon sweaters with national pride. Everybody seems to forget that this country was born in revolution, and that the individual, to be free, must first turn upon himself. After that, on others. And, after that, on the Establishment. It's all going to end one day anyhow; who do I think I'm kidding by running in place 1,500 times every day? I was driven out Thursday night by a 410-pound Dial-a-Cab driver named Horowitz and called Tiny by his unimaginative friends. We had a good chat. Cab drivers usually rap with me; they pay me obviously heartfelt testimonials when I disembark. Many of them refuse the tips; in forty-five minutes we have become friends. I'm something of a phony about this. Weeks pass, I get the same driver again, and not only don't remember what we talked about the last time but don't remember him. Though sometimes I do.

Two frozen beef-filled green peppers baking in the oven. I've become like Dick Seamon; I eat not to enjoy but to live: the twenty-first-century nutriment-pill taker born ahead of his time. What amazes me is that I lose no weight and keep my good health. Haven't been sick once since our split, not even a cold though plenty of cigarette hangovers. And here's a guy who subsists on instant breakfasts, TV dinners, beer and Valium. All quite economical, and apparently a balanced diet. If I'm in the mood, I can take as many as seven Valiums with no apparent aftereffect but an alarm-clock grogginess that eventually wears off. You used to tax me with having insomnia just to be beastly to you. Within that theory, try to account for its persistence. All of which reminds me again: how near we were, and yet how far. Highly conditioned behavior on both sides; the past's victims. It's a crying shame your mother—*or* mine—didn't kick off years and years ago. Now that I no longer send *my* mother money (except a big hunk from the book advance), I hardly ever write her, and, in candor, have few feelings about her at all. This presumably makes me a shit; children are supposed to go on cherishing their parents forever. Who says? Parents.

Working down through my second G-bottle of beer. A quart is thirty-two ounces. A regular bottle is twelve ounces. So, when I finish this one, I will have had five bottles plus two ounces, plus the four glasses at Franzl's; roughly, the equivalent of nine bottles in five and a half hours. Under two bottles an hour. I guess I can just drink beer forever, or until I die. Just learned last week that one of the guys at *Time* drinks a quart—not a fifth—of the hard stuff every day, and has done so for years. Yet it doesn't really show.

Finished Phil's book, skipping a lot, and crying like a baby. It's all so nakedly sentimental. I think I borrowed money from him yesterday just to see someone I knew; I didn't really need it. I'm now drinking beer, and fingering the hem of a pillowslip—that pacifying hangover from my pneumonia summer. It's absolutely black; I've permanently released it from bed duty for this assignment, which is probably symbolic thumb-sucking. So is beer-drinking, isn't it? This has been an endless though not a lost weekend. I did great gobs of exercise yesterday—you wouldn't believe how much— and more today; read a good book (Phil's) and the Sunday *Times*, finished the crossword puzzle, cleaned the kitchen, watched bits and pieces on TV, made a new friend (though casual), did all the laundry, smoked, slept, dreamed. One of these days I suppose I should put the wolf parka you gave me in cold storage, or sell it. Which makes me think how many loose ends there are in life. And how much we are possessed by our possessions. (Not an original thought. Emerson had it first. "I say I keep a cow," he wrote, "but the cow keeps me." Or words to that effect.) Since I have so few of them now, I am scarcely possessed by mine. The TV and the typewriter belong to the office; most of my silver to Savarin and assorted mid-town Manhattan restaurants from which I've lifted spoons and such from time to time; the Taiwan earthenware to you. Hardly any point in locking my door. I do appreciate having the Beetle, which is an instrument of liberation, but the finance company still owns more of it than I do. If I ever pay it off, and if I ever get rich, I'll give it to Allen. Might just do it anyway.

Dare I go to the head candler in shorts? Monday's a good day to wear them to the office since none of the brass are in. What's the point in consultation anyway? The point, I guess, is to summarize your emotional problems, which have reached a burdensome if not a critical state, before an impartial and qualified auditor who will then determine whether you need psychotherapy. I know I need it—everyone can use it—and can't afford it, so why go? What good did $150 worth of consultation do you? The fact is, I do have something to talk over with a shrink: a plan of action—or, rather, a non-plan. More of this later. You're a clever gal and have probably already guessed. Odd thought: with a beer at hand, and writing to you, I feel at peace, rather the way I feel on the station platform, waiting for the train. I never miss a train, and once I figured out why. If I get there, say, ten minutes before *it* does, that's down time—*my* time. I can relax. I have nothing to do, no one to see, no commitments, no levies on my thoughts, until the train comes. For ten minutes, my whole world's at rest. You know that, too. There's been a lot of such down time in my life lately but of a different sort. I'm not facing things, I'm putting them off. If I take Valium for example, I don't have to confront sleep, which to me is a contest; the decision has been chemically taken out of my hands. This candler, as I told you, comes warmly—affectionately—recommended by a girl I know. She's not interested in *my* problems but in ventilating hers before a sympathetic person. She does most of the talking and I most of the listening. The relation is nevertheless rewarding to me. These days, *any* relation is rewarding. It isn't any concern of yours now, but I should say for the sake of honesty that there's nothing in our relation beyond good feelings. By all her standards I'm ineligible; if I weren't, I don't think she'd come near me. That's put awkwardly, but you can figure it out. Well, she has mentioned me to the shrink more than once, because I figure peripherally in her life now, so he's probably taken a pre-position on me. It's probably wrong, or dumb, but I don't keep my impotence a secret; maybe I'm unconsciously (*sub*consciously?) proud of it. After all, it can't be a secret, can it, in Act III? I don't go around advertising it, but to confide something to one person at *Time* is to let everybody know.

For instance, I presume you knew I had a roommate for two months last winter, which was an unmitigated disaster. Her idea, incidentally, not mine, but for reasons I won't go into, I simply couldn't turn her down. I knew it would be a disaster, and warned her it would be, and it was. The poor girl had an idealized notion of playing house, and of course reality demolished the whole thing. I don't think any two people can live together in one room; besides, as you can testify, I'm not the easiest guy to live with anyway. That was my first and last exercise in do-goodism—and that's not quite honest either. At the time her suggestion came along, I would have grabbed eagerly at the steady company of Frankenstein's monster.

The shrink is going to get a torpid patient tomorrow at 7:30 A.M. Working on my second quart of beer, and will certainly have a few more when I go to Franzl's for chow. I amaze myself sometimes. How do I get away with it—all those cigs, all that beer, and yet all that exercising and industry too? And at my age? Do you feel any better for not smoking? You claim not, but I do hope you stick to it. I would quit, and maybe yet will, but what for? Lately, I've had a few sharp chest pains, nothing I haven't intermittently experienced before. I've wondered idly if it's one of those modest coronary warning signals that no one should ignore. When they occur now—not often, and of very brief duration —I try to apply to them the description that Jim Lebenthal gave to *his* heart attack. It felt, he said, as if some Italian restaurant had planted an *osso buco* in his chest. Well, it's never felt like that to me. Anyway, when one occurs, I'm not really distressed. I think merely, all right, if it's a heart attack it's a heart attack, and if it carries me off, what the hell. You wouldn't necessarily be on easy street, but I'd be. It's a feeling comparable, somehow, to waiting for the train.

God knows what prompted this thought, but do you think you'll ever be remarried? I know I never will. Outside of you, I'm just not interested in women my age, and I'm not presently chasing women of any age. Nor are they chasing me. Franzl's is no pick-up joint—I've never met a woman there— and I wouldn't consider haunting a joint that was. I did meet a thirtyish flack for show-biz accounts, but she turned out to be either scared to death of men or a Lesbian—possibly both. That connection ruptured after three or four meetings. How's *your* love life? You won't think me sincere, but it would be nice if you ran across a man who suited your specifications. I sure as hell didn't, and neither did Ed, your first husband. I would say that, for self-serving reasons, I hope you do meet and marry a Mr. Right, but it just wouldn't be true. I think *I* was Mr. Right, warts and all. Mr. Near-Right. Mr. As-Close-As-You're-Going-To-Get. It's the way I feel about you. Some time, if we remain in communication—correction, if we *restore* communication—tell me what you and that head candler talked about those three times you saw him. I can guess why you went. But I kind of liked the guy, and I'd like to hear what he suggested you do. Maybe you've told me and I've forgotten. I'd like a complete transcript. Remember when it dawned on me why you'd consulted him and I asked you why, and you replied, "It's none of your business"? If you meant that, then it *was* none of my business. Your mind was already made up. That's totalitarian justice.

This phone hasn't rung in three days. I'm not annoyed, just impressed. It's a comment of sorts on my life, like my mailbox here, which never spouts anything but bills. Never, for sure, a line from you. Incidentally—and don't ask me why this sudden new train of thought—I got cleaned out at the office last week. As a try-out senior editor, I got Mike Demarest's office after he left to make a million bucks (or Bunnies?) at *Playboy*. I hang my coat now in a closet outside his office; and though I usually keep my wallet in a pants pocket, on this day it was in my coat, I think because it was too much effort that morning, after drawing it out to show the conductor my commuter ticket, to put it back where it was. Some trains I ride now seat five people—nnn aisle nn—where four feel crowded. Anyway, they got the wallet with about $40 in currency, plus over $2.00 in change from another pocket, plus my keys from another. They also heisted the TV set from my room, but that was recovered on the premises, as was my wallet—credit cards and documents intact but the money gone. Since I hold *Time* responsible for lousy security, I'll gradually recover the $40 on the expense account.

I must go or miss the dinner hour at Franzl's—the chef knocks off at 7:30.

I've been to see the head candler. It develops that I'm in a state of depression—nothing I didn't already know. He wants me to take what is called the full psych battery ($150) and also to see him again. He understands, of course, that I haven't the money to go back into long-term therapy. At my age it's rather pointless anyway; the concrete has set. He's also going to put me on an antidepressant that is reportedly quite successful. I got the feeling that my depression is deeper than I realized, though he didn't quite say so. I can guess the combination that brought it on: the book, which is an oppressive extra assignment, on top of everything else; your leaving with the kids for East Hampton all summer and possibly for Vail in the fall; and trying out as senior editor, which alerts all the old judgmental anxieties. I don't think I'm doing too well either, and I know I don't much like it. You can't imagine the difference between a good writer and a poor one. I've got one good one—only one—working for me.

Another idle weekend, but I don't feel pent since I'm on vacation. My stint as a try-out senior editor is over, probably for good. HAG called me on Friday afternoon to tell me this, but what he had to say was somewhat ambiguous. He said that I'd probably be interested in knowing how I'd done; that I'd done all right; but that on return from vacation I'd go back to writing for the "Behavior" section, and that, for reasons that had nothing to do with me, *Time* was not replacing Mike Demarest. His sections would simply be parceled out among the incumbent senior editors. Apparently the current economy wave, which has already carried off four writers, is breaking over higher ranks as well. Henry did say that I would still fill in, from time to time, but I'm not sure I want to. If they're not going to be handing out any more general's stars, why bother to reach for one?

Had the full psych battery one morning last week—takes about two hours. I was hung over and slightly nervous. The interpretation will be available Thursday, but of course I'll be gone. The series ends with a hundred incomplete sentences—"Men are . . ." "I was most anxious when . . ."—that sort of thing. One is supposed to complete them with the first thought that comes to mind. Towards the end, I ran into this one: "Mothers are . . ." and guess how I finished it? Like this: ". . . not quite women." The shrinks ought to have a field day with that one.

Your mother called the other day—or did I tell you? Very petulant. Simply had to have some more of the money I owe her for financing your round trip to the Mexican divorce mill. Some old couple is driving her up to the Cape. I guess I'll have to send her a check.

The kids are over to sack out on the apartment floor. I've got a dozen ears of the first local corn for dinner tonight. We'll supplement that with fried chicken. Tomorrow morning we'll leave very early for the George Washington Bridge. I have a 7:30 shrink appointment, and after that we're on our way to Wisconsin. Couldn't have left earlier in any case because the campsite doesn't open up until Wednesday for us. If the weather is fine and the bass bite, I might just stretch this time out by a week. I need the change, and it's going to be a busy fall and winter. I've just turned my back on the book. There's a convention of sociologists the last of August that I'll make *Time* send me to (it's in Washington) and I'll get started again after that.

It's going to be a tight squeeze in the VW, even more so after we reach Appleton and pick up all the camping gear; from there it's eighty miles north to Ephraim. I sure haven't prepared much for this trip. Just assuming, for instance, that I can find the Jersey Turnpike from the George Washington Bridge—and for that matter, that I can find the bridge after the head-candling session. Once on the Jersey Turnpike, though, it should be no problem; just one turnpike after another all the way to Chicago. I had to clean the apartment for the children; astonishing what a mess I let it get into. But cleaning up is really easy, there's so little space—and so little furniture—in the room.

We're back, the four of us, and sitting around my apartment like utter strangers. I'm tanking up on beer, Allen is dining on his fingernails, and Joe is taking a tub rather than a shower because, he says, he's too tired to stand up. There's been a great to-do about getting back to East Hampton that has soured the evening, which is being consumed by hostile silence. Another bit of evidence that the generations simply don't mix. I can sense the distance; all that my sons want is to get out of here; the social obligations involved in being with their father, now that the fireworks have been bought and the Wisconsin excursion has ended, make them very uneasy. They have nothing to say.

The first day without them, after all that togetherness, was miserable. Solitude my sole companion and all that. I didn't even feel up to going to Franzl's, so bought a fifth of gin and some vermouth—the first hard liquor I've ever had in the apartment—mixed and drank three stiff ones, ate two pieces of leftover Finger Lickin' chicken, hit the sack at nine, slept the clock around and woke up feeling healthy for the first time in God knows how many weeks.

You'll get an account of the trip from the kids. I think they had a good time, but they're not overly communicative so it's not easy to tell. We took our time coming back; left Ephraim Friday about noon and made White Plains Wednesday at five in the afternoon, with stops in Appleton (I spent an hour with mother), Waupaca, Winnetka, Toledo (the same Holiday Inn as two years ago) and Winchester, Virginia.

When I look back now, the vacation takes on a rosier glow than it had; in retrospect, it seems more fun than it was. It really wasn't much fun. Maybe the kids will tell you otherwise; they kept busy enough, and the fishing wasn't all that bad, and the weather was mostly fine, often too hot, but the holiday never really came to a head. To cap it all for me, I began to feel old for the first time. Another illusion smashed. Camping out was a dirty bore; I had the only air mattress, but couldn't sleep anyway. Our borrowed sleeping bags were too efficient, you had a choice of being too hot inside them or too cold outside them. The tent was pitched in the open so that, about six each morning, the rising sun turned it into an oven. No matter when we went to bed—usually quite late— I always waked at six. One night we all went to a trout boil in Egg Harbor—potatoes and big lake trout sectioned and boiled in huge cast-iron cauldrons, cole slaw, rolls and Door County cherry pie, $3.50 per capita—but I don't like lake trout that much, and boiling accentuates its fishiness. Door County is not as unspoiled as it's billed. There are isolated spots, like Whitefish Bay, a beautiful sandy Lake Michigan beach twenty minutes south of Ephraim, but the water is numbing, just like the Atlantic off Maine, and I'm not much for just sunning. The public beach at Ephraim—for that matter, at all the little resort towns—is a miniature Coney Island at midday; it's where everybody goes. The car is still full of its sand. In fact, I've got a carful of mementos, each of which makes me a little sad: the jar of Spanish peanuts, now spilled; Crackerjack prizes; road maps for all the states we passed through; the receipt for the motor hotel room in Winchester, Virginia, that had an indoor swimming pool scarcely bigger than a puddle; gum cuds in the ash tray; empty paper bags. Kind of hate to clean it out. This will probably be the last vacation I'll ever take with the children. They think they're grown up, you know, and they are; they've outgrown the stage where they can show affection, or even need, for parents. Still, they're children too. As last time, the detour to Virginia for fireworks was the high point of the trip, and this time I let them shop. Coming and going, we hit every single establishment. The journey itself, for me, the route, was such a faithful replica of the one we all took two years ago that I found myself looking for our tire marks on the turnpikes. I kept bumping into us, in what I now look back upon as a happier time, even though I realize that the marriage was over by then, as dead as my job. It's true what they say: we remember the good things, the bad things fade. If you had any handles on you, I'd probably grab one. The alternative, the only alternative I can think of, probably won't work out the way I expect it to. It seems a shame, in some respects, to let a nineteen-year investment go just like that. I think that was what I meant when I asked you many many months ago why you were so willing to give up without a fight. You had no answer to that—from which I can only infer that you saw nothing worth fighting for. Ah well, the results of my full psych battery are in the head candler's hands by now and I'll find out when I see him next week just how sane or dotty I am. I don't expect to get my money's worth out of this last venture into psychotherapy. I can almost guess what the tests will reveal. Nothing I don't already know, or suspect. Nothing terribly bad.

During these three off-duty weeks, I've been astonished to discover what a dreary product *Time* is. I bought and consumed each issue; not cover to cover, but selectively. It's really quite dull. Very self-conscious, very look-at-me-doing-what-I'm-doing. The thought of going back Monday curdles my milk.

I am having a noodles and chicken TV dinner. The noodles are listed first, by law, because there are more noodles than there is chicken. The prospect of eating this crap doesn't entice me, but no matter; for some curious reason I shot up to 182 pounds on the vacation, maybe because I didn't exercise, and can afford to lose some. Prices are not low in Wisconsin, except for beer, which by the twenty-four-bottle case can be had for as little as $2.50; that's only a dime more than a six-pack costs in New York. In resort areas, they've got to make it in a hurry, and Door County has a very short season; really only two months. So up goes everything. You wouldn't believe what they get for chicken: 59 cents or more a pound.

Your phone call came this afternoon. I didn't really expect you to return the call last night, but just in case you did, I put the phone out of order—a trick I learned from Steve Kanfer, our cinema critic. You dial zero, stick a pencil or something into the hole to keep it there and then take the phone out of its cradle. I'm not surprised about your mother. It's fortunate she has enough money to indulge her final years. The nicest thing she would do for everyone involved in her life, herself included, would be to die, the sooner the better. The same holds true of *my* mother, who has taken a slightly different course. But the parallels between these two self-centered, idle old women are striking. Both of them possessed of that curious old-woman charisma that makes the casual wayfarer in their lives admire the shit out of them. I've concluded that they play to this particular gallery; certainly not to their husbands and their children. You'll no doubt weep buckets when your mother finally turns up her toes. It's the drill. But my mother's death is not likely to weigh heavily on me, except in terms of the residual guilt in which, all unconsciously, she immersed her offspring practically from birth. I don't really want to go to her funeral, since her death will cancel my last obligation to her. I would attend it purely for the sake of form, for those chronological peers of hers in Appleton who will muster for the occasion to gloat and count the house. "Aha! Son John is absent. That dirty unfilial shit."

And that poor, marvelous, dead old woman who deserved more from her children, including enough Child's mayonnaise to float in, than she ever got. My absence, in fact, would gratify so many aged mourners that it could be considered an act of grace not to disappoint them by appearing.

I was going to stop smoking this vacation, and didn't, and admire you inordinately for having laid off since last February. You *must* feel better; in any event, nobler. I wonder whether I really want to stop. Often enough, in jest, I've said that I don't stop because if I did, I'd live longer. Old age needn't be a liability, but the examples of it ready to hand—your mother, my mother, for instance—don't encourage emulation. I'm not bold or smart enough to define happiness, but this much I know: whatever it is, it *isn't* what our mothers are. They're both miserable. I could throw up whenever a total stranger, like the woman behind the desk at Appleton Memorial Hospital, gratuitously observes what a wonderful old lady I'm trying to check out of one institution into another. On what in hell does she base this judgment? I'm sorely tempted to inquire, but of course you can't get a straight answer. Or else you'd get a wounded look; how sharper than a serpent's tooth it is to have a thankless child.

Off to Franzl's for beer, on top of three healthy martinis. You think I'm a lush, but how wrong you are.

A short entry. Amy Machriston has left Herb and the girls for what Herb calls "a second-rate shithead." They've known each other for years. I heard about it from Herb just today, when I drove into New York for want of anything else to do and looked in on him in the Seagram Building. He's quite upset but under control; from what he told me, I doubt that he'll get her back. She seems to have turned resolutely away from everything that was, almost as if she'd deliberately erased the past. Her paramour, whom she'll probably marry, is in his mid-forties and has never married. I sympathize with Herb; it's quite a jolt; you can see it in his eyes. At the same time I find consolation in it too. There must be a virus that breaks up marriages. At least he has the children, and of course he's obliged to and will pay her nothing, so that he's in good financial condition, at his income, to rustle up another spouse. My own treasury has deteriorated, what with the Wisconsin journey, which cost more than I reckoned it would, and dismal news from *Time*'s profit sharing. Our investors, on a falling market, did rather poorly; my stake in it has dropped from $43,000 last year to $34,000 presently—a loss of $9,000 or nearly 25 percent.

I dread going back Monday. Lots of missing faces, and some silly new economy measures. One must now requisition copy paper, and I would guess that pencil-stealing is out. In the mail was an invitation from Irv Horowitz to lecture in a course of his in communications at Rutgers. The assignment frightens me, but I guess I'll have to do it. It comes on an awkward day—Thursday—and carries no honorarium, just travel expenses, which I'm sure *Time* would pay anyway. Somebody copped my typewriter while I was gone; left me an old junker that doesn't work. I'd like to get my own back; I'm used to it and its action.

Back to popping Valium. I took none along on the fishing trip and regretted it. Once there, never slept a single night through, and fell far behind on my sleep quota, or have I already told you that? Tonight for my solitary dinner I got fresh corn and tomatoes from the Meadows Farm and a small steak from Gristede's to tease a jaded appetite. Worked, too. Ate with zest, after the teeniest of martinis to set the juices flowing. Tomorrow night I'll try Franzl's beer as a soporific; ate lunch there yesterday (a sandwich washed down with

Michelob) and went back after dinner for more brew. Doesn't seem to hurt me, not even my kidneys.

I really miss the kids. Their company for two and a half weeks was like a new lease on life. The depression took a complete holiday, but recurred the moment I deposited them with their respective friends. They were effusively grateful on departure, but I think it was mostly an act. Urge them not to sell their fireworks. It'll be a long time before they get any more.

Since my vacation tan has faded, I drove over to Gretchen's today to recover it, but the sun failed me. My apartment house has a roof that could do duty as a solarium except that it's graveled and I have nothing, like a beach chair, to lie on. I met the house fag in swim trunks in the elevator. He was off, he said, for a swimming pool four miles out of town that is open to all Westchester residents. I should try to find it.

Gretch and I had a nice talk, and she fed me a beef sandwich and beer for lunch. As she no doubt has told you, she's thinking of blowing the Westchester scene for Malta, to write books and run a modest *pensione*. I endorsed the idea and told her of mine, which is not too dissimilar. You may have got an inkling from the kids; I don't believe in secrets any more, and have always been something of a blabbermouth. Andy was there, looking more like Linda in his long hair. He has possibly the noisiest bike around. Gretchen makes $10,-000 a year reporting for the *Patent Trader* and casing books for the *Reader's Digest*. Think how well *you'd* do, Ann, if you were really interested in making money. You'd be nearly as well off if I were to die in harness—not just now, but, say, after we've broken Uncle George's trust. The real estate market is depressed right now I'm told, but you'd be better off anyway to rent the house for a while, at least until the market recovers. I should think you could get $500 a month for it furnished, more likely $600—which, with $125 or $150 coming in from the rental unit, makes $9,000 a year gross. Not all profit of course, but meantime you're paying only 5½ percent on the mortgage (mortgages are up to 7 percent or better now) and increasing your equity all the while. Gretchen says she could get $49,500 for her house right now, and thinks that's too low. Yours, with pool and a minimal face lifting, should bring $100,000 on a normal market. *If* Wall Street recovers its poise. *If* Nixon isn't reelected.

Back on my exercise regime and feeling the better for it. Did 1,500 runnings in place and 200 sit-ups today.

I think it's the solitariness that gets me down the most. Man isn't designed to live alone. Gretchen made an observation this morning that I can affirm: solitude feeds on itself. Those weren't her words but convey her meaning. When there's nothing to do and nowhere to go, you find yourself not going anywhere and not doing anything. You don't feel like doing anything. I could work on the book, wash the car, clean the oven, scare up some company, go calling, read. Instead, I sit around with the TV on writing this endless letter, playing with Westchester County's filthiest pillow slip and, as now, sipping a martini (another tiny one—I haven't much gin left). It's ten minutes to six. I killed my appetite for dinner by polishing off the rest of the tomatoes and corn so I'll probably snack at Franzl's when and if I get there. It's become a beautiful warm day again but it might as well be raining for all the good I'm getting out of it.

I have thought about returning to you, assuming that I could, but I don't think it would work out on either side. You're not the forgiving kind, and I'm not penitent anyway. I'm reasonably confident that you don't want me back, just as I'm reasonably confident now that you didn't want me in the first place. Seldom has anyone put up more resistance to marriage than you, right up to the altar and beyond. I can guess how you interpret that resistance now—as rational. Somehow you knew or sensed the marriage wouldn't be compatible. My sharpest memory of our wedding day is not a sweet one. That may have been the beginning of the end, though it was some time coming. At the intellectual level I blame you for nothing. After all, I did marry you. I got into something I obviously wanted to get into. I qualified then, and perhaps still do qualify, as one of those guys who will suffer a string tied around his big toe, who really believes it when a girl says that a bed invitation, like the one extended to me one Christmas before we were married, is just that and no more. At the heart, or feeling, level, I don't deny some resentment; I'm sure you nurse a good deal of it for me. With just such a little extra effort, on both sides, it would have worked. It kind of worked anyway. Maybe it's just because the memory retains pleasure and rejects pain, but I look back with considerable fondness over all those years we had together, and, in many ways, feel married to you still. Even though I am the shithead of record, I can't make the first move toward a reconciliation; it has to come from you, and I know it never will. I'm not looking for a successor, because I have other things in mind, and hesitate to do so since I'm not in a position to guarantee consortium to any woman, but I keep thinking I should at least get back into circulation. Early last spring Wendy Fernbach called me at the office, said the right things about the divorce, and then in effect indicated that I was an eligible unattached man whom she would like to invite to her do's. At the time, I had the roommate I told you about earlier. When I said as much to Wendy, her interest declined at once and she suggested I get back in touch when that temporary arrangement was over. Which, of course, I could scarcely do. That roomie, by the way, is back where she came from, pursuing the scholastic life. She's a lovely girl but a thorough emotional jumble—like me in some ways: common, garden-variety sex problems. Of course, I'm a fine one to talk. I was still writing *Time* book reviews under Bobby Baker the last time I balled with a woman (a way of putting it that you will doubtless find offensive). Maybe we can get together some time to discuss our separate excursions into infidelity. I cheated on you, as the custodians of conventional morality so disapprovingly put it, more than you realized, but I never considered it cheating really. The equipment doesn't deteriorate with use, affairs have nothing at all to do with marriage, and what you don't know can't hurt you. In any event, those days are over for me, at least until and unless some wise counselor picks the lock. Solitary experiment—no need for detail—indicates either that my resistance is terrific or else that I am old before my time. As I've said, this doesn't in the least deter me from getting into bed situations. But it sure as hell deters the woman. I understand some of the psycho-dynamics of it. Holding out is hostility, isn't it? I'm depriving the woman at the same time that I'm depriving myself. I'm sure I unconsciously deliberately held out on you—just as you unconsciously deliberately held out on me. But you're simply incapable of accepting the latter half of that equation. You still feel that a wife is well within her rights, during the early stages of marriage, to cry and accuse and carry on like a banshee whenever, in intercourse, the man reaches a climax first. The rationale being that he's doing it to her deliberately, frustrating her sexually out of pure malice. Just as you used to say that I wielded my insomnia like a weapon to interrupt your sleep. These positions, needless to say, were the ones I resented, with some justice I think. It's true that we stack the deck in our favor but I feel, nonetheless, that the marriage and I never really had a fair chance. You had a point to demonstrate, and you demonstrated it. Towards the end, I doubt that you would have noticed the total and absolute absence of Grosser. His dereliction, in fact, helped confirm your point.

I'm reaching the bottom of the gin bottle and will not, on any future occasion, re-stock another one. As a matter of fact, I don't think I'd drink one half or one tenth as much if: (1) alcohol didn't put an insomniac to sleep, and (2) my life were in balance. Contrary to your impression, I am amiable in my cups; the reason you feel otherwise is that *you* have the drinking problem, not me. I didn't grow up with parents who consistently overindulged in ways that threatened the security of little girls; I didn't learn to take a punitive attitude towards drink. My associations are as positive as yours have been conditioned to be negative. Drink relaxes me, relieves tension, bathes bleak landscapes in a rosy glow and puts me to sleep. If it came in pills and were not cumulative in effect, the likelihood is that a doctor would prescribe it and you would accept it. Or maybe you wouldn't. When I was on Seconal, I remember, you responded to the pre-bedtime stupor that barbiturate sometimes produced in about the same way as you did to the effect of three martinis. Someday, perhaps, someone will finally convince you that I'm much too disciplined a person to be an alcoholic. I am, you know. But the time has come and gone when such wisdom, belatedly striking your mind, can do you and me any good. How we do deceive ourselves to make things seem the way we think they should be, rather than the way they are.

The situation at *Time* is very unsettled. I'm back in my old office, with a substitute researcher who knows nothing about the "Behavior" section and is not in the least interested in being of service. The story list left by my predecessor is weak; none of the stories worth a line in *Time*. What's more, no queries have been sent out to our correspondents in the appropriate bureaus. I begin from a dead start with stories that need a week to ripen. Nor is anyone around to clue me in. The senior editor (Bob Shnayerson) worked Saturday on a cover for the "Education" section and so didn't come in today. Last week's "Behavior" writer is assigned to "World" this week and so he wasn't in either. "World" writers work a Tuesday-to-Saturday week. I needn't have come in myself, but it was better than rattling around the apartment. I had all day a sense of uneasiness and detachment, as if *Time* and the job don't matter any more, if they ever did. I could have begun familiarizing myself with the list, but didn't, except in a perfunctory way. But the day wasn't a total loss. I filched a knife left behind from Saturday's catered dinner, a stack of paper hot-drink cups and some disposable plates. I've probably got more tableware than you have if you don't count your *repoussé* silver; but none of it matches. I've popped Valium again, so I'll sleep. One night Valium, the next, beer. Broke the pattern on the vacation, but not the need. I don't want to lie awake for hours in apartment 2-A contemplating the lunar landscapes of my life. Watched the movie *The Train* on Channel 4 which I've now seen for the third time; Burt Lancaster managed to get through the whole thing without changing expression. I realized for the first time the German colonel was Paul Scofield. I don't need another Valium, but will probably take one as insurance. Saw Phil and Loudon Wainwright, but neither had much to say. Phil is being *Life*'s managing editor this month, an unforgivable demand to make of a heart-attack victim. The dear fool—and I mean Phil—ought to know better.

It has occurred to me that I really love my children. But they're grown-ups now and don't much want to chum around with the old man. Understandable enough. All the same I miss them. Maybe I try too hard to woo them. Maybe I consult their desires too deferentially. Maybe I should just decide to do things and then do them without a preliminary discussion.

My limited collection of friends are off on vacation, so lunch prospects are on the meager side. I lack even the ambition to make my lunch: I'm getting like mother, who hasn't done much of anything purposeful since Dad died. Notice I don't capitalize mother any more. I did it for years automatically, without thinking, as if she were a category all to herself.

Saw the candler this week and see him next. The psych battery interpretation was in and we spent the hour going over it together, each with a copy in his hand; I asked to keep mine, and did. I didn't find it too illuminating. It's very jargony, with many painfully obvious deductions, some wrong, some confused, some confusing. For instance, it states that I have "homoerotic impulses"—whatever they are. The candler assures me it's not related to homosexuality, and I must say I agree. Also, I apparently confuse sex with aggression; this may bear on my root problem (pun intended), but the candler didn't really explain. In fact, he explained very little—there goes $150 down the drain. I'm seeing the candler again, but I think it'll be for the last time.

I'm to senior edit again. HAG didn't even have the grace to inform me; I heard it first from the rumor factory and then, a little annoyed, checked it out with him personally. He said something silly about the editing experience being good for a writer, but I know, and I think he knows that I know, that my only function is to plug a hole left by an absent senior editor, in this case Shnayerson. So I told him that while I was willing to do the company an occasional favor by filling in, I was also of an age to consider the primacy of my own interests; that it was, after all, more work and more responsibility and that I preferred writing anyway. He agreed to the validity of my point, but it was left there, inconclusively. As I've said, I would like the title, which has some meaning in the trade, but I'm not at all excited about doing the work without it.

While I was gone, Rollo May sent me a belated thank-you note for my story on him, but it never reached me (though it did get to the Letters Department and make the Letters Report). It was addressed to Mr. George Coffin and dictated to his secretary, who typed it for his signature, presumably following standing orders: "Rollo May, Ph.D." I suppose I'll have to reply—but how, without embarrassing him for getting my name wrong? And should I sign it "John Koffend, B.A."?

Phil called Tuesday afternoon and asked me over to his mother's uptown apartment, where he and Kathy stayed the week, for cocktails, and then to dinner on the town. I think he feels sorry for me. Present: the Wainwrights, Shana Alexander and some British free lance whose name escapes me, and Mary Leatherbee. We ate at The Sign of the Dove, whose cuisine has greatly improved. No one offered to divide the check, certainly not I. It must have cost Phil easily $100-$150. We had a lot of drinks at the apartment and at dinner too. I got a little bombed—but so did nearly everyone else —and lapsed into my forensic mood. One subject, on which no one agreed: mothers are not necessarily lovable. His book has not been widely reviewed (the *Times* has so far ignored it) and has not sold out its first printing of 25,000. I doubt now that it will, and I'm ashamed (not really) to say that that perversely pleases me. Maybe I really am a son of a bitch.

Bought Caldor's cheapest beach chair today ($6.99) so that I can sauté myself on the roof. It has everything Jones

Beach offers except sand, water, hot dogs, orange peel, life-guards, and crowds. As far as I know I'm the only tenant who exploits this natural sun deck. Good day for sunning, too: ninety-three degrees. I'll go up again tomorrow. Also, just for the hell of it, made up a bowl of your potato salad. I meant to produce only a modest amount, but in the end there was almost enough for a church picnic. Well, it's a one-course meal: potatoes, apples, radishes, cucumber, celery, eggs, little onions and mayonnaise. Perhaps I've told you that I don't eat by the clock on weekends. Today I had instant breakfast at eleven, a can of salmon at four and ham and eggs at 6:30, plus a huge piece of chocolate cream pie.

Jocelyn called me at the office this week—Jocelyn Bannon. I think I know why. She said that after dropping out of my life like a stone she felt guilty about it and got into psycho-therapy for a while. I told her she'd done nothing to me, that I had my eyes open and that I'm over twenty-one—and I think that's why she called: to hear me relieve the last little shred of her guilt. Hearing from her didn't affect me one way or the other—but why would you care about that?

I did take more sun Sunday and have turned Cherokee brown. It occurs to me that male and female tan-seekers do so from almost opposite motives: the men to look more masculine, the women to look more feminine. No, that can't be right. Anyway, I do look healthy. Franzl's as usual Sunday night, though my capacity for Michelob seems to be declining; I can no longer drink anywhere near fourteen seidels (I've had more than that on occasion) and no longer try. Maybe ten last night, at two sittings separated by dinner in the apartment: potato salad, ham and chocolate cream pie—the same again tonight.

I've no ambition these days and the head candler says

that's a symptom of depression. I need some new connections, a sea change, a radical shift of direction—in short, a new life. The old one wasn't so unsatisfactory, come to think of it, but I'm sure we can both agree that it had lost much of its point. I wish there were some way of determining, beyond the shadow of doubt, what ingredient (or ingredients) was missing from our mix. It seems a pity to have come so close, to have lived together so long, without ever being able to know whether the marriage was faulty to begin with, whether it ever really had a chance. You remember how I've talked at times about the things in life that can't be won by striving? Like sleep, and being yourself; to try is to condemn yourself to failure. Maybe marriage is one of those things. What good would it have done our marriage if both of us, or either, had tried a little harder? And tried a little harder to do what? For instance what good would it have done me —or you—if I'd tried harder in bed? As Masters and Johnson say many times over, (and I'm sure I'm repeating myself, but then the psych battery tags me as obsessive-compulsive) there's no way in the world a man can will an erection—and no way in the world, if his head doesn't interfere, that he can prevent one.

I'm going to have Burt Stark look at my mouth—nothing detectably wrong though I have one back tooth that's been temperature-sensitive for a year, don't dare chew on that side. . . . I also have to get my glasses changed. It's been four years, I think, and the fine print is finer than ever, even with corrected vision. If I lost my glasses now, I couldn't work until they were replaced. All this by way of preparation, and just in case I do have something in mind—an un-plan, you could call it—but I don't suppose I'll ever do it. Everything's attributable to the effects of solitariness, the traumatic rupture and the middle reaches of middle age. I haven't learned yet not to resent it, and so to resist it. Have you? The woman I may have mentioned, Barbara Smith, a very pretty Slavic girl of forty who models in the garment district, confides everything and anything to me. I don't particularly enjoy being pigeonholed as the old, sexless male friend, however affectionately regarded. The only other woman my age that I could conceivably be interested in is you, and that's because I know you, loved you, and love you still. Or I think I still do. How in the hell does one know? What do people mean when they say they love you? And why do they have to say it at all? Perhaps the definition of love relates to the definition of alcoholism, though it's not a perfect analogy: someone you love is someone you can't do without. But the same applies to the doctor and the cobbler, and besides, there's really no one you can't do without if you're forced to. People say they love, but they can never explain why, either to themselves or the other. But granted all those difficulties, whom do *you* love? Could you list them? No doubt you can extend the list. And mine? In no order: the kids, you, Frank, my sisters Mary and Jean, all the Kunhardts, my old man dead twelve years (didn't realize it till after he died), Jocelyn Bannon (really quite a gal), Barbara Smith, Martha and Loudon Wainwright I guess, assorted people on *Time* of whom HAG is emphatically not one—and, I might add, inappropriately, Valium (because it puts me to sleep) and beer (because ditto, and because it also knits up the raveled sleave of care, to originate a phrase). Conspicuously absent from both lists: mother. Maybe Franzl belongs on my list, but that would confuse love with gratitude for his having admitted me to a society for which I don't really qualify. I make an effort to fit in at Franzl's and the effort must show. These people are just as intelligent as I am, but in different ways.

They tolerate me, accept me most of the time, and may even like me; they also know I'm not one of them. Last night I brought Franzl what may have been a love offering: a jar of my potato salad. He wasn't there—sleeping off too much beer at the Bavarian Club's annual picnic under a torrid sun—and his cook, spiritedly defending his own territory, told me Franzl despised mayonnaise in potato salad and I'd be wise to pack it straightaway home. But I demanded he put it in the refrigerator, and later, when Franzl came back, he took a bite or two and pronounced it "good"—as one tells his hostess that he's had a marvelous time when the truth is somewhat short of that. We do say to people what we think they want to hear. It's part of the small-group behavior that Erving Goffman has explored so resourcefully and with such great discernment in his books. I made potato salad. I offered some to Franzl. End of social transaction. I shouldn't need his approval; that's another transaction, linked to the first but separate. I write a story for *Time* that satisfies me. End of *that* transaction. If *Time* criticizes or rejects the performance, that, too, is another transaction. I screw you, and find pleasure in it. End of transaction, or nearly. Your pleasure in being screwed is your lookout, or nearly, and not mine. Of course it's never as simple as that, but we (I don't necessarily mean you and me) tend to confuse roles, motivations, objectives and rewards so thoroughly as to interfere with, or greatly complicate, what is fundamentally almost as simple a transaction as I've described. I don't pretend to be an authority on any of this, and don't want to be either, but I'm not sure we stupid humans ever do anything right. We're gifted spoilers. Now I know what I'm doing here—what the psychologist said I do: intellectualizing as a defense in what he calls "sexual areas." If you talk about it, you can talk it away.

I'm in La Grillade waiting impatiently for my dinner companion, Fred Golden, and you're in the city and I wish I were with you. Stayed up late and got up early to meet the candler at 7:30. Then a dreadful day editing—not over yet. One more story to masticate tonight and another tomorrow. I hate it. Almost totally unmotivated; it must be advancing age. I either want a comfortable familiar rut or a real quantum change. *You,* incidentally, were not under attack last night over the table at the Plaza. *I* was. You're so G.D. positive, though, about everything. I need you nakedly, and you don't really need anybody. I'm absolutely famished for human connection, and for surcease.

There it ends. Fred arrived, as did the "Books" section secretary, Arlyn Minor (you don't know her) who has been let go, and later somebody else joined us, forget who. And somehow I got stuck for $18 of the bill. Not all of it mine, though I did have four martinis; in fact, you might say I got through the week on booze; Friday night too. But nothing today, and nothing tomorrow either. Screw Franzl's, I'm sick of going there. No mail all week.

Sorry I missed your good-bye call—or did I say that? It must have been because you won't be seeing me again. Now you know about Pago Pago. I can't keep secrets. There's better than a fifty-fifty chance that I'll go there.

Page missing here, somewhere. To hell with it. I have the will for only a few lines. Nice of you to call and say good-bye; sorry I missed it. It hasn't been easy, life without you. All I said that night was true. We may get together again in heaven or hell, but I guess not in this world. I'm finishing a beer, then to bed. Thank God this week is done. I lack the energy to brush my teeth. The apartment is a slum and my lungs are a ghetto. Anything is better than this—anything.

Anything. Anything anything anything anything. Pago Pago, here I come.

The head candler and I are quits, at his suggestion. Except in extremis, I won't see him again. Prognosis, summarized: I am in a deep depression, due mostly to a need for warm and reciprocal human contacts; I have probably been a depressive all my adult life for reasons that go way back and that he hasn't had time to trace. Depression stubbornly resists ordinary tête-à-tête psychotherapy, and so he agrees with me that prolonged treatment of that sort will probably do me no good. Psychic impotence is also quite intractable, and about all I can hope for is to find a woman I like of surpassing patience, compassion and understanding. Fat chance. He has me on a regime of what he calls pharmacotherapy (he tends to talk like a textbook), which means three kinds of pills. One is an antidepressant that has chalked up a good cure or relief record. He says that I have four chances in five of responding to this drug, in which case I will definitely notice the change: no sense of depression, a more cheerful outlook on life, and even possibly an increase in libido (depressives are depressed all over, down there too). Then a new sleeping pill—name forgotten—which produces no hangover and is noncumulative; if two capsules (my dose) put you to sleep, you will never have to take more, as is the case with the barbiturates and Valium. And, finally, some hormone pill, Android, calculated, I presume, to help generate and sustain an erection on suitable occasions. I am most interested in the efficacy of the antidepressant; this bout of depression has knocked me for a loop, though for unfathomable reasons I can perform as effectively as ever on the job. It's when I'm alone that hopelessness stares rudely at me.

I caught a minor note of hostility from the candler the last two sessions. It could have been projection on my part. I can detect hostility when none is there. For instance, toward the end of our last session, when he was going over what I was to do (report periodically on the effects of the drugs, seek another appointment if I urgently needed to see him), he said, "I don't want any more money from you." His way of responding, I guess, to my repeated observation that I just couldn't afford to go on seeing him, and of saying that the weekly appointments had come to an end. It struck me later as hostile. There are gentler ways of putting it. In fact, did it have to be said at all? He also asked to see you, to hear your side of things, just as your guy, you'll remember, asked to see me. I told him that I didn't think you'd come. Was I right? I don't think you're interested in a reconciliation. If you are, you've given no sign of it. I have ambivalent feelings about it, which I may tell you about sometime. It's something that shouldn't be said until I'm dead sure that a reconciliation is totally out of the question.

Speaking of hostility, I fielded a naked piece of it one day this week—and, strangely enough, didn't recognize it until hours afterward. A girl I've known for years—it doesn't matter who—but never screwed, invited me to her apartment for dinner. It's way uptown. I've had such invitations from her before, but only since being plagued with psychic impotence. The invitation implies a bed situation, and I have been in bed with her, though not often, and never with any success. She knows of my problem. She's also married, but it's a funny kind of marriage; no children, her husband is far older than she, and they've both spent years in therapy, he at her insistence. I don't think she loves him. She's a rather wary and withdrawn woman, not a mixer, has formed few alliances, of which I'm one, possibly because we've never demanded anything of each other. Anyway, I went to dinner (her husband was out of town, naturally), not really intending to spend the night (no razor in my briefcase, no change of clothes). But after a couple of Chivas Regals I changed my mind. As I say, the invitation was already there. We stayed up quite late and then I took her husband's place in bed. I was anything but tight, but I could feel the scotches, which tend to disarm my anxieties. There was the usual foreplay, which got her ready. She was rather passive—or rather, ungiving; I did all of the touching. Grosser stayed completely aloof from the proceedings, that dirty uncooperative son of a bitch. I hadn't really expected anything else from him, so I wasn't particularly upset—not consciously anyway. After a while, we separated and composed ourselves for sleep. Soon I felt her leaving the bed. "What's the matter?" I said. "Where are you going?" She said, "I'm going into the living room to masturbate." In short, savage hostility. I simply didn't recognize it then because it was so uncharacteristic of her. She didn't go into the living room; we talked a bit, and it came out that, like me, she was in a depressed state, but for different reasons. She had a good cry, which is also not like her, and then we tried to sleep. But I was thrashing so much that she left the bed again and curled up on the couch. I guess insomniacs and kinetic sleepers should be limited by law to single beds.

The ferocity of her statement didn't occur to me until the following morning, at work. I told the candler about it and he agreed. That episode, plus leaving him, plus his rather pessimistic though realistic assessment of my psyche, all combined to plunge me more deeply than ever into melancholy. There were other factors. A thought hit me during the last session and I shared it with the shrink. Wasn't my dream of copping out to Pago Pago a form of suicide? Yes, he said; I was drawing down the curtain on everything that had gone before.

I'm off for a week in Washington and a national assembly of sociologists. *Time*'s paying, naturally, but my true objective is to reenergize myself for the book Steve and I are obligated to write. I may not do it anyway; never have I been less interested in doing anything.

Back from a three-martini lunch with Grace Parkinson that has radically altered my attitude towards her, this unattached and somewhat formidable woman who has been a platonic friend on and off for years. The alcohol, which I didn't particularly want or need, dissolved all inhibitions. And once more I was confirmed in my conviction—perhaps prayer would be more appropriate—that the whole and maybe only point in life is to go on talking, to keep the conversation going, that as long as you do that it doesn't matter what you say. Over the years I have stereotyped Grace as one of those jib-nosed, stern career women who draw a circle around themselves and dare anyone to step across. She had a livelier sense of what she wouldn't do than of what she would—for her ad agency or for men. I couldn't have been more wrong. The lunch was all shared confidences; and it turns out that she is as sexually accessible, and eager, as ladies half her years and twice her topography. In short, we're all the same. If we recognize differences, they're of our own manufacture. To discover this facet in Grace was tantamount to accepting the fact emotionally that human equations form at every conceivable level, that just because you aren't attracted to someone doesn't mean at all that they're not attractive. All of which is not very profound, but Jesus Christ, what a lot I have to learn. And the older I get, the more I have to learn. If, before today's lunch, someone had said to me that Grace Parkinson was sleeping all over Manhattan, I would have laughed derisively in disbelief. It turns out to be true. She met a man on Sunday, went to bed with him on Wednesday (no dice, though, he's got problems) and is seeing him again Saturday. While I sit up in White Plains on weekends and launder myself in self-pity, Grace is up and about looking for phalluses attached to eligible, or at least congenial, males. Thus do we learn. And how do we learn? By talking, by sustaining the dialogue.

I'm on an American Airlines flight and waiting for takeoff to Washington for four or five days of an American Sociological Association convention that will be very useful to the book Steve and I are pledged to write—should I ever write it— and secondarily useful to the magazine. They've got more than their money's worth out of me. I've ordered two martinis because Washington, unless memory fails me, is dry on Sunday—and so is my mouth—a rather annoying side effect of the antidepressant pills (Tofranil). One associates a dry mouth with terror and anxiety: the speaker unable to speak, the lover suddenly informed there's someone else. I can't detect any significant changes in the right direction, though last night, for the first time in God knows how long, I fell asleep naturally, without the sedatives that medicine and Franzl dispense. Popped right off at ten and slept through to 8:30, even though I'd had plenty of sleep the night before. Perhaps Tofranil was responsible, except that the long undrugged sleep didn't refresh me. I could sack out again right now, at 3:30 in the afternoon.

Steve will be in Washington on the cuff. I'll sneak him onto the expense account whenever possible and will put him up if necessary at the Sheraton Park, where I'm staying.

I'm at the Park Sheraton or the Sheraton Park—with people in lapel name tags darting all over the place, connected to each other, a comfortable ambiance. I know no one, and feel very much the outsider. I daresay you've never had the feeling, you with your outgoingness and self-sufficiency. I keep thinking, there must be another lonely stranger here, preferably of the opposite gender, who is as eager as I am to relate. But it's like one bullet trying to find another in the dark. I did run into Irv Horowitz from Rutgers, whom I know. He was friendly, but this is his crowd, not mine. In this context, I began to wonder how I would do in a scene like Pago Pago, where I would have no connections at all. If I can't make them here in civilization, with connections in the phone book, what am I going to do in the capital of American Samoa, 8,ooo miles from here?

This hotel has a pool—quite a nice one. I didn't bring a suit, but I think I'll buy one tomorrow, on *Time,* and spend these next four days goofing off. After all, I'm a lame duck; my days on *Time* are numbered. The "Behavior" section is conveniently pre-killed next week. Everything going on at this symposium is canned so I don't really have to do anything. You may be unable to understand how my attitude has changed. I just don't care any more. The candler has reduced me to a chemical formula: so many antidepressants, so many Android pills for Grosser's recalcitrance, so many capsules for sleep. One more prescription and I won't even have to breathe. Well, compared to the pharmacological determinants in my present life, plus the diurnal exigencies of *Time,* Pago Pago still looks pretty good. I don't accept myself in the present scheme, and I don't think they accept me. The value of Pago Pago, among other considerations, is that I'll have to sink or swim. It's bad business for you, I know, but you and your mother will work out some kind of arrangement. As I've said before, you can have my profit sharing and what the estate will produce. All I intend to take out is severance pay, assuming I can get that, which will provide me with something like $14,000 to make it in American Samoa. If I saw any other course I'd take it. But I see nothing else. The kids will respond to adversity, and your mother's fat, combined with your initiative, will keep the wolf from the door (a really original mixed metaphor).

Two days into the sociologists' convention and already running down like a cheap clock. Steve charged into the academic metier with all the enthusiasm of his twenty-five years and a natural affinity for eggheads. He likes to strut before them, and is indeed impressively bright. His intelligence, in fact, dismays me. He's all but convinced I'm going to let him down on the book—a distinct possibility—and has committed the (to me) unpardonable indiscretion of confiding my confidences to him (depression, doubts about the book, etc.) to Irv Horowitz, Herb Gans, and God knows how many other convention delegates. Today he fell into a sulk about it, threatened to give up and return to New York, tell the editor at Putnam that I'm dropping out. A form of blackmail. The fact is, I think, that if he'd hung around Manhattan immediately after we'd sold the book in March, then we'd both have got right to work on it and the momentum might very well have carried us along—and me through a very bad fit of depression. Unrelieved so far, incidentally, by the Tofranil, the daily dose of which I'm gradually increasing on order. All I recognize so far are some of the side effects: dry mouth, constipation, blurred vision. Too much to expect, I guess, that a chemical could warm an emotional climate so perdurably gloomy as mine.

Because of all this, I think Steve is retiring me from my role of surrogate father. He appoints them everywhere; Horowitz is one, Gans another. I'd hoped to be restimulated by the convention, but the papers I've read and heard so far have been distressingly commonplace, and I'm very down about everything now, even Pago Pago. There *are* options. I've proposed several to Steve. One is that, from the depths of his scholarship he do the book, and I would do the re-writing and editing—in which case, of course, we'd have to reapportion the take. Another would be for me indeed to drop out entirely and pay him my share of the advance. This would involve a rather elaborate stratagem at *Time*: I'd have to get them to fire me, so that I'd get severance pay (which I'd keep, and from which Steve's money would come); you would get the profit sharing and, as I've said before, my cut of Uncle George's estate, if and when it comes through. I don't know exactly why, but the book terrifies me, in the same way, I guess, as the society of sociologists. As the psy-chologist said, I appear to be losing confidence in my intel-lectual powers—words to that effect. I didn't believe it then, but I'm beginning to now. Never have I felt such an outsider.

It's a shame too, because this week in a way could qualify as a vacation. The weather's been sunny, and there's that pool. But all I feel is guilty, guilty at getting bombed last night at a dinner I hosted for some sociologists, guilty at smoking too much, at being here under false pretenses and riding the expense account to boot, at running into Ruthie Galvin from *Time*'s Boston bureau, patrolling the same con-vention—guilty, guilty, guilty as charged. Guilty even at being fifty-two nearly fifty-three; you said I've become quite gray. Steve said that when he was in Waupaca with Fooey and George (Steve's from Waupaca, you know), he made three predictions about me: that I'd drop out of the book, quit *Time* and commit suicide. I'd say his betting average is either .667 or .000. If I don't quit *Time* I'll certainly do the book, and I doubt that I'll commit suicide in any event, even though it is tempting. It's kind of an unplayable ace in the hole, something in hand against utter psychic defeat. I don't really expect much of Pago Pago (or do I?), but if that were to turn really sour, maybe then I might play the ace. Maybe. But I doubt it. What I want is for someone to take care of me.

The pills aren't working. I am almost totally immobilized by depression and guilt, overwhelmed by a sense of inadequacy. Wallowing in it, drowning in it. Why must I take myself so seriously? Why can't I accept myself for what I am instead of worrying about what I'm not? I thought this morning, lying in bed late, that sleep is a refuge to me now, in the same way that death would be. The hotel room is a refuge beyond which lies a stormy sea of critical sociologists. The hotel is a refuge from *Time*, the same as being here is, the same as weekends are. At breakfast, Steve pointed out a young man and said, "That's Wheatley of Princeton," and my viscera turned to ice. His class at Princeton will form one of the chapters of our book. The fear is that I won't be able to monitor it; that I could not then and there introduce myself. I can't write the book. I'm cheating *Time*. I'll probably get away with it, but still I'm cheating just by being here, frozen into inaction. I need help, and I don't know where to go to get it. The future seems unbearable. I begin to understand now how people can crack up. But I can't sympathize with them and I can't really sympathize with myself. I equate my condition with weakness and weakness is wrong. I should be strong. I should be able to get a fresh grip on myself, as they say, face my troubles, conquer them. I should be able to take *some* course of action, but what? But I mustn't go on like this. This is like probing an open wound.

Steve and I flew back at noon on Eastern's shuttle and tomorrow I go in for a one-day work week. He has seen the results of my psych battery and, on the strength of what he says is a comprehension of analytic theory surpassed only by Freud, sought to explicate some of it for me. No need to repeat his diagnosis, which was quite on the mark but broke no new ground. He did remind me of a pattern that I've been aware of, intermittently, since high school: my past is littered with half-baked pies. I'm not a doer, but a half-doer. This is one sign of the passive personality and, I take it, of the depressive. Guilt is a sign of passivity; anger in-turned. The divorce and this siege of depression are of course related, but in more than the obvious ways. That action of mine was in its way a full-baked pie; this depression is punishment for that action. Why I recoil with great anxiety from doing the book requires a more complicated explanation. I can sense it without being able to find the right words. I am afraid to succeed—but I don't quite understand why that's so. I am also furious at Dad for having let mother crush his balls and furious, too, because, partly through his example, I got mine crushed too. Damn near anyway. I was still writing book reviews under Bobby Baker the last time I came inside a woman and that's more years ago than I like to reckon. I did settle the Oedipal issue, according to Steve, but not without scars to show for it still. And then nearly every factor in my emotional life mitigates against sex, possibly by subconscious design. I drink—and drink is a depressant, of the libido and everything else. I take tranquilizers; ditto. I am a depressive; twice ditto. Small wonder, really, given the magnificent cooperation of my conscious, which assures me that I will fail before I do, that Grosser just lies there like a noodle, neglecting his duty. It would be a miracle if he could do anything else. I am seriously thinking of giving up drinking not so much from guilt but from the desire to give Grosser all possible help. I'd like very much to get back into the woman business. I told this to the shrink—I had to call from Washington to report no results on the Tofranil—and from his tone I could tell he's heartily in favor of the idea— my knocking off the sauce. I'm also considering a kind of one-man Operation Bootstrap. Miserable as I am, and much as I may enjoy the misery, it doesn't after all get me any- where. It's not going to be easy, and I may, at first, have to do it mechanically and also take some drastic steps, like quitting *Time*. And even like going to Pago Pago. I'm also going to stop bleeding all over the place. This won't be easy, because complaining—about the magazine, for instance—is all but second nature to me now. Most important, I'm down pretty near rock bottom; it's going to be a long and arduous climb back up to being somebody again.

I'm not sure there isn't some malice in Steve. I don't quite trust him—as I do Phil, for example, although my relations with these two males don't bear comparison. I like Steve, obviously, more than you do. You felt he was some sort of subversive or maybe unhealthy influence. I detect, or think I do, a streak of arrogance—or whatever—that compels him to put down anyone who threatens him in any way, that compels him to say, I'm better than you are. Much of this per- haps comes from his fears that I will default on the book. Anyway, I'm bored with talking about it.

Jocelyn Bannon called just an hour ago and invited me out for a drink. I agreed to go, and now that I have, I will. "As a friend," she said. The call didn't stir me in any direction beyond idle curiosity. I haven't seen her since February. But now as I write the butterflies begin to flutter.

No mail waiting for me; just three bills, one of them for- warded by you. How are the children? I try not to think about not seeing them, perhaps never again.

Your letter came today. You're quite right. I did miss the August 1 payment, trusting that your rather casual attitude toward money would blind you to the oversight. In which case, I would have been $500 ahead. But you'll get it now. You must understand I'm not resentful at having to support you and the kids; it was what I was doing, after all, when we were married. But I have no fat at all in my bank account, except for the half advance for a book I now realize I may never write, nearly all of which is gone anyway for mother, repayments to your mother for the cost of the divorce, the vacation trip to Wisconsin, plus occasional extravagances; and that was one way to build up a little excess. Anyway, it's more or less academic now: what I owe you, the children, *Time* and society. I have just about decided to leave *Time* for other ways and other shores. Your mettle, as well as mine, is going to be tested as never before. There's an almost driving urgency in me to do this. On a small and far more insignificant scale I'm saying, or trying to say, with Luther: "*Hier stehe Ich, Ich kann nicht anders.*" Notice that I am, uncharacteristically, writing uphill: one sure sign to a graphologist of optimism, an elevation of spirit, of hope. I feel none of that. I'm dining—or, rather, drinking—alone at La Grillade on what by *Time*'s reckoning is Saturday though it's really Friday: all sections closed early in anticipation of the Labor Day weekend. Hence there were no readily available dinner partners, I dreaded consigning myself to the solitude of White Plains and so am here, drinking and eating alone. Working on my third martini; also three at lunch plus a cognac with my coffee. And, in between, a full complement of exercises. I begin to realize, though, a certain compulsion to my drinking—not that of the alcoholic but that of the lonely and slightly desperate man. If one can qualify so unqualifiable a state.

The meeting last night with Jocelyn was irresolute. She had suggested picking me up at eight, an hour that immediately became the fulcrum of the day. I prepared for it as for a first date: showered, shaved, sprinkled myself with after-shave lotion, put on a tan Chipp summer suit over a Brooks Brothers yellow sports shirt, arranged the collar just so and then presented myself at the dot of eight on the street corner my apartment house overlooks. She came by soon enough, in a new air-conditioned Mustang, and ferried me to a bar in Mamaroneck, presumably for the sake of discretion, where she promptly ran into a married gal of her circle doing much the same thing: out with somebody other than her husband. I was informed after a trip to the ladies' room, etc., that her friend can and does repeatedly wade through a fifth of vodka about as rapidly as, say, a youngster drinks orange juice. Jocelyn and I sat at the bar and talked like outsiders about a failed arrangement that has affected, directly, at least nine lives. The place was one of those bars where you can't see three feet ahead of your nose. We were alone. There were people in adjacent rooms, but none in ours. Both of us very self-conscious. At first I tried to pull off the strong-man act: no wounds, no hard feelings, the game—alas—is over. We drank an execrable stinger or two—so bad that I switched to beer. The silences, when they occurred, were charged. I forget much of what she said, and of what I said, but does it really matter what she said? She said, for example, that she will never again invest herself emotionally in another man. Her marriage is dead, stone cold dead. They get together in bed, but rather in the same spirit that she does the housework. I don't mean to imply that they don't both enjoy it—they undoubtedly do—but just that it has become over the years a form, just as not screwing, in other marriages, becomes over the years another form. Jocelyn now comes and goes as she pleases; Guy might kill her or at the very least lambaste her, if he knew beyond any doubt where she was going and what she intended to do. But she doesn't tell him and he doesn't ask. I asked her what she said to Guy before heading out for her rendezvous with me, and she said, "Nothing." He doesn't ask. He doesn't want to know.

The evening, as you may have gathered, was very inconclusive. I am not—or, rather, I *am* a stubborn man, and I wasn't about to reestablish even at her initiative an alliance that has been formally over for eight months and actually for longer than that. Still, I can't help thinking: why did she call at all? Why look me up? *I* haven't made a move toward her. Why does she? I'm sure it's terribly unfair to talk all this out with you, but after all it does bear on things. See if you can understand this: I wouldn't come back to you on your terms, but I would gladly—eagerly—come back to you on mine. We're not likely to. We're two proud and stubborn people, and I've drawn a new chart for me that, if I have the guts to act on it, will sever forever any connection with my past. I feel that I have to do it. Right or wrong, willy-nilly, I have to do it. The alternative is the same form of living death to which circumstance and I, as the agent of circumstance, have consigned myself ever since I was able to think.

What I'm doing now is hanging around long enough to-night to justify a Dial-a-Cab. Two martinis, no more; one more and I'd be on my kettle. I'm eating to eat—in this case, sweetbreads with mushrooms and onions (not bad) and canned green beans plus a flacon of domestic white wine at La Grillade—no appetite to speak of. Give me three meal pills and I'd take them instead. You'd like the sweetbreads, though they do loom imposingly on the plate, like a dish the restaurant doesn't want to reduce to leftovers tomorrow.

The juke box here—what an anachronism!—is addressing us in the minor key. Low, sad, inconclusive harmonies designed either to make people hug each other more tightly, or move apart. I repeat something I've said before: you're the only woman my age I'd look at twice. Does pride keep us apart, or apathy? We've both had time to weigh the advantages and benefits of the single life. I don't deny them, any more than you; but at our age I can't see the benefits of solitude. The truth, I *think*, is that I miss you as a woman, not just as my wife (there's an element of bullshit in that). But still it can't be denied that you have used the time off from marriage to do things and go places prohibited by marriage.

I guess I'm drunk, though it's not easy to define the state. Certainly the sober side would instantly recognize my condition—but who says we must check out our judgment to them? And, anyway, even accepting their judgment, I do no harm. Offend no one with my conduct; depart quietly, sleep, awake with a sense of guilt that no one else has to share. But alone; I give no one offense. One can say, what a stupid way to live, and I won't knock it. Still, *I* can say: how stupidly my judges have lived and how stupidly I have lived within their verdicts. I smoke more, drink more, pine more, than when we were married, and maybe all this is rushing me to the grave. But is it such a dreadful place? I'd rather be there, in many respects, than here. Errol Flynn lived fifty wastrel years and enjoyed them; I've lived fifty-three years and enjoyed nothing beyond a few widely separated moments in the course of which I stopped thinking about myself. By a strange and unplottable route, this gets me back to where I am now. I'm going to quit. I'm going to shit all over the rules. I'm going to drop totally out.

In a Milquetoast way, my salvation has begun. The duty facing me on my return from Washington was to query the field widely on an upcoming "Behavior" sensitivity-training cover story Friday, on a subject that I know next to nothing about. I decided to make sense for a change, and to be strong. I went up to see Ed Jamieson, sitting in for HAG as managing editor, to tell him I couldn't possibly compose sensible cover queries without first acquainting myself with the subject. But Ed, as usual, was incommunicado. Only his secretary answers his phone. I have fantasies of Ed, in which he removes neither his vest nor his mask in the shower, commands his secretary to call his wife and tell her that he won't be home to dinner. So I didn't get to see him. Instead I wrote a note—a cop-out, I guess—that conveyed the same message: I wanted the cover date postponed to allow me time to digest the background on the subject so that my inquiries to *Time*'s field points would make sense. No response to that, of course. Hence, for lack of response, I will postpone the cover myself. I figure it will take me three to four days of reading to compose the queries, and I will take at least that long. If the system objects, it will do it no good. I'd love to get fired anyway. Let them fire me.

I may be killing myself—which is an overstatement. Bombed three days—rather nights—in a row in Washington: Sunday, Monday and Tuesday. Then bombed last night seeing Jocelyn, though for me I had very little to drink. And bombed again today. I will not lie; three martinis and a cognac at lunch with Fred Golden; two martinis with Fred at Ho Ho's before dinner; two more, one white wine and a cognac dining alone at La Grillade. Now, in the apartment, I'm sipping vermouth—the only intoxicant in the place. That's a lot of booze. I need none of it. I'd prefer the endearing, nonalcoholic elegance of female friendship. I don't want to be passive. Drinking is passive behavior. But I think I need an ally, and an ally I haven't got.

Well, at least no liquor today, but nothing accomplished either. Staring me in the face are the cover on sensitivity training and at least one 5,000-word chapter for the book. Except for direct duties at *Time*, depression has paralyzed me. It is almost too great an effort to rinse the few dishes I use, or to thaw dinner. Tonight, instead, I ate a few crackers with bacon and horseradish goop, a stalk of celery, some peanuts salted in the shell with half a bar of chocolate-covered halvah. I won't die of this diet, I suppose, and I might even stay healthy.

If there were anything else to do but haunt this apartment, there'd be less temptation to haunt Franzl's. There is welcome relief from anxiety at the bottom of the glass, and everything makes me anxious now. What's going to be so different in Pago Pago? That makes me anxious, too: to step off in the middle of the South Pacific with no contacts, no job and enough money to last me maybe for a year. I've never finished anything important in my life, have I? Except when the decision was not in my hands, as, for instance, completing college. When it was my decision, I dropped out. Graduate school. That first *uncompleted* novel that I lost— conveniently. Two more—*uncompleted*—from the leave of absence. It was Steve who reminded me of this pattern in my life. I can't finish anything. "I don't even think you could commit suicide," he said. "If you ever did, I'd be sorry, of course; but I'd be proud in a way, too. At least you would have finished something you began." My mind is a blank tonight; that's part of depression too. You said in your letter that you don't know what depression is. I don't understand the psychodynamics of it either but it has something to do with passivity and with anxiety and guilt. It's a real downer. The guilty one becomes so because he cannot vent the hostility and aggression he feels towards other people; he must turn it against himself, as guilt. Something like that. Depression only *seems* to disappear in congenial company. I don't feel it, for instance, sailing on the Sound with Fred Golden or dining out with Barbara Smith. But it's knee-deep in this apartment, like the dust. It simply is true that only you can help yourself. It's a matter of deploying your own resources, no matter how exhausted. In my case, they must be near the exhaustion point. I wonder what I'd do in a real *crise*. But I can't think of one worse than this. As Fooey said, to be divorced is worse than being dead, because you have to live with it for the rest of your life. I daydream sometimes about our getting together again, but it wouldn't work. Just a year gone out of our lives—not quite a year. Something impels me to escape, to run away and hide. This is of course the death wish only faintly disguised.

I've heard from Gretchen, who invited me for Sunday lunch with Anita Feagles, Beth Day and Beth's agent Max Becker. Gretchen spread us quite a table: chicken salad, fresh rolls, quiche Lorraine and coffee Bavarian cream; better than I've done since the last time I was asked out. Beth has a book on schizophrenia coming out in January and another in the research stage; Anita's sold one, titled *Attics*, that she describes as the dirtiest juvenile ever. Everyone at *Time*'s doing books; Mayo Mohs, Fred Golden, Steve Kanfer, and so on. Makes our little commission from Putnam seem insignificant. Max agreed with me that if Steve Englund and I limit the book to the new sociology, it probably won't sell enough to recover its advance. I've thought this from the start. My objective was a potboiler with just enough scholarship to wow the reading public. I don't give a damn whether a sociologist would flunk it as a dissertation, and I certainly don't care whether informed readers condemn it. For that matter, I'm beginning not to give a damn about anything.

The society of Gretchen *et al.* has wrought a salutary change in my emotional climate. The depression has gone underground. In celebration, I've acquired five G-bottles of Schaefer's from the nearest deli and have broached the first. When I'm feeling up, I drink to stay up, and when I'm down, to get up. I also drink to sleep and, now and then, for socializing. It may or may not be noteworthy that my $150 psychological profile was absolutely silent on the subject of booze. Moreover, I took some heart from an article in the Sunday *Times* magazine that said four martinis in a man about my size produces a blood alcohol content of only .06, well below the accepted legal definition of drunkenness (.15), as in drunk driving. And I almost never have four martinis. Three is generally my limit. The drunk, though, justifies his consumption, no matter how copious.

If someone were to construct my personality from this place, he might not have an easy time of it. The suits hanging in the closets, some with Chipp labels; the Bermuda shorts draped over the open closet door; the Brooks Brothers shirts —all this, of course, would fix my gender and, less accurately, my dimensions and my income. What would the cheap beach chair folded against the wall reveal? Maybe the truth: that I like to lie in the sun. The mess could indicate many things: (1) that I am untidy; (2) that I am a bachelor; (3) that I am probably out of action as a man, because who would dare seduce a woman in this squalor? Of course, I could be one of those cheap bastards who always insist on going to her place. The typewriter and the Sunday *Times* hint at a certain literacy; the tenant could be a writer of some sort, most likely a free lance. The limited shelf of books transmits an ambiguous message: Stella Standard's *Cook Book;* Erving Goffman's *Asylums;* Kunhardt's *My Father's House;* Herb Gans's *The Urban Villagers;* Jane Howard's *Please Touch;* Braden's *The Age of Aquarius;* Williams' *The Tragedy of American Diplomacy,* and *Intellectual Origins of American Radicalism,* by Lynd. Obviously, something of a brain. But that would be wrong. And an outdoor type. Wrong again. That stack of fishing rods in the corner belongs, not to the tenant, but to his boys. What to make of the deck of cards, with a Confederacy motif, on the floor? He must be a thrifty man: witness the miniature mail box bank on the Herman Miller dresser, gravid with quarters. (Not quarters, though the bank is designed for them; pennies.) To the discerning pharmaceutical eye, valuable tips in the selection of drugs on the card table—another clue in itself, that. Valium, a tranquilizer. Tofranil, an antidepressant. Dalmane, a noncumulative, nonaddictive soporific. Android H-P, for male hormonal deficiency. Jesus, that tells all. The guy is not young, else why the need for monkey glands? He can't get it up any more, and worries about that. He worries about everything, and lives in a lather (Valium). He's depressed (Tofranil), and because he is, he can't sleep nights (Dalmane). What does the bathroom tell us? Not much more, except a reaffirmation of his slovenly ways (the bathtub hasn't been scrubbed for weeks, obviously, the bath towel smells offensively sour). An aspirin bottle, half full; three toothbrushes; a used tube of Pragmatar (he's had ringworm, athlete's foot or crotch rash, or all three). A Trimcomb haircutter is illuminating: whatever the tenant's income, he has to pinch pennies, cut corners by mowing his own hair. What does the kitchen have to say? Refrigerator inventory: four and a half quart bottles of beer; three quarts of milk; half a pound of lightly salted butter; a jar of herring in sour cream and some bacon-and-horseradish dip; apple, grape, pineapple and grapefruit juice, a few cans of Borden's Frosted drink in assorted flavors; leftover applesauce; leftover grease; mayonnaise; three overripe eggs; several bars of halvah. In the hydrator compartment: limp celery and three or four desiccated oranges (about five months old, in fact). In the freezer compartment: TV dinners, cheese cake (eaten into), chicken a la king, creamed chipped beef, frozen breakfasts, Eskimo pies, some individually wrapped chicken legs and thighs. Go through his few effects, jumbled in the dresser. A divorce decree in Spanish (*ole!*). A storage guarantee on a wolf parka. A car-insurance policy. An "agreement," signed by the tenant, his collaborator, and G. P. Putnam's Sons, to write a 90,000-word book by April 1971 under the provisional title of *The Sick Society*. Hand tools and shoe-shining gear. A modest collection of savings stamps books. The uncompleted manuscript of an untitled novel. An unfinished letter to his former wife (this we know from the divorce decree) exceeded in length only by the one Mark Twain wrote to a friend, just a few months before he died, complaining that a young woman and her paramour, both in his employ, had bilked him out of thousands. And I almost forgot: a glassine lid of grass in the front closet. What do we know about the tenant in 2-A? I take back my original observation, we can gather quite a lot.

In this environment I have become something of an eremite. I guess I want to be alone, no matter how much I say I abhor it (and I do abhor it). Gretchen's lunch broke up about 3:30, whereupon Anita asked us all over later for drinks. But I declined. Why? Two reasons: I wanted to do my exercises, which necessitated going back to the apartment, and I had half-formulated plans to go to Franzl's. With these observations recorded, I begin to feel the depression moving in again like fog. Why? I don't know. But all at once I'm sad again. This is really an impoverished life. What in the hell would I do, for instance, if *Time* didn't claim my work week? What if I lost my job and, at my age, had to find another one—another one like it? What if I had enough to live on, but just enough to live on? Would I sit around on my can as now, writing this exercise in futility, doing crossword puzzles and commiserating with myself? I sure as hell am my mother's son. That's been the tenor of her life ever since the old man died. That's why I think, as an act of resurrection or salvation, I've got to take a leap from the known into the unknown, no matter what the cost to those I leave behind. All of it scares me, and activates my guilt: leaving *Time* after fifteen years, abandoning my responsibilities, flying 8,000 miles to nowhere. But I've got to do it. I've got to do it. I've got to do it or go on living in the most pointless, unrewarding and dreary way imaginable to me. Now it doesn't interest me to go to Franzl's, though I suppose I will. Tomorrow is not a working day, and I can do what I've been doing for years: put off all decisions until tomorrow. Tomorrow I'll tackle the book or do something positive. Tonight I'll just drink too much beer, smoke too many Camels, and breathe.

Time is hurrying by, hastened by beer. Halfway through my second quart and feeling nothing at all. Because of Gretchen's lunch I'm not hungry and will probably eat nothing, unless perhaps a late and undigestible snack at Franzl's. It's 7:30; I've been drinking beer since, say, five. It's just something no-account to do. I do indeed envy you your industry. Whatever the divorce meant to you emotionally, you went right on with your busy-bee ways—indeed, got busier. I've never been able to operate that way and never will be. I tried. I did a lot of things, while young, that were self-assertive, though maybe the steady grain of passivity showed through. And I have glorified the past. I guess everyone does. You're probably the only one who knows that that scar on my cheek was self-inflicted; and I'm not absolutely sure I told *you*. For all other inquirers, I confected an elaborate story that reflects some credit on my manhood, though not a hell of a lot; I've told it so often that I now half believe it myself. Just as I say that I lost that front tooth in a fight with Wally Klein in and out of the Y pool in Appleton; not a word of truth to it. And that, for reasons you're familiar with, I challenged in San Juan a crewmate aptly nicknamed Tarzan, was knocked unconscious and awaked minus pants, wristwatch and billfold in some back alley. Bullshit, all of it. I can't recall a single serious fight in my life, certainly none that *I* sought out. The nearest thing was a so-called "grudge" fight in high school with Lester Schultz, which was staged in the gym one afternoon after school and attended by most of the student body. I forget what the grudge was, or even if there was one. But I'd picked my adversary with great care. He was one of the school's precocious smokers, with a concave chest, poor posture and muscles like pudding. We went three rounds in balloon gloves, and naturally I won. Immediately after, and still today, I decided that Lester had agreed to the match as a favor to me. And you would have to be me to figure that out.

My past, my youth, are littered with a lot of little lies like those. I don't think any big ones, but that may be only because I am a very small figure on a very small canvas. I wonder if I told you any, and if you told me any. If a lie is anything short of the whole truth, then of course I've lied to you many times. I had to lie—conceal—about Jocelyn, too, and the other alliances of less or no consequence, just as you had to lie to me about yours. At one time or other, I've probably lied to everyone whose path paralleled mine just long enough for each to sound the other out. I'm not talking about white lies either, all those necessary to keep society going; but self-serving lies, calculated to reinforce the desired false image or to get you out of a tight spot. Every one of my expense accounts is riddled with lies, but whose isn't? I know why we tell lies, too. Because we're afraid the other won't take us the way we really are. And since the other fears the same, we go through life like characters out of Graham Greene. Read his *The Ministry of Fear* and you'll see what I mean. Aren't the kids, in one way, saying this? Cut the crap, cut the role-playing and do your thing (i.e., be true to yourself, or at least try). Now it's eight. Two quarts of beer—sixty-four ounces—in three hours (180 minutes) or, roughly, one ounce of beer every three minutes. Sounds innocuous broken down that way, doesn't it? But I'll have more at Franzl's, and I'll pay for it tomorrow. Last night Valium (four) gave me nearly a clock-around sleep, from eleven to ten, which is more than anyone needs or should get.

I have the feeling that part of my new fuck-it-all attitude is just childish ducking of responsibility. But who defines responsibility anyway? The past. If you can ignore the past, you have no responsibilities whatsoever except those related to yourself. The past bids me: stay on the job; earn enough to keep you from want and send our children through college; live selflessly, and sparely, on what's left over for me; work harder than ever, and earn more money so that I can get back into the business of contributing to my mother's support. Etc. etc. etc. If you're not rewarded here, you will be hereafter. Grateful and brainwashed survivors will put flowers on your grave. The alternative: drop out. In either case life will go on, for me and everyone else involved. No one is likely to die before his season, unless he willfully changes the timetable; sticks and stones may break your bones but names can only hurt you. Besides, death pays all debts. A shithead exists only in the eyes of the beholder. I'll bet the moneylenders sleep as serenely in their tombs as does Jesus, wherever the hell they tucked him away, and it is incontrovertible that the rich have more money to spend than the poor. If that seems glaringly obvious, just bear in mind that money *can* buy you peace—an anesthetized peace no doubt but still peace—whereas poverty can't buy anything. Money, power, and what they signify—that's what this life is all about, and no one has ever returned from the next. If there is a next. I know God-damned well there isn't—and I recognize the anomaly of invoking his name to say that there isn't. But that's all part of the abiding dilemma: both the believer and the atheist need God.

That paragraph strikes me as a trackless wilderness. Have cracked the third quart. You may be able to detect this from my composition, but I'll bet not from my script. Either the years or beer, however, are beginning to exact their toll. After those four days in Washington and after three martinis, etc. Friday at lunch, I ran in place only 1,000 times and did only 100 sit-ups, and today it took great effort to perform my customary quota (1500 and 150). But I did. And I'll do it again tomorrow. I've given up trying to do as many push-ups at a crack as I have years, and have settled for forty or forty-five at a time so many times a day. This is still pretty impressive for a man of my age and habits. Something compulsive about it too. Bobby Baker once caught me exercising in my office and asked me why I did it. To stay in shape, I said. "Why?" he asked again. And I couldn't answer him.

Wish somebody would call. You. Anybody. Franzl's appeals to me less and less, but I know I'm going out; the walls are closing in on me. I'll take smokes and play my silly little game: leave them in the car and see how long I can do without them (about an hour). If I were just a bit more looped—and I'm really not looped at all, just logy—I'd brush my teeth and hit the sack. But then what in Christ's name would I do on Labor Day morning, beginning at the ungodly hour of seven?

Christ! What a head of depression (dismay really) this morning. Did go to Franzl's for five beers, no chess, nothing to eat. Home about midnight for another quart of beer, gobbling peanuts like a starving man. Then tossed and writhed and turned all night, waking up with cold sweats and unremembered nightmares, the bedclothes tied in knots. Haven't been out yet today, and it's past one. Paid bills, including the $500 I owe you from August 1, cleaned hell out of the kitchen, made a stab at cleaning the rest of the apartment, too, but gave up on that, and took two loads of white laundry down to the basement. Lunch is in the oven—a frozen Swanson breakfast of French toast and sausage patties—and I'll have that with a banana and milk for health's sake. You can imagine the feeling of loneliness in this still-strange setting, this hateful place where I know no one, and with friends out of the recently expired past only twenty-five miles or so north, doing all the Labor Day things we used to do too before the split. Old Johnny One Note, that's me these days. The mood seizes me, builds up momentum, and then it's like a tailspin: almost impossible to pull out. My lungs are on fire, anxiety gnaws at my vitals, all I can think of doing is issue a broadcast appeal for help. I guess it will just have to be Operation Bootstrap, as Steve recommends, but I don't know where the muscles are coming from. I don't know, either, how much of this is histrionics, or whether I really am resourceless as a result of this emotional low-pressure front. If I go outside and get into the car, where is there to go?

If I stay here, as is likely, what do I do? I simply cannot bring myself to work on the book. It's not warm enough for sunning, and too late in the day anyway. Summer's over, the year is beginning to die. I did my exercises yesterday, but can I do them today? And what's the point? I can't think of *Time*, the job, the upcoming cover, the commitment to Putnam; my mind draws a veil over all that. Only Valium works; the Tofranil tablets don't lift my depression, the Android don't make me horny, the Dalmane don't put me to sleep. (That's not bad grammar; the "tablets" in each case is implied. But what do you want—good grammar or good taste?)

I've been sitting here pondering what positive action I can take to haul myself out of the dumps. The dumps. There's an apt metaphor—the trash heap, for discarded and unwanted things. Years ago you said, during one of our arguments, that you couldn't really consider divorce because I couldn't get along without you. You were probably right. I've been trying to look some truths smack in the face; they're not comforting to behold. It's tempting to go overboard, to sell out completely, to agree with everything the psychologist said of me in his analysis of the tests, and everything Steve said. It's tempting to give up. But I've always been harder on myself than anyone else has, and somehow I've got to look more approvingly, or with more acceptance, on the construction that adds up to me *qua* me. Popeye says, "I yam what I yam and thass all I yam." But I edit that to fit myself: "I am what I am, but it's never been enough and never will be." Steve applauds the strength that, after nineteen years, asked you for a divorce, but that may be only a measure of his hostility to you and yours to him. I wonder now, naturally enough. I did, I know, marry a mother among other things; I looked to you for that. Had I resolved that dependency need in the proper season, then I wouldn't have had to carry it past its season; and then, of course, I would never have married you. Because I married you out of that need as well as others. If I'd been surer of myself, armored with a stronger sense of self, then I would not have wanted to surrender some of my self into your self. I wanted a commanding mother figure, and I got one. Note that the psychologist describes me as a passive-aggressive. That means, as nearly as I can determine, that my aggression is sublimated as passivity. It's the weakest expression of self, though of course the victim can't be blamed for choosing it, it's the only defense he knows. Much healthier to the self, I should think, to overaggress, though not very useful either. You do have to get along with the boss, but not to the point of self-abasement. I took some pride in my antiestablishmentarian posturing at *Time,* and at other companies before that one. Like my well-earned reputation for being the magazine's house grouse. I remember years ago, before the war, when I was working for Kimberly-Clark in Neenah—some dumb clerical job in a bay of clerks—and Bill Wright, my boss, called me in and announced that my six-month probationary period was successfully ended, an occasion he was observing, he said, by raising my pay from $95 to $100 a month. Without thinking, I said: "What am I supposed to do now? Get an erection?" He almost canned me on the spot. But posturing was all it ever was, especially at *Time.* I complained, but I stayed. One should do one or the other but not both. I have never played fair to myself; I don't know how. I equate sexual potency with aggression (which of course it is) and so with violence. So says the psychologist. And hence if I confuse all women in bed, including you, with my mother, and my aggressive feelings toward her border on violence, it seems clear enough, doesn't it, why Grosser lies down on the job? If all this is so, and I have no idea whether it is, then when mother dies, it follows that I will be overwhelmed with guilt. Not remorse, guilt. Right now, while she's alive, I can't imagine that reaction to her death. Right now, I don't want her to die—or, if I do, don't recognize the desire—but would it affect me much if she did? I can't hope for a sudden and magical liberation of feelings upon hearing the tidings, when that time comes. Like Fooey, the damage has been done and is irreversible. So I've been wondering what I can do to release myself from the springe, and the best I can think of is some action that will force me off course. Negative actions: quit *Time*, beat it to Pago Pago, drop out, in short. A stronger psyche would examine prospects with a clearer and less pessimistic eye, but then a stronger psyche wouldn't have got into this fix. The positive courses are plain enough to me, but I don't know if I have the strength to do them: honor and fulfill my contract with Putnam, no matter how many hours and weekends, how much agony, that may take; stay at *Time*, keep my trap shut, and try to work more effectively than ever before; build a new life on the basis of what I've got left in resources and years—or swallow my pride and ask for a reconciliation with you. If only you weren't such a prideful woman yourself. I dread the thought, though, of the painful and protracted effort to give birth to a book that was ill-conceived to begin with and that is not likely to sell; I dread staying on *Time*, half alive and half dead and only half engaged, while the last few good years go irretrievably down the drain. I hate the status quo, long to change it and seem to lack the will. I want to dig a hole and hide in it— a womb wish if there ever was one. I want at least one person totally and unmistakably on my side, locked, with me, in the mutuality of our dependence, our affections and our concerns. I'd like to be strong, but failing that, I'd like someone around who won't make a federal case of it if I'm not.

The Valium's working and I must go to bed, at 9:30. There's a noisy party on somebody's balcony outside, but I can muffle it by closing the window and turning on the air conditioner. Good night.

I'm getting a doughnut; going to have to lay off the beer. Noticed it this morning when, the day being cool, I put on a winter-weight suit and found it embarrassingly snug around the belt. Of course, it might not be beer either, just age.

Have been plagued with recurrent chest pains at night, strong enough to wake me up groaning. Doubt it's the ticker; my guess: it's a side effect from one of my numerous pills. The Tofranil, as I obviously can't stop telling you, has been a keen disappointment. Despite an ever-increasing dosage my depression deepens. As for the chest pains, you know I wouldn't mind if they were symptomatic of serious trouble. I know now—at least I'm, say, 98 percent sure—that I could never take my own life. I haven't the strength, not even to contribute indirectly to self-destruction as does the alcoholic, as your first husband did perhaps when his car rolled down that cliff between San Francisco and Carmel. But if some uncontrollable outside agency, like a bad pump, were to make the decision for me, I know I wouldn't mind. It's one way out.

I can't take Valium every night so I'm drinking again. Egad, maybe I *am* a lush. Do I come across as one in this letter? If so, pick out the drunk parts. Most of it was written stone sober. What got me started today was an aggravating delay on the Penn Central—I got off at 179th Street or thereabouts, walked at least a mile looking for a cab, was picked up by a total stranger who dropped me at Fiftieth and the river and I cabbed to Time & Life from there. I had taken practically a dawn train to get an early start on a four-day work week and arrived, hot and fuming, after ten. Then Gilbert Cant invited me to lunch and we lay-analyzed each other over the barroom equivalent of sodium amatol (is that right?)—martinis. Three each. After which all my exercises and a considerable amount of work. I have been overruled on the sensitivity cover. It's up for week after next because HAG is fearful *Newsweek* will catch wind of what we are up to and beat us to the draw. The whole thing would be ironic if it weren't so God-damned infuriating: (1) we're inexcusably late with the story, which "Behavior" suggested doing last December; (2) since last February our "Color" department has been shooting T-groups and feelie work-shops all over the country. Had I known then, I could have begun boning up on the subject in my off time. But was "Behavior" told? Yes—last Friday, the day I got back from Washington. I've been wading desperately through the raw material ever since, including great gobs of the weekend when I wasn't feeling too sorry for myself and of course I still have a section to write this week. You'll be pleased to hear (at least I'm pleased) that I complained to no one. Or mini-mally. One reason is that I'm trying not to care. It would suit me fine if I disappointed *Time* enough to be fired. One way or another, I'm going to collect that severance pay.

But, God, what a dreary life it is. I've come almost full circle from where this letter began. Would I do it all over again? Answer then: Yes. Answer now: No. I don't greatly blame your shrink, but if he hadn't said what he said the time I saw him, things might have come out another way. "For a man to get satisfaction from his marriage and his job—those aren't privileges. They are rights." I took him literally. If only he'd injected a Teutonic note of caution, I might have thought twice before committing myself to that skittish colt Jocelyn

—and winding up with neither her nor you. What would have happened, do you suppose, if I hadn't made the move? My guess is one of two things. Either you would have got a divorce or both of us would have got back into therapy—and hang the expense—to see if we couldn't rescue the marriage. Boy, I can tell you this, Ann: if you ever took the initiative I'd jump at the chance to try again. But you won't. And I haven't the nerve, and maybe not the will, to take the initiative myself. Maybe I will though, in the near future. Because I can't lose either way. If you're willing to try a reconciliation I win—don't I? Because maybe that's what I want. And if you reject me, then I'm free. Then there's nothing at all to hold me here anymore and I can say stop the world, I want to get off.

I should be doing something more useful than this, like reading the book I brought home, one of half a dozen I must plow through for the sensitivity cover. But industry doesn't appeal to me. I guess I've already begun the dropout process. Nothing seems very real anymore. I feel like a stranger wherever I go, even at *Time*. Whatever the rhythm of my life may have been, I'm off the tempo, a beat ahead or a beat behind. Nothing counts. Things still matter, but nothing counts. I'll go through all the familiar motions in this upcoming cover story, including panic, but it won't count. I live now in unconnected pockets of time, in each of which all the other pockets fade or disappear. I know that's schizoid, whatever that means. In the apartment, as now, sipping a martini in the slipper chair, writing to you, frozen macaroni and cheese in the oven, I don't think of the magazine or tomorrow or even, except in a dream way, of my un-plan to cop out. That's this pocket, and inside it time stands still. I do keep in touch with reality, but perfunctorily. I bought a fifth of gin tonight but I also bought a loaf of bread, and I put the butter out to soften, and I will remember to make sandwiches for tomorrow's lunch. I don't miss trains, and I say and do the right things at the right times. But in this pocket I am one me, and in others the *Time* me, the me socializing on those rare occasions when I'm asked out. I am other me's, and all of these me's have very little in common. Once having mastered the social rules, one can walk blindfolded through life, and that's part of what I'm trying to say. Another part is that I have divided myself into fragments—the true schizoid—that relate to those stagnant time pockets and don't overlap. Like, getting off the train tonight, I could almost feel the *Time* me changing into the White Plains me and I drove off, before entering the Wedgewood, for a fifth of gin and a loaf of bread. A loaf of bread, a fifth of gin and thou/ Beside me, singing in the wilderness/ Ah wilderness were paradise enow! Khayyam. I once memorized some one hundred of Fitzgerald's verses, years ago, and wish I could recite them still. My favorite, then and now, if I remember it right:

> Ah, love! Could you and I with Him conspire
> To grasp this sorry Scheme of Things entire
> Would not we shatter it to bits—and then
> Re-mould it nearer to the Heart's Desire!

Doesn't that make you want to weep? My dinner is almost done, and I can already tell I'm going to wake up groaning with chest pains tonight. I have about as much interest in eating as I have in screwing. It may be modestly significant that at Gretchen's Sunday I ate as zestfully and almost as much as a horse, and could have eaten much more than I did. This puzzles me. If it's merely a matter of having someone else prepare my food, then I would eat at restaurants with hearty appetite; but it depends more on the occasion than on the food. It's all too much for me. I'll figure it out in the next life. I don't feel too down now, thanks to gin. Isn't that awful? But sometimes we have to pay through the nose for peace of mind. And we all pay different prices. The grave's a fine and quiet place, but none I think do there embrace. Who wrote those lines? But, with a bit of Thomas, they say it all:

> Do not go gentle into that good night,
> Old age should burn and rave at close of day;
> Rage, rage against the dying of the light.

I'm showing off, am I not? Now I know something else: I'm going to call someone tonight out of sheer need. It should be you, and it would be, except that I can't pass the muster of my mother, waiting thirty years ago at her desk in the hall upstairs for her wayward sons to stagger back at any hour from Jake Skall's liquor dispensary on Appleton's South Side.

My teeth, I think, are going to hell. This once would have concerned me, but Gauguin was no prize either in the South Seas. Syphilitic, consumptive, his smile corroded by caries, his digestion defiled by the local fare (he dined regularly on canned peas sent out from France, can you imagine?); nevertheless he did his thing, though a fat lot of good it was to him. Where now his paintings sell in six figures, then they sold in three. He died counting himself a failure. But at least he did it. He defied the rules, broke and ran. The fact that his art is now widely acclaimed is totally beside the point. He did what he felt he had to do. And the nonentity ignored by history because he lacked the talent, or the desire, to leave a posthumous record, is Gauguin's equal. Anyway, what good does it do anyone to live after he dies? Better to live when you live. And now, I wonder, what curious association, prompted by that previous sentence, planted in my mind the architecture of a riding stable in Appleton, just south of the

Fox River and the second set of locks, on the left and ascending side of the Oneida Street hill? It's gone now, but for me it's still there, and abruptly my memory restored it to its place in the past. I took horses out of there, not often; and it exerts no urgent claim on my memory. I remember nothing about the horses I rode or with whom I rode them. But I can see it all the same, an unlovely hillside building saturated with sunshine, just across from the fairway of the Riverview Country Club's second fairway and just north of a tavern owned by the father of one of Riverview's cadre of caddies, a runny-nosed young man whose name completely eludes me. He's probably behind the bar this very night, having replaced his pa, who died of a ruined liver, and is now dispensing for 50 cents the eighteen-ounce stein of beer that cost me a nickel thirty years ago.

Hoo boy, have I screwed up tonight. Called everybody I could think of on the phone—in no order. And what news! My last winter's roomie is getting married. It will never work, but let them try. I called Dick Seamon and he proposed I fall sick tomorrow and go sailing with him. So I'm going. It's something I've never tried before—to goof off on *the* important writers' day. I'll pay for it, I suppose, but it was his initiative. He didn't have to suggest it. I didn't get Leon Jaroff, who is my boss this week, to tell him I'm going to be ill tomorrow; but I tried, and anyway I feel great about busting the pattern. Let them can me, it's worth $14,000 to $16,000. I've lost nearly all interest in *their* goals, and am focusing on mine. If I could get you tonight—and I'll probably try once more, in vain—I would ask you without salesmanship or overture: will you take me back? And you would say no. Wouldn't you? And that would be that. Try to imagine how liberated *I* am trying to feel in this new role.

I should have filled it long ago. I am no longer umbilically tied to *Time*. Duty orders: go in tomorrow, write your one story, do it well, make them appreciate and approve of you. The heart says (half drunk): go sailing with Dick, be you. I doubt if you can appreciate the enormous, though admittedly conditional, sense of liberation this inspires in me. If drink is the factor, then *Gott sei dank* for that. Now I'm going to bed, but not before calling you once more. I won't get you, but I'll try.

A quick note, all I have time for. I called you all day today too. I just wanted to hear your voice. You won't want a reconciliation, but I have to hear it from you. I called the shrink today, on orders, to report the effect of the Tofranil—nil— but he still extends a modicum of hope. I may not have reached my dose level, which must be approached with gingerly care, and am to amplify it, and will. I said you did not object to seeing him, and he seemed pleased by that. He wants to see you, and I want him to. But, Ann, don't lead me down any dead-end trails. Go to him, if you will, impelled however modestly by the possibility that we can try it again together, or don't go to him at all. I have had all the rejection I can handle, imagined or real—and the difference is microscopic. I'm on the verge of an irreversible decision, and tugged in both directions. I want very much to know that I'm needed, and if you don't need me, and never did, then that's that. I have to know. I don't have to tell you not to fake it. You won't. I can't beg and I won't. It has to be there in you; if it isn't, then it isn't. And if it isn't, then I've got to chuck this whole bit and sink or swim somewhere else. You were and are my only wife. I made no panic, intellectual decision to be married; I did pick you, and only you, never anyone else, and I climbed one hell of a lot of steep mountains to arrive in Sun Valley in March twenty years ago. I won't demean my relation with Jocelyn, and neither will I pretend penitence about it. She offered me something I wasn't getting anywhere else, and I needed it then as I need it now. Maybe I *am* down on my knees. I just don't know. I do know that the solitary life is not for me, that I had more years and more experiences and more ups and more downs and more sun and rain with you than with anyone else in the world, and that to pretend I can cut all of that out of my system is like saying that I can get along without my heart. I would never be able to say all these things to you in person, but don't you feel them? Can't you tell? Can you really get along fine without me? Were those nineteen years together nothing but a bad trip?

I'm very tired, having stayed up quite late Friday and spent the night in town, what there was left of it. So tired that even after a two-hour nap Saturday afternoon I went to bed about 8:30 and slept till nine. Dick Burgheim saw me at a farewell party on the twenty-sixth floor for a departing researcher, and asked me to dinner downtown in the apartment of a friend. I got very loaded and I stayed much too long. About one, I called a woman I've met since the divorce and prevailed upon her to put me up for the night. I had the VW in town, and though I could have driven it out, I didn't want to. As it was, we stayed up till past four, mostly talking but also making a little preliminary love. She refused to let me sleep in her bed, but I went in anyway; and was surprised when Grosser, in the course of a timorous campaign of mine addressed to her upstairs equipment, began to stir. With some encouragement and assistance from her I might have got back in the business; drink may be a depressant but it's also a powerful uninhibitor. But I didn't get any or much;

just a kind of what-next passivity. After a while I left the bedroom and finished the night on her couch. I had meant to work in the office Saturday—on the sensitivity cover, not the book—but instead I stuffed my attaché case full of things to read and drove out to White Plains.

There's no point in your going to the candler if you go just for my sake. It would have to be for ours. You'd like him. He would at least, seeing you, get perspectives on me and our failed marriage that I can't supply. The consultation is crucial. I will see him again after you've seen him (if you do go); and then perhaps it will be easier to decide whether to mount a campaign for the marriage or to beat it the hell out to Pago Pago. I had lunch with Brad Darrach Friday; we talked about some of this. He wanted to know whether I'd ever done a really shitty thing. I couldn't think of any. Then he said, "Think of a really shitty thing to do." And in the silence that followed, he said, "It's hard for you to think of something, isn't it?" And it was. Aggression is one of my problems. I can aggress in small and peevish ways. This is one reason you found me so difficult to live with, and researchers in years past so difficult to work with—but not in the self-assertive, Popeye ("I yam what I yam," etc.) ways that count. If I could, then no doubt Grosser would listen to gut-level orders and stop obeying those countermands from the head. And, if I could, I would no doubt have a different attitude toward my work and toward *Time*.

You wouldn't think I'd be sleepy after all the sack time I logged last night but I am. Maybe it's the antidepressant, which I'm on again, with an increased dosage, after a two-day layoff (I ran out). It's a God-damned expensive medication: $7.50 for less than a week's supply. They'd better work, and soon; I can't afford that just for a dry mouth. Breakfast today: pineapple juice, two bananas, milk and instant coffee. Dinner last night was one of those frozen beef shish kebabs, vegetable salad, a whole canteloupe, milk, and a bar of halvah. Nothing at all to drink, though I have gin, vermouth and two quarts of beer on hand. I may polish off the beer. Planned lunch menu, if I get around to it: peanut butter and jam sandwich (because I have to use up some bread), leftover vegetable salad, the last two bananas (which won't keep another day), milk, and a couple of Drake's Yodels. Planned entertainment for the afternoon: TV (old movie or Mets game), exercises, a letter to mother. She's out of the rest home and back in her apartment; a woman comes in five hours a day, for $1.25 an hour. Or $1.50. Frank told me all this over the phone one day last week. He's going to be in New York the end of September and I'll see him.

I really must be getting old. It was a chore doing 150 sit-ups. So maybe I'll have to do another set to prove that I can. Except to get the Sunday *Times* I haven't been out all day. I wonder what the apartment-house staff think of me: coming home at all hours by cab, leaving at odd times in the morning, something of an anchorite. And one night, after I'd taken the phone out of its cradle so as not to be disturbed by calls in the morning, some White Plains police, along with the super to let them in, opened my apartment door at what must have been 3 A.M. to see if I was all right. Apparently it had been reported—by whom I can't imagine—that my phone was mysteriously out of order. When I assured them rather grumpily that there was nothing wrong they withdrew. I rarely speak to or even see anyone here. The super, having had to let me in occasionally when I locked myself out, is the only person who has seen the inside of my room.

I should get out more often, if only to get in practice for Pago Pago, but what's there to do and where to go? Nothing much seems worth the effort. One gets ingrown living alone.

People become objects. I suppose I have more acquaintances now, and it may even be that more people like me. I never cared a good deal for the Westchester crowd and forgot many of their names from one party to the next. But I'm still a non-doer. Martha Duffy asked me to a bon voyage party at ten Friday morning on the Michelangelo. They're sailing for Naples—or, rather, they've sailed. She also pointedly said I was one of only three *Time* people invited. I said I'd go, but I didn't. So now I'll send them an apology to Porto Ercole, above Rome, where they'll visit Essie Lee, Alwyn's widow. He died this summer. Did you ever meet him? A tall, gaunt, leathery Australian with a Mephistophelian beard. He and I were fellow book reviewers for a while. A misguided near-genius who misspent his talents. When I heard of his death it meant nothing to me. I retain two memories of Al. On both occasions he was drunk. I guess I was too. On one, trying to show me his and Essie's Manhattan apartment late one night and lacking a key, he put his fist through a glass door pane. On the other, he and I had shared a Carey Cadillac one Friday night. Essie and Al then had a country place in the Yorktown area, not too far from the Martins. On the way out, there was nothing for it but to stop at a roadside tavern which was clearly one of his haunts; all the help knew him. We were there for what seemed hours while the Carey driver waited outside. Alwyn was on one of his bouts, which would go on for weeks and months and then abruptly end. At last I persuaded him to leave, and our car turned down a lane, not quite wide enough for the beam of a limousine, that snaked for moonless miles through a jungle of pines until we came to a clearing of matted grass beyond which, a hundred yards or so off, I could just make out the silhouette of a house. We got out of the Cad, the driver too. "This is all mine," said Al, and flung his arms wide to embrace this piece of northern Westchester. The gesture threw him over backward; he went down like a man shot. As I recall, after being helped to his feet, Alwyn staggered away under his own steam; I don't think I got to see the house.

I still owe your mother for most of the divorce itself. I keep only haphazard track of this obligation and would estimate that I've paid $350 of a $900 debt. For that matter, I still owe Sam Newhouse most of what I borrowed from him for that ill-fated six-month leave from *Time,* without pay. Totally unproductive, so far. My agent thought he'd found a buyer—a paperback house—for the Jonathan Doe novel I wrote then, but the deal fell through. He still has the manuscript. On the other hand, there's always the likelihood that I'll never finish anything. Certainly not the sociology book. Maybe another one I have in mind and am well into. If I ever sell (complete) anything, then I can dust off the unfinished crap from that long-ago leave and collect something from them. You'll get your share. I've lost nearly all desire to be financially fat; the most I want of life now is to have what I do make sense and to be fun. I won't even demand relief from my enforced celibacy, mainly since it's so unlikely. Screwing is nice, but at my age unnecessary, however nice. That model I've mentioned, Barbara Smith, who is very outspoken, once recently said she had a very improper question to ask of me and then changed her mind about asking it. But I made her. It was: in view of my psychic impotence, what do I do when I get horny? I didn't answer, but I know the answer. The fact is that I almost never get horny. Maybe I should seduce a sixteen-year-old, and perhaps it would work—if there were any complaisant sixteen-year-olds around. But Humbert Humbert cornered the last of those accessible to dirty old men. Anyway, I don't get full erections except when totally off guard, i.e., asleep. I will sometimes wake up with one, not as the result of a stimulating dream, but I can't remember the last time I had what doctors call a nocturnal emission, it's been so many years. Emission is by no means impossible, to make a very bad pun. But this hang-up goes back years, as you know better than anybody, and now, even though it doesn't exactly throw me, it's become a thing. They say (don't ask me who *they* are) that Samoan women have no emotional or sexual hang-ups at all. Maybe that's what I need.

The beer, as usual, is bringing me peace. What I'd really prefer to do tonight, if my preference were consulted, would be to take you alone out to dinner, not necessarily at Franzl's —Nino's would do—and talk about us. Or talk about any-thing. I do crave your solitary company, but God knows why. I wish we were still married but living apart. Not like your parents, which was a crummy arrangement. We'd be man and wife, mother and father, but still free. Free and tied both. The human animal was never designed by evolution to be monogamous. But he needs a more or less permanent connection with someone of the opposite gender, one stronger and more abiding than all the others that are bound to occur, and do, in the course of a normal lifetime. If I were able to say all such things to you face-to-face, or bet-ter yet, act them out, then this letter would not be necessary, divorce would not have been necessary, and contractual mar-riage wouldn't have been necessary to begin with.

It was nice of you to ask me over for dinner, but I begin to quail now at the prospect of an evening with my former family. How many times have I felt compelled to discipline my tongue, which is perfectly capable of making unslurred sense after a whole lot more than two G-bottles of beer? In all the years with you I never took charge, and I should have. I should every now and then have done mildly shitty (not peevish) things. Or did I? It appears so simple to me sometimes, but with you it never was simple. "Ann (a call from the city), drop everything and come into town." "Why?"

"Because I want you to, I want you here." "Why?" "I don't know, but come." Or: "Ann, it's going to be a late night and I'm taking a room at the Winslow. Come on in and spend the night with me there." Or whatever, along those lines. I find it significant, though inexplicable, that since the divorce I haven't spent a single late night at a hotel. Not one. I always beat it out to 2-A by cab. *And,* ninety-nine out of a hundred of those late nights I was alone.

It's six and I'm about to shower and shave. I know beforehand the evening will be guarded and strained and that, if the kids vanish after dinner, we may end up with a row.

How right I was. As far as I'm concerned, tonight settled it. You made it quite clear that you're happier alone, that a reconciliation is simply out of the question, and that the decay and ultimate death of our marriage can be attributed largely if not entirely to me. We are simply, irrevocably and irreparably incompatible. I will not and cannot accept your critical judgment of me. You say that now, in the single state, you enjoy not being forever criticized and judged. Well, I wish you well in this fantasy of a dream state—where all around you approve and applaud everything you do. It becomes pointless, in view of all you said and didn't say, for you to see the candler. I haven't the faintest desire for you to see him on behalf of me. It also becomes pointless for *me* to see him again, since your spirit is built of flint and you will not allow for the possibility—won't even entertain the possibility —that we could under any circumstances get together again. Now I have no choice but to put into action my plan to try something else. I don't know whether you expect me to go on pulling down from *Time* the income that sustains us all. I sure as hell don't need it; and if you do, then learn how to get along without it. Maybe you think you can make it without my contribution, and maybe you can. You're sure as hell going to get the chance to find out. Everything that happened tonight confirmed me in the conviction that you don't want a husband and all that entails. You want a pay check, and the form of marriage. Well, now I'm really going to be shitty, by your book. I have no choice now but to blow, and blow I will. Every God-damned time I tried to open a door tonight, you pushed it firmly shut. Don't ever ever do anything out of pity for me, and when that's your motive, have the grace to say so. I'm good and mad, and the strength of it, I pray, will carry me out of my fears and reservations into a new life. It may be no better than the last one, and it may be worse, but at least it will be different.

It's not easy for me to remember, after all, that I was the demolitionist of record. I keep thinking of it as something caused by an outside agency, possibly even you. I feel the victimized one, when of course the world of morality would render another verdict. I feel it was *you* who left *me*. You would have in time. In honesty, you will agree to that. And in a very real way you did leave me. This may be the rationalization of a born loser, but the evidence is there: the quick trip south of the border, the decisions—none of which I heard from you—to spend the summer in East Hampton and to move permanently out west (it's only because you couldn't rent the house that you're not there now); the steady rejection of all my timid overtures, culminating in what you said last night. Now I truly believe that the marriage is dead. And how long has it been dead? How many years? Did it die when you moved out of our bedroom because no one can sleep with a restless insomniac? Or when at last sex ended for good? And when was that? I remember occasions, not so very long ago, when I could and did express in other ways what Grosser refused to say. A moonlit night on the porch of a cottage during our first trip to Wisconsin two years ago; several times in your bed in the guest room. And the alacrity with which you gave me up—I keep coming back to that—as if I were no loss at all, my defection itself just a transitory blow to your pride. Nineteen years down the drain just like that. You mystify me. To go to a psychiatrist not because the defects in our marriage bothered you but because they didn't. I can't believe that's honest. You're deceiving either me or yourself. And don't forget, too, that that consultation of yours could be construed as a gambit in the game that led to separation and divorce. At the time you knew nothing of my affair. I honestly don't know whether our thing ever would have come to a head without your psychiatrist, who set me to thinking about what *I* was getting out of my job and marriage. I was living in a dream state then when anything seemed possible: to leave you and *Time* and live with Jocelyn on the little money both of us could earn—at what kind of work didn't matter and I didn't care. I just wanted out, and still do. I wanted to feel appreciated, to get back a whole lot of lost identity. As for our quarreling, my criticism, *your* criticism too—I think your memory has embellished the case against me. I got as good as, if not better than, I gave. You weren't constantly criticized, as you seem to think you were. I was often tempted in the heat of an argument with you—none of which I ever won—to tape the next one and play it back to you. You were the decision maker in that family: to send Bob to prep school on *your* money (as if money has any personal identity); to put in a new bathroom; you picked all the new furniture; criticized me endlessly for wasting time on weekends washing and polishing the car. Maybe I asked for all that. Maybe what I did want was not a mature sex life but a mother. But who the hell knows? I tried, and I went on trying long after you stopped trying. And then I, too, stopped trying.

I have the feeling too that the time to move may be nearer than I think. Omens here and there. Signs. Before I left for Washington, a letter arrived from the editor at Putnam's, politely inquiring how the book was coming along and asking to be advised by letter or phone. I put off answering it until after we got back from the sociologists' convention, then pleaded that as an excuse for being late responding—a good way of hinting that we were hard at work on the book, which we weren't—and otherwise fobbed him off with a couple of paragraphs that didn't lie but didn't quite tell the truth either, and that permitted (invited) him to assume everything was moving along on schedule. This afternoon I got another letter from him that I didn't dare open. I left the office, in fact, without opening it. What if it asks for a look at a chapter or two, no matter how unpolished? We have nothing to show. What if it makes some other impossible demand on us, like coming in for a chat about progress? I am painting myself into a corner, making it impossible *not* to go to Pago Pago. And terrified at the prospect. I've lost the knack that I once had in my youth of doing bold things and bringing them off. And if I can feel that New York is an unnegotiable distance from Wisconsin, as I did all the while the kids and I were there, how am I going to feel in Samoa, 8,000 miles from all I know? This little studio prison may seem, in retrospect, like a cocktail party or a salon. What's driving me there is an aching, allover need for relief from pressure. But I may find more pressure there than here. Sometimes I think I haven't the guts to go. At other times I try to reason myself out of it (which is easy, since it is an irrational thing to do), but mostly I long to do it as the life prisoner longs for death. It isn't the being there that I'm after, it's the going. It's one way of screwing up big. And it may take me to that relatively calm and airless realm that T George Harris reached as a *Time* writer: the realm, he said, that lies beneath despair. I'm not there yet, and maybe I can find it in Pago Pago. It's certainly nowhere around here.

Five more Valiums down the old gullet, which, along with all the rest of me but my emotional constitution, will be fifty-three day after tomorrow. Don't the years pile up quickly on the downhill slope? It seems only yesterday that our San Francisco vacation was spoiled by that call from *Time* in New York telling me that I'd be hitting the campaign trail with Vice-President Nixon. And yet it was 1956, fourteen years ago, and I was a callow thirty-nine. Don't remember much about that vacation except that we shopped at Gump's for those wine goblets, thinner than eggshells, that the Giffords gave us as a wedding present, ate at a quaint restaurant up Telegraph Hill, and in Chinatown and at Fisherman's Wharf. What the hell else did we do? Were we there a month? I remember better covering the Republican convention that summer, going up by train and staying up late drinking in the club car with Loudon, sharing a hotel room with Barron Beshoar, and picking up a girl late one night, taking her home and screwing her, stealing out after dawn without waking her, and sneaking back into the hotel room without waking Barron. Really pooped the next day, too, but what does it matter now? As someone has said, we can catch up on our sleep in the grave. Seeing Art Weaver in the Nebraska delegation and Wendy Fernback, then Miller, in the stands. I remember very well, though, our trip to Omaha the following year in the brand-new MGA. You will recall you chewed me out, but good, for trading in the Hillman on that. Seems to me you were always chewing me out for something.

Two more chest-pain attacks today, one rather strong one on the night train. They don't upset me, but maybe I should take an office physical before cutting out. I haven't had one in more than a year.

For the first time in all my years with the magazine I've stayed away from work—and on my writing day too—with a hangover. Why should I feel guilty about that? But I do. Dick Bush is in town, on his way back to Tokyo. I invited him to dinner Tuesday night, and thus it began. We met first at the apartment of some friends of his, the Lowerys, who were once part of the American community in Tokyo but returned stateside six years ago. A good many martinis there, then Dick and I left for dinner at the Paul Revere Room in the Lexington Hotel. More martinis, and I, like a fool, picked up the tab. And from there by cab to the Oak Room at the Plaza, for too many stingers on the rocks. I guess it was a true bender, though I remember every moment of it, including the cab ride out to White Plains, setting the alarm for nine and falling into bed just after three. When the alarm went off I reset it for ten, got up again and called in sick. Leon Jaroff wasn't in so the message was relayed to him. He called back after eleven (waking me up incidentally) and I mendaciously explained that I'd been working late on the Robert Ardrey story, began to get sick to my stomach, called a cab and threw up all the way home. In actuality I don't have a hangover at all. The old me, rousing groggily at nine, would have dutifully gone off to work, done my story quota, worked till eleven or midnight. There were, in fact, extenuating circumstances. I was supposed to have been off this week, boning up for the cover; but then on Tuesday it was postponed and so I was faced suddenly with having to whack out a this-week "Behavior" section from next to nothing and, of course, I had to see Dick and that meant drinks and a long night. I'm holing up here for a day with no company but a guilty conscience. I smoked so much yesterday that my throat is raw as liver. I'm now smoking my last cigarette, having doused the rest of the pack with water and dropped it into the garbage. It's 1:30 now and I've had nothing to eat but a glass of pineapple juice and coffee. Perhaps the punishment includes really getting sick. I'm capable of it. Where and how and why did I ever learn to hold such a low opinion of myself? And after all, what's so terrible about what I've done? Got drunk, stayed up too late, and voted myself a day off—the first such in fifteen years. It's either a harbinger of worse to come or a one-shot that won't ever be repeated. I know one thing, though. I'm going to knock off this two-fisted drinking. You may be right: If I'm going to drink at all, it shouldn't be martinis. Besides, drinking is self-indulgent and I've been doing too much of it lately. I don't really think it's a habit, but I won't know, will I, unless I try doing without?

I'm to call my head candler, I assume about your appointment. I'd told him you would see him, but that was before our talk Sunday. It seems rather silly to me now to say that there's no point in your going because you're not interested in a reconciliation. So maybe I'll call you and talk about it some more. Now, suddenly, I'm overwhelmed with f.f.a.—free-floating anxiety. Maybe I'm coming apart. Sometimes I think I am, that I'm poised on the lip of an emotional decline.

The shrink can see you at 1:30 this coming Tuesday afternoon, after which I'll see him early Thursday. I've arranged to have your consultation put on my bill. His office is way north. You'd better drive, it's the easiest way to find it. You just come down the Saw Mill River Parkway, and just past the George Washington Bridge, almost immediately past it, you'll see a turn to the *left* marked Presbyterian Hospital. Well, I'll tell you the rest of it when I next call. I don't know what good it can do, but what harm can it do? And at least he'll hear your side of it. This has been some day. My fifty-third birthday, by the way. I didn't remember yours either, did I? It's kind of sad the kids forgot, but there's no reason why they should remember things like that. I wrote "occasions" first and then erased it. This is no occasion. The nicest thing that's happened all day is that Barbara Smith called. Somehow she'd heard that I was "sick." I'll bet at *Time* they all really believe it too. They don't know what a bullshitter Koffend is. But I do. I've watched TV, read the *Times,* developed a bellyache and bawled like a baby at a movie titled *Bus Riley's Back in Town.* And, naturally, predictably, inevitably, went out and bought a pack of Camels. This one-day layoff is going to cost me in more ways than one. I'll probably have to write the whole section tomorrow. They're short of writers and anyway they're not the kind of stories anyone can take over. But what the hell, it'll all be the same in a hundred years. Tonight I've got to knock myself out with Valium and go to bed early. Simply can't stand much more of my society today.

A letter to the shrink, drafted late one night on the eve of your visit to him, and, for obvious reasons, never sent.

I have a fairly good idea why this form of communication, which admits of no give-and-take. I've read the evaluation often enough to understand how (if not why) I deploy my intellect as a buffer and a shield. My wife of nineteen years is coming to see you Tuesday—that is, if the appointment time suits her convenience. She hasn't committed herself on this because I haven't talked to her since the appointment was made. I seem to have been wrong in my *a priori* judgment about whether she would see you at all. When I talked to her about it, after having first raised the possibility in a letter, I asked her why she had agreed to go at all, and I ventured the observation, before she had a chance to reply, that unless she were going for her sake or for ours, there was no point in going at all. She would not agree, even after prompting, that reconciliation was a possible motive; she allowed me to believe that her reason for going was to help me, and she also suggested that I pay half the cost. As you know from my call, I will pay it all. I am not optimistic about her consultation with you. I still harbor the suspicion, which is lifelong, that *they* are invariably right and I am invariably wrong. I told Ann that she would like you, and I am certain she will. If you are sympathetic to her during the hour—and I have no doubt you will be—she will probably burst more than once into tears. Her emotions lie very near the surface, where emotions belong. In one hour, however, I doubt whether you or anyone can demolish those defenses that compel her, in my opinion, to regard marriage as a clash of wills which only the woman should win. I could be dead wrong about this. We warp the evidence in favor of our predispositions, and I am predisposed to believe in this case that our marriage failed before it began. At one level, I know how kind it is of you to find room in a crowded schedule for my former wife, and for me. It could signify a genuine interest in solving an emotional impasse, a genuine interest in the principals involved. But I have a lot of trouble accepting anything like that. I know people are good, but I don't really believe it. What I really believe, I think, was crudely stated years ago by a friend. "Turn your back," he said, "and people will shit on your plate." He may have been, and probably was, wrong. But the fact is that I have seldom since turned my back.

I have decided that this communication is intolerably self-conscious and therefore should not be sent. It's all part of the grand mis-design. One must piss in dark corners, draw the shades to make love, wear masks to hide emotions, smile through tears, honor one's parents and be strong. But what if life is just the opposite of all that? Try to sell that bill of goods to children, those blank slates on which we inscribe all the bad tuition that got inscribed on ours. Somebody has got to bust out of the vicious circle, and the really strong ones do. They know who they are. To them, the Other is important, but as a mirror mostly, surely not as a model.

So you're going to see the shrink on Tuesday. And so you resent my dropping into "your house," as you call it. If you faced the kind of weekends I do, you might understand why I drive up most weekends when you're there. It's a familiar scene. It's where I lived as husband and father for ten years, and I know every square foot of it, from the peeling ceiling in the back hall to the bullet hole Bob put in the living room ceiling when he accidentally fired Allen's pump gun. I know the chairs and the rugs and the books, most of which I've read and many of which I've reviewed, and the rusted chrome switch plate by the Sears Coldspot, which has now outlasted our marriage, and the stain from raccoon pee on the stair carpet and the red hand I painted on the frame of the basement door, and the dog's dishes, and your collection of wheeled objects. You'll be gone soon enough, or I will. Until then, I'm so aware of the house and of all of you, and so trapped in this apartment, that it's all I can do not to invite you to dinner at Franzl's, or anywhere. God, how I miss the old life, even just as it was. I'd be better off if I were in the woman game, but that is something of an obstacle in my private life. That and impecuniousness. Perhaps old Grosser will learn to lift his head again as I lay off the sauce. He's the soul of inactivity now. I gave him a fair chance the other night—something right out of Portnoy —but he showed no interest at all.

Thrilling afternoon to look forward to. I've done my grocery shopping and my exercises. Soon (it's after three) I'll take my shirts to the laundry, pick up the morning *Times* so I can do the crossword puzzle, turn on the TV, heat up a TV dinner, and then wait for bedtime to come. I'm not likely to sleep. I was dog-tired last night, went to bed at ten and slept through to 11:30 the next morning, feeling none the better for it. The tenor of my days appalls even me, who am not by nature or inclination an activist. Being alone so much of the time is hard on the spirit. I can understand now why some convicts prefer the chair to life imprisonment. The latter is what I've sentenced myself to by my crime of last year. In Pago Pago, I would of course be even more alone and maybe I couldn't take it. I can't take this either. I know you're a new Ann, an Ann who has lived a separate life now for nearly a year. You're not the Ann who was my wife. If only the phone would ring. If only someone would call. If only I were going out to dinner tonight with a friend or to a friend's house. I want to call any of my old friends and say, I'm lonely, may I please come over? But out of sight, out of mind. I don't ever see them on the train because they get on farther up the track and sit in the back cars, and I get on in North White Plains and sit in the front. With strangers. I should get out of here and live in New York, but I can't afford the penalty or to move the little I've got. Barbara Smith gave me a paperback book for my birthday, Philip Slater's *The Pursuit of Loneliness,* inscribed: "So we can pursue it together—and lose it. Happy Birthday. Love, Barbara." But she'd forgotten too; it came late. And the kids forgot. And you didn't, after all. When Frank comes to New York, would you come to town for dinner with both of us? Silly to ask you here. I'll ask you in person when he comes.

Have brought home a stack of reading to do this weekend but probably won't get to it. Maybe if it's warm I'll take some up to the roof. The kids don't really miss me, do they? No more than you. Or Phil or Loudon or Kathy or any of my former "friends." At times like this, cooped up in the apartment with the blinds drawn, the sound of traffic on North Broadway, an occasional audible movement from one of my neighboring apartment dwellers, I think of them doing all their customary togetherness things, scenes I once inhabited. You tell me nothing of your life unless I ask, and then so little. I want to see the children, but I must be careful there. My need for them is greater than theirs for me. I try to think up fun things that would tempt them but they all cost so much money: Coney Island or that other amusement park in New Jersey, deep-sea charter fishing off Montauk, which would take a weekend and a small fortune. They've seen all the movies. You think (and have said) that I don't want to see them, but it isn't true. They're past the age of the simple amusements that sufficed in the past and well past the age when they could be satisfied just with Pop's company.

There sure is a lot of misery in the world, nearly all of it self-engineered.

I must begin thinking of the loose ends to be tied before I leave for Pago Pago. *If* I go. Nobody, you too, really believes I'll do it. There's the car for instance. I can leave it in the parking lot here but I must send you the key. Owed: about two years of fifty-dollar monthly payments. There's nothing in the apartment worth salvaging, unless you want the Herman Miller dresser and the rug, and possibly my pans and tableware. One of the boys might want back the tools I repossessed, particularly the electric drill. You'll have to get into the strong box for the Farmers Underwriter shares, which are worth something; you don't even know what bank. I'll tell you all that and send you the key. There's one at home but you'd never find it. I'll send you a key to the apartment too. I intend to leave owing a month's rent (which they recover anyway from the initial deposit) so if you want anything of what I leave behind, you'd be wise to come and get it before anyone here realizes I'm gone. I plan to take all my summer suits but none of the winter ones. They're not worth anything. The typewriter is *Time's*, but I think I'll crate it and ship it to me in Pago Pago, c/o General Delivery. I'll need it out there. My attaché case—worth $40 new and still usable. Now as to cash. You're not going to be too well off, unless your mother pitches in or you have a rich man on the string. I'm going to keep all the severance pay. That ought to support me in Pago Pago, even without a job, for three or four years, though I'm guessing at the cost of living out there. The money in the profit-sharing fund takes about three months to release, and has to be released to me. Whatever that may amount to you'll get it all. I would estimate a net of $30,000, which may be on the high side. That's enough to keep your household going for two years.

Then, the estate. At last report, it seems we're very close to home there. We may have to shell out as much as $10,000 to buy off the sole remaining survivor, who's entitled to some of the trust's earnings until her death. But whatever my cut of that, it's yours. You may realize, after inheritance taxes, $40,000—and it could be a whole lot more. And $40,000 would keep you going another two years. Remember, once you get these big hunks, they're not income, and therefore not taxable. Now, you'll lose *Time*'s free life-insurance policy, which is worth double my salary (more under certain circumstances), or about $60,000. That is automatically canceled when I leave. I have two $5,000 double-indemnity policies with Aetna, each of which has some small cash-surrender value. The annual premiums on both are about $500 a year. I will probably stop paying those premiums when I leave. If you want me to be worth something to you dead, you'll have to keep up the payments yourself. I'd investigate the possibility if I were you, but I'd investigate even more carefully what they're worth to you now. The Farmers Underwriter shares, which I haven't looked into for a long time, may be worth as much as $5,000. When and if I get to Pago Pago, I will continue to be honorable in my dishonorable way. That is, if I get a job, which is very likely, I'll send you half off the top of whatever I make. I have two writing projects—neither one of them, incidentally, the new sociology book, which I've just about decided to flush. One I consider very promising. If it delivers on its promise, you will certainly get your half—again, right off the top. I'm trying my best to be realistic about a very surrealistic bend in my road. I don't discount the possibility that on arriving in American Samoa I will fall flat on my ass or turn beachcomber or legitimate lush. Fifty-three is one hell of an age at which to pick up stakes, move 8,000 miles, and hammer them down again. I may wind up weeping in the consular office, whatever they call it over there. I may just walk out into the South Pacific surf one day and go down with the sun. But if that's to be my end, I'm likelier to do it in a more chicken way. I haven't had Seconal for years, but if I can swing it, I plan to take along a lethal dose, just in case. Now, I also have about $1,700 cash in the checking account—the residue, principally, of Putnam's advance. This steadily dwindles. I have towering obligations to American Express, most of them incurred during my week in Washington but some since. Whatever is left in that account at the moment of decision I will also selfishly keep, to get me to Pago Pago mostly. Silly as it may seem to you, I am sustained by the Pago Pago fantasy and doubt that I could live without it. It's my keeper, the custodian of sanity and the antidote for all else that is wrong. And all else is wrong. I'm smoking like a choked chimney, boozing it up, unable to cohabit with a woman (or a God-damned knothole, for Christ's sake) and so consistently unhappy that I can confuse oblivion with bliss. I would rather sleep than live. When I get out to the South Seas I'm not going to wow anybody, but I haven't wowed anybody here either, have I? And the threads are frayed and fraying more all the time. Breakfast today: pineapple juice and ersatz coffee. Lunch: a small bowl of cereal and milk in "your house." Nothing since, except some martinis from that leftover bottle of gin. I don't even want to eat dinner but I will: a Mexican TV plate, plus a piece of stale chocolate cake. And on this starvation diet I have somehow managed to run in place 2,000 times and do 300 sit-ups with feet unhooked. I have the last of the gin in my glass, the TV dinner in the oven. If I'm tired enough after consuming both, I may just go straight to bed, though it's likelier I'll beat it out to Franzl's, even on a Saturday night, to take an unaccustomed whiff of humanity. Either that or call one of my fair-weather friends and dump myself like a foundling on his doorstep.

I told you my roomie of last spring was getting married. Well, she's married now. And today came a letter from her, in that wide-open, first-grade writing that tells so much —tells me anyway—about her.

One can sense the anger seething beneath the surface of the letter. Last night, on the northbound commuter train, a strange and indefinable event occurred. One of the sub-conductors seized the middle of the aisle to recap an episode earlier in the week. He announced that some other conductor on this line had stepped off the train and died—presumably of a heart attack although this wasn't said. He then conveyed gratitude to all those commuters who, on request, had helped fill the hat passed down the aisle by some colleague of the dead man, for his widow's sake. Whereupon the hat was passed again. I noticed that most people gave— small change, but they gave. I gave nothing. I didn't know the deceased. But the incident gave me pause. Did all the givers know him? Doesn't the railroad union take care of its own? Were these quarter-donators donating willingly? Or was this one of those impositions laid on the quick by the agents of the dead? Am I missing something? Should I have kicked in with a fin, and if so, for what? Is everyone else but me in step?

I relate the one event to the other. There isn't the slightest doubt—in my mind at least—that without the two difficult but illuminating months she spent with me, the roomie would never have married. In a way I set it up. I didn't want ever to marry her, and don't. She's a fine girl, as I've said, but her life style is penitence, and a little of that goes a long way. Like a fool, I laid much of this on while she was here, and so she was delighted to go. Maybe her husband whom I know and love, can accommodate her riddles. I would classify him, from long experience, as a man capable of getting along with a professional heckler.

Back from half of Sunday with you, washing and polishing the car, helping you with the Sunday crossword, watching the kids dash in and out on their mysterious errands— almost like old times. It says something about the poverty of my life now that this was the best Sunday I've had since Wisconsin. I've got my life properly screwed up now. Steve and I are way behind on the book and probably won't write it. This leaves us $4,500 in hock to Putnam. I'm torn between coming back to you—which is by no means certain —and running off to Pago Pago. I'm afraid to ask you. Last night at the Kunhardts, after you left, we got to talking about you (just Kathy and Phil's sister Edie and me) and Kathy said she's suggested a reconciliation more than once and that you invariably say no, you're not interested, you have grown to like living by yourself. I'm not absolutely sure I want to come back either; it would re-consign me to the old life—by which I don't mean you but the rat race, the silly Westchester crowd, the God-damned commuter train five days a week, late nights, and nothing ahead but sixty and the modest income of retirement. Meanwhile, *Time* itself is sliding downhill. It all seems more than I can manage, and yet it adds up to nothing at all. If only there were some way to make a new life together. The children have to be educated, of course, but we could take chances. Get out of the pattern, find another one. There are dozens of things I'd rather do than write for *Time*. Teach, for instance. Do we really need that big house and—between us—something like $36,000 a year gross? It still sounds like an awful lot of money to me, and yet it covers nothing.

You made a shrewd guess. I *am* drinking more—just about every other day. I hadn't meant to yesterday (nothing the day before), but after all day in the apartment I was keyed up so tight that I polished off the last of the gin—a third of a fifth, I'd say—and then carted a six-pack of Budweiser over to the Kunhardts and drank most of that unassisted. I think these recurrent chest pains come from over-smoking while drinking. I'm smoking more too, two packs most days. I hope it's not lung cancer (or do I?) and the chances are it isn't, but it's got to be something. I'm really tired of living on drugs: tobacco, liquor and beer, Valium and the pill regimen the head candler has put me on. In the last two days nearly twenty-four hours of sleep, though none of it unabetted. The same tonight. I feel I must knock myself out with Valium: I can't stand my thoughts in the dark. I'm getting old, I'm fifty-three, my hair is mostly gray, the exercises are harder to do now and I don't do them as frequently. I loathe my work (that's not quite true), I hate myself, and I really can't see any way out. As usual, I've put everything I've got on your visit to the head candler on Tuesday and mine on Thursday, as if two fifty-minute hours with a shrink will solve everything. It won't. It won't. That's always up to us, and I'm not equal to it anymore. Time stands still when I'm asleep, when I'm writing you, as now, or when I spend a few hours at the old home as today. Then nothing else counts, or matters. It *is* the womb wish, isn't it? What in the hell was it that arrested my maturation? There's something obscene about being a fifty-three-year-old boy. I wish there were somebody who could tell me what to do. Maybe what I need is a self-improvement program—no matter what—and then stick to it—no matter what. Boy, have I got free floating anxiety right now.

It's 11:30, I've been reading Slater's *The Pursuit of Lone-*

liness, which I recommend to you. The Valium is beginning to take hold. Good night, my wife of nineteen years, good night.

Just a few lines while the frozen Italian dinner (lasagna) is thawing and my laundry is tumbling two floors below (I didn't do it Sunday after all). I'm dying to know what you and the candler talked about but I guess it's best to wait and hear it from him Thursday. A researcher invited me to a preview of Bob and Ray last night. It's funny, but very brief—8:40 to 10:20—and I'd say you'd have to be a Bob and Ray fan to like it, especially at $8.50. The crowd reminded me of a theater night in Omaha, all fat frumpy women and *Lumpenproletariat* men. Scarcely any young people at all (my escort is fortyish and just a friend). I did catch a cold from Sunday but a mild one, just a tickly throat and what could pass for postnasal drip. What the hell *is* p.n.d. anyway? I never really knew. Light week so far at the office, everything having been written last week. I've been spending my time boning up on the h.p.m. cover (human potentials movement; my day for initials I guess), which is not going to be any fun to write. The subject doesn't grab me. Besides, we're much too late, everything's been said. Hot today, wasn't it? Got up to ninety, a fitting exit for summer's last day. Wonder if you cried, as I predicted. I'll ask the shrink.

Now that I'm off the Tofranil my depression appears to have lifted some, but perhaps it's just buoyancy left over from Sunday with you. Queer how much that meant to me, I'm famished for company. I'm still convinced that a bad marriage is better than none.

Lunching tomorrow—business—with Jane Howard of *Life,* who wrote *Please Touch,* a tour of the human potentials movement. I don't really need her help—I've read her book—but I thought, why not let *Time* set me up for a lunch date. She called me first, last week, on something about having to make a lot of speeches on the subject, and would I send her all the files that came in to *Time's* cover. She could have got them anyway, by asking just about anyone, without going through me.

Today I asked Arnold Drapkin, who's an officer in the *Time* chapter of the guild, if there's a way to assure my getting my severance pay. He said there was, definitely, and will explain how first chance he gets.

Incorrigible. Lunch with Jane Howard (martinis and lay therapy) and dinner with Fred Golden (martinis and man talk). I kept busy with the cover, but the day lacked all direction. Slow death. Its painlessness—and it's not exactly painless—is quite beside the point. Its aimlessness is quite *to* the point. It's 11:30 now and I must rise at six, full of Valium and the lingering effect of gin, to chauffeur the VW in to learn what I can guess—that you're not interested in remarrying, least of all me—and to inform the shrink that there's only one way and one place for me to go. Well, as I've said, one breath, one step at a time. As long as it's Wednesday, why worry about Thursday? And so forth. Thursday can be an infection that should not be permitted to defile the day before. So say the gestalt theorists anyway. The past is dead. The future is yet to be. Long live the here and now. One more smoke and to bed. If I didn't look so much like Everett Dirksen I'd wear shorts tomorrow. The weatherman predicts more ninety-degree weather. I nearly wore them today, and would have if I hadn't had a lunch date. But anyway I can't tomorrow either. At four, I'm seeing a director of the Esalen Institute, suitably enough at the Elysee Hotel. Stuart Miller's the name; he has a Ph.D. in something. How did your session go? Tomorrow will be my last. I've invested a lot in them, with nothing much to show for it. We'll see.

I'm at Franzl's. I saw the shrink this morning, two days after your appointment with him, and now at last I understand that the marriage is irretrievably, irreparably, and forever over. We try to live on illusions, which die hard. Until this morning, I nursed the illusion, past all credibility, that the mistakes of the recent past were correctable, that none of it really had happened, the bad dream would fade in the sun, the witch doctor at Presbyterian Hospital would wave his magic talisman and everything would be just as it once was: you at twenty-eight, in your red velvet dress, gracefully posing for your husband's Speed Graphic in the apartment in Omaha next to the filling station, a congealed and glossy memento of the long ago past. He was quite straightforward with me. He cast loose my last mooring. It's not fair to say he did. *I* did with a cold chill in my heart that persisted until I had a martini with Andrea Svedberg at her suggestion, in the Monkey Bar at the Elysee Hotel (a place you might remember because we once had a pre-theater drink there, years ago, with Jean and Jack Ames). Andrea and I had come from a four-hour talk upstairs in room 403 with Stuart Miller, a director of Esalen, and his wife Sookie (the spelling is a guess), about the sensitivity cover I must write week after next. It will be the last cover I'll ever write, which you may have gathered from the cryptic note I sent you today with your check. I think I knew all along that the course was irreversible, but hope, like the king in chess, does not easily die. The candler summed up what you'd said: that you're not going to remarry, least of all me, that any thought of reconciliation is therefore folly (I think he added something like: unless you were forced into it), and that if I hadn't made my move last fall, you would soon enough have filed for divorce against me. After one martini and now two Michelobs, the finality of your position, and the fact that I was already dead without knowing it, doesn't have the shock value it did this morning at 7:30. I can accept it—what choice anyway? It is, to be sure, the ultimate rejection; nineteen years of marriage to me and a year before that of crumbling your resistance to marriage have been as nothing. If you have any feelings at all for me now, I can well imagine what they are (and they're not what you may think I think they are), and I don't want to hear them. I thought of calling you, but what would be the point? It is finally over, ended, nothing left. It came out with the needle on zero. As I indicated in my note, now I know what I must do, and I am going to do it. I'm squared off with the shrink. I've asked for and got a sizable and renewable prescription for Valium which I will accumulate, if possible, and take with me. No more antidepressants. No more Android— Grosser can hang his head from now on for all I care. I think I made it clear to you, Ann, before making the appointment that if reconciliation was out of the question there was no sense in your going. You should have told me that it was. So you went under false colors and I'm not going to pay for it. Indeed, I mean to blow in a blizzard of due bills. Let them find me. I haven't had much to drink tonight, and I am, whether you believe it or not, going to consign that indulgence to the past I'm fleeing. I'm going to leave a lot of useless baggage behind. I told the shrink this morning that I like to drink, and I do. He said it was destructive, and it is, but he doesn't know everything. He didn't choose to argue or defend a piece of candor from me: that I couldn't believe he was genuinely interested in my problems except professionally, as the mathematician is interested in theorems. Our connection is professional, not human. It was our last time together, but he hurried me out on the dot of 8:20 with a warm scoutmaster handclasp and an injunction to keep in touch. Why would I keep in touch with him?

I had my talk with Arnold Drapkin. It develops that the only way I can assure severance pay is to lie down on the job, and in my case that could take months. Should I lay it on the line with HAG, he's got me. By announcing my intention to resign, I thereby forfeit all severance rights, if they want to play by the rules. But it's a chance I'll have to take. Surely after fifteen years of competent commitment from me, they're not going to stick at $14,000 or so.

Everyone here at Franzl's, where I happen to be, is apparently better adjusted to life than I am. They're all happy, or act so, and I'm not. This feels like the most uninspired segment of this long letter to you, and yet its subject is a turning point, one of those road bends that, once taken, carry you beyond every familiar landmark and landscapes that you can draw with your eyes closed. The people here no doubt think I'm nuts, sitting here at a table writing (What do they think I'm writing?) though Frankie Mondschein (true name Francois Clair de Lune), the cook, came out with his glass of spritzer, deposited it on my table, his butt on the facing chair, and reminisced at length about his past (he once cooked two years for the "21" Club).

I sent this note Friday to HAG, and in true HAG style he hasn't responded to it:

Before you last took some time out from your residency here, I suggested we have lunch after you got back. May I now propose Tues. or Wed. of next week?

If lunch is impossible, then please consider parting your schedule any time during either day long enough for me to say something that can be said only to you.

Stilted, isn't it? Yet it was the third version; the first two were even more so. I'm off regular duty next week to prepare for the cover. It's a good time to see HAG, and to begin burning bridges. I will tell him that I want to leave, and why, and that I must have my severance pay to make leaving possible. Otherwise it would be terribly awkward—it takes about three months for the profit sharing to come through—and also meaner to you, and it's already mean enough: my stake would have to come out of the profit sharing. I could be a hell of a lot meaner. There's nothing defensive in my saying that. No matter what lien I agreed to on the money due me from the profit-sharing fund, it's my money and can be given (or sent) only to me. If I chose to be really beastly, how would you go about collecting any or all of it from me in Samoa? I wanted to tell Henry *before* doing the cover, out of curiosity, to see if just once in my life I could write a cover without getting into a lather of anxiety. My days on *Time* are numbered. Telling him makes me a lame duck. So my cover performance doesn't matter, or shouldn't. It could conceivably make a difference in my attitude and it will be edifying to see if it does.

When I called Thursday night from Franzl's, you were correct in saying that I'd been drinking, but wrong in your implication that I was drunk: one martini and two beers were all I had. I should have persisted in talking to you anyway, but I'm a trained seal by now. Your criticism and your imperiousness chasten me. I feel guilty without good reason. And besides, as I suggested, what is there to say? The thought of going to Samoa does terrify me. It's likely to be a disaster, but I know that I have to do it. I drove to the house this morning after having a haircut, and ate a bowl of your new cereal. It *is* good. The ghosts are beginning to gather. I surveyed that familiar scene with an expatriate's avid eyes—the pool, the flaking paint on the flank of the house by the sliding door, the overgrown grass, the Japanese maples, the torn and bulging front door screen. I padded barefoot down the asphalt drive to the mail box and padded up again with your mail, among it my letter with the last check. I unwrapped *The New Yorker* and looked at the cartoons and read Penelope Gilliatt on Buster Keaton. All these being among the meaningless and yet so meaningful trivial patterns of which so much of my life has been composed. I was not in a sentimental mood or all this might have got to me. But now, in the apartment in the middle of another Saturday afternoon, it does get to me a little, like an old snapshot from one's youth. It's not quite three and I've taken two Valiums because I feel over-smoked, unhealthy and tense and know I must deny myself today, and tomorrow, and for as long as I can, the release of drink. I don't think it will be a deprivation, or even particularly difficult to do. Once I set my mind to something, I tap a rich lode of self-discipline. I did drink yesterday, but as the unwilling victim of circumstances. The Esalen people are almost paranoically upset about the color art accompanying the cover and called me late Friday afternoon to insist that I meet them for dinner to tell them what can be done about it. Nothing can be done, and nothing will be done, but I didn't tell them that. I didn't have to go. I could have pleaded pressing closing-night duty, but I'm really not a bad guy and so I went and did what I could to restore their composure. We ate in their hotel after drinks in their room. It was 11:30 before I broke away, and so I looked in on the usual Friday night pour in the "Business" section of the twenty-sixth floor, downed a glass or two of foul and acid red wine from a gallon glass jug, and shared a Dial-a-Cab north to Westchester with Marshall Loeb. Arnold Drapkin was among the wassailers. He agreed I should level with HAG, expressed his confidence that there'd be no trouble about getting my severance, and assured me that the guild would make an issue of it if I didn't.

I ate well yesterday but have no appetite today. I am sick at heart, I don't know why. Everything seems so pointless and that includes Samoa. The Valium are hitting me and I feel light-headed and a little dizzy. Nothing in my larder tempts me. But then in *The Ipcress File*, which I saw on TV the other night, Michael Caine went for days on end without eating anything at all.

You seem resigned to the fact that I may be leaving, in a terminal break. Or maybe you don't believe I'm going to do it. Scarcely anyone does. I know that I am. Almost nothing could dissuade me now. What could? A reconciliation per-haps, but that's out. Some unimaginable counterproposal from HAG: say, like a year off, accept a few South Pacific reportorial commissions from *Time* while I'm there and, after a year, if I have second thoughts, come back. I have only half an idea what they think of me, how highly they esteem me. I could be pleasantly surprised, but since that's so rarely been my experience in fifty-three years, I'm expect-ing nothing and certainly am not going to hold my breath. The Valium, instead of making me peaceful, is making me groggy. Would you say it's a form of drinking? Yes, you would. Why do I expect you to call tonight? Wishful think-ing, but somehow I do.

Even the seconds are dragging now. I'm waiting for five o'clock to come so that I can watch an old Laurel and Hardy movie on TV. Then dinner. Then *Mission Impossible* at 7:30. Then what? Something equally enthralling. Has any-one ever led so full and exciting a life? No one to call. I saw the Kunhardts last Saturday, can't very well invite myself over there again. I have a cigarette machine now and roll—literally, punch—my own, not to save money, though they come out to 20 cents a pack, but to give me something to do. I don't manufacture ahead, just one at a time. The thing works rather neatly, and you can't see any difference between my product and a tailor-made. There's a filter tip and everything. But they smoke hot.

An eternity later: 8:30. I went to bed, but the willies climbed in with me, so I've given up and will let Valium do the job. Now that I'm assured a six-month supply I don't have to worry about running out. That's the candler's prescription: renewable for six months. Odd. "You mean," I asked, "that I could if I liked renew it every day for six months?" "Well, not quite," he said. "The dosage is for two tens a day, so the druggist would be a little suspicious if you renewed too often." He must have his reasons; he must know I won't be here six months hence. Phil called and invited me to lunch *chez* Kunhardt tomorrow. Maybe you'll be there. It's something to do besides the Sunday crossword. I'm on my third week in the same sheets. My bed smells like an East Village pad. I bought an Air-Wick and keep it unstoppered to compete with the scents of the unkempt bachelor's digs. I'm used to them, but a visitor might take offense. But then I don't have visitors.

My life at least now has direction. I know what I'm going to do and can think and plan that far ahead. No farther. It will be necessary to let you in on some of the logistics, if you want my spoons. You can just drive the VW away. We can change its registration after I reach Samoa because I'm not leaving American soil. I see myself as an aging beach boy with the towel concession. Or a night desk clerk at a tourist hotel. Or a reporter for the Samoa *Times*, if that's its name.

I'll take my *Time* identification card with me. There are lots of things I can do as long as I'm not particular about the money, and I'm not. Your half of it won't help you much, but you'll get it. I wonder sometimes what the kids will think of this, and have tentatively decided that more than anything else the move will impress them. I won't be completely out of touch, but unless I hit big on some private project it's likely to be a long time before I see them again. They'll just have to grow up without me. They've been doing it anyway. So have you. If I read my psych battery correctly, the psychodynamics of my youth don't apply to theirs. It may be that you are a castrator, like my mother, and that I was castrated like my father (or came to marriage half castrated to begin with), but I fought back some, raised my voice in anger, fulfilled some if not all of the obligations of the male parental paradigm. In none of the boys do I see the young me, keeping the maternal apron strings taut if never quite actually breaking them, busting out of the family exercise yard, going away to college, putting to sea, doing my best to escape the templates of the suffocating and oppressive familial mold. They needn't necessarily have been psychically blighted by the conduct and example of their father. If you want to put it on a basis of weakness and strength, which I think silly, I wasn't the weakest father in contemporary history if I wasn't the strongest either. Phil obviously worshiped his old man and his book, *My Father's House,* is a hymn to him. But Phil works much too hard, far harder than I ever did, and lets *Life* take much too much out of him. I'll probably survive him even though I'm ten years or so older, and even though that's no great accomplishment. He rules his children's lives. For the most part I've let my children run their own, though I've made some unforgivable mistakes. The spirit of today's younger generation has been a liberating force too; they don't buy the form as unquestioningly as we did. I may still be a conservative, but never have I been as conservative as you. In Pago Pago I will be nobody, or at least as nobody as a man can be with fifty-three years of personal history. Who knows? This impulsive decision of mine may awaken sleeping resources in us all. I don't worry about you. You're a strong woman, and will come up with new and workable arrangements if only because you have to and are emotionally incapable of sitting still, standing by and falling into funks. You may even get remarried as a calculated step. After all, your decision that it was high time you had an affair preceded your first affair. Your head's decision that it was high time you got married preceded your marriage, and led to it. Had you even met Ed then? Or was he one of the first qualified prospects that came along after you'd made up your mind? No invidiousness intended in all this, or do I deceive myself? Am I disappointed in you, and bitter? A little, maybe, but they're not the motive forces in my decision to clear out, which was prompted not by head but by heart considerations. Someone just rang my downstairs doorbell, a man. "Who is this?" he demanded. "Who do you want?" I said. That may have been the third time my buzzer has buzzed in a year.

I'm sitting naked in your mother's slipper chair in the center of the room, both the TV and the air conditioning off, smoking a bit too much as usual and itemizing the dirty laundry on the parquet floor, which is a measly quarter of an inch thick: six pairs of socks like dead black snakes, a pair of dirty Bermuda shorts and some clean skivvies, a clean T-shirt and two dirty short-sleeved shirts. Also my Linus blanket the pillowslip, a sweater, and a pile of unsorted but clean laundry on the coffee table—at which I have never had coffee and never will. When my roomie was staying with me she sat on it and broke it. It bellies now like a balloon spinnaker. On the chair that I use as a table, match-

books from the Monkey Bar and the Red Coach Grill, a
salt cellar, a *Time* pencil, an invitation to cocktails next
Sunday from five to seven (I'm tempted not to go, for
character-defect reasons that wouldn't concern you). All
kinds of pink gnur under the bed, which has seen a lot
of service but hasn't bounced in years to the energetic
rhythms of intercourse. I suppose it never again will. Maybe
Grosser will end his lengthy sit-down strike in tropical
Samoa, but I don't count on it. In a pinch, I can always tell
female connections down there that I have Jake Barnes' un-
fortunate affliction: a missing vital accessory. They won't
believe me, but in a way it's the truth. You know what I'd
really like to do? Ask someone to share my sleeping problem
with me tomorrow night. But who? I'd say, "I'm not a good
sleeper, so would you let me come over and not sleep with
you?" I'd ask *you* here, but my place is a noisome mess. The
carmine lavatory bowl is whitewashed with Crest toothpaste
spit; the toilet is full of cigarette stubs. I guess I *was* impossible to live with, wasn't I? What was that you told the
shrink about my college diary? Put it to my credit that I'm
as embarrassed about it as you were when you read parts of
it. Incidentally, I want those two volumes back. They and
my tool chest were all that were really mine in the house.
I don't know why I want them back but I do. Curious
dinner: three frozen pirogens filled with sauerkraut, a
chicken breast, a Tootsie Roll and a small can of mixed
fruit. Not unbalanced really. I grow less and less interested
in preparing meals for myself. Another Camel and then
to bed.

The Kunhardt lunch fell through. Peter was seriously injured playing football at Groton yesterday—several broken
ribs, possibly a ruptured spleen—and Phil and Kathy left

in the middle of the night to be with him today. Surgery is necessary to determine the damage to the spleen. If there is any damage, the spleen will be removed since we don't need it anyway. I was told all this by Loudon, who called this morning. Now I'm going there for an early and nonbibulous supper. I had some doubts about accepting because I'm not really interested in an intimate Sunday night supper with the Wainwrights. Although I told Loudon I'm not drinking much any more (a fib of course) I may have a few before leaving. I've thought a lot about all this. With a few under my belt it's easier to communicate to you in this letter, my thoughts expand, I enjoy people and life more, free floating anxiety is partially anesthetized. So why swear off just now? That may only be the rationale of the smoker who, having laid off for a week, lights up just to prove to himself that he can now take tobacco or leave it alone. The Wainwright supper invitation has supplied a tension to the day that is uncharacteristic of my Sundays. With 6 P.M. just a few hours off, I feel pressed into action: do my exercises now, read some of the literature on the human potential movement that I brought out as homework, worry about the impending cover (a favorite activity of mine, worrying) so that the week antecedent to writing the cover will be spoiled before it begins, call you and tell you to send the next jury-duty notice back unopened with this legend added to the envelope: "No longer at this address." I'm supposed to report tomorrow, but I'm not going to. I don't want to stand jury duty, and I can't anyway with the cover coming up. Marshall Loeb just called to ask me to drinks and dinner tonight. My God! Three social invitations in a single day.

Among the possessions of mine you'll get will be the S&H trading stamp books you gave me for Christmas, and also the Plaid stamps from the A&P that I've been saving for almost a year. It was last October 12 that I announced my decision to leave you for Jocelyn; on the same night she told Guy. How soon after that I physically cleared out I don't remember. And the date of the divorce—November 21—is one I must look up on my copy of the proceedings in Ciudad Juarez, all in Spanish so that I don't know what it says. I don't even know on what grounds you divorced me. I see it now: *incompatibilidad de caracteres.* My God, there's a translation! I never noticed before. I've just read through it unmoved; it happened too long ago, and the legal event of that day in Mexico runs a distant last, in impact, to all the events leading up to it. So typical of you, incidentally, to combine a Mexican divorce with a weekend shopping trip. You've never told me much about the experience. I'll bet in a way it was fun. The English copy is full of typos, and does not in every respect agree with the Spanish text. The latter says I am to pay you 45 percent of my income, after child support has been deducted; the former says 50 percent. Well, soon the whole thing will be immaterial. How long will it take to wind up my affairs and leave? Two months? Three?

Too bad you'll miss dinner with Frank Wednesday. He's been in town some time but hasn't been able to get hold of me. He's been calling the wrong extension—Mike Demarest's—and I'm back at my old number. If he tried the central switchboard—well, you know from experience what an obstacle course that can be. Bad news about the estate. The old lady wants 10 percent of the estate, about $25,000, to clear out so we can get the rest. Our top offer is $10,000 and that's too much. So maybe we'll just have to sweat out her death. I think she's eighty-two, but she's ornery enough to live forever.

I'll have to take what you said when I called tonight: that

my version of what the head candler said you said is "substantially correct." It becomes important. If there were any chance you might come back to me, it would make a difference, I think, in what I plan to do. If there isn't—and it appears there isn't—then I must do it. I can't honestly stand much longer the way things are now. There may be more sensible things to do but I can't think of any. This solitude is corrosive. It's beginning to invade the office. Because of moves and transfers, there are more empty offices than occupied ones around me, and the occupants are not acquaintances. Tonight I stayed fairly late because I just didn't want to go out to White Plains and be alone. But by six o'clock I was alone in the office anyway: not just my corridor but the whole floor to myself. Closed and locked doors all about. I know I am obsessed with my lot, but that's one of my problems—I'm an obsessive-compulsive. The shrink held out little hope of relief from this; the defenses have been in place too long; they're part of me now like tattoos. He agreed the antidepressant pills had had a fair chance and didn't work. He agreed, too, that long-term analysis—not classical Freudian, but analysis—might help some, but that it would be a long and difficult haul over a stretch of years. Three sessions a week at $40 each, or $120, of which *Time* would pay maybe 60 percent. But I can't afford the difference: $48 a week, or nearly $2,500 a year. You really don't seem to understand how broke I am, or care. Well, I care. The net of my last pay check was $843, of which I sent you $577.70. From the difference, $265.30, I must pay $195 rent and $51 for the car and $34 for the commute. If you'll add up just those three items, you'll see it's a deficit operation for the next two weeks: $280 to pay out of $265 and change. Considering everything, you've got one fine deal, but it's not going to last. You can just pay that God-damned hospitalization yourself. I owe Aetna $150 or so on one of my life insurance policies. It's overdue. I don't know where the hell I'm going to get it. I've been cooped up in solitary for a year now, and the rich irony of it is that if I hadn't sentenced myself to it you would have. So I suppose I should take solace from that. I did it to me, strictly speaking. I have no right to be bitter, but you can bet your ass I'm the bitterest resident of White Plains, if not Westchester County or the Western Hemisphere. I am not such a schmuck as you think I am or I think I am. I'm just a very unhappy middle-aged man with emotional problems too big for him. If you think this sounds like drunk talk you're wrong. Nothing at all today. I'm not making any promises to myself on this score, but I know what I'm going to do. For Christ's sake, I can't afford to drink. If I could only sleep. But my stomach is hollow with anxiety, and I can't risk lying in the dark alone. If I could only find a woman to live with who would take me as I am—but I'd have to be able to take her, too, and I'm pretty particular. That would at least solve the loneliness. I had hoped for that with the roomie, but she wasn't the one. Nor I for her. It was almost worse than being alone, but as soon as she left I missed her. God, Ann, I miss you too. It's just plain loneliness, I'm sure, but I never knew how dreadful loneliness can be. No doubt I'll be even lonelier in Pago Pago, but maybe there I can find that wonderful kingdom that T George Harris discovered and that I've mentioned to you: beneath despair. If I could find it now perhaps I wouldn't have to go. I'd give everything I have for one whole day of emotional peace. Mephistopheles could strike any kind of bargain with me now. I'd sell my soul for very little— peace of mind, just peace of mind, for the rest of my life.

As usual, I've taken pills, and they're doing nothing to me. I've had two. It's 10:10. At eleven I'll take one more. I wish someone would invent a sleeping potion that is cheap, nonaddictive, non-cumulative, and hangover-free. Valium comes nearest, but where once two tablets worked now it takes four or five. Loudon thinks I'm nuts going to Pago Pago. It's the place not the plan that he disputes. Why Pago Pago? Why not Des Moines? Or, more sensibly, some small town in this country where the living is cheap. Waupaca? I have thought of that. But it's part of what I want, or need, to get as far away as possible, halfway around the globe. That in itself says this is it, this is the very end of the road, you can't go back. It would be just my style to get over there, have a heart attack and die. Or lung cancer. But I've scheduled the office physical that I passed up last spring. Loudon doesn't think I'll get my severance pay, but he was boiled when he said it. I wish there were someone at *Time* to whom I could confide before going to HAG, but there isn't. Dick Seamon might break my confidence by passing it up the chain of command. It is taking a chance. But I'll go anyway. I don't want any farewell party either. I just want to fade away, a legend in my time. I'm something of a legend there already. Boy, does the hole close in fast after you've gone. Who misses Mike Demarest? He wasn't even replaced. George Love— the indispensable George Love? Not a tear or a trace. Barker T. Hartshorn, whom I always thought of as Bockerty Hartshorn? Bob McLaughlin? Cranston Jones? All gone, all forgotten. And my God-damned siblings. They know how sorely I crave personal mail, and I wrote them all after our vacation, and not one line from any of them. You might have considered it too, you know. One letter from you in a year. It's the little things that count now. To open my mailbox night after night and find nothing in it is to suffer a major disappointment. I haven't your gift of reaching out for people. After all your years with me you must know that. (Why did ticking off all those departed *Time* staffers remind me of my brothers and sisters and that they owe me mail? Queer, the associations of the mind.)

So much to tell you and so little time for it. This is the second late night in a row and I must get to bed. Now I discover that getting severance is not going to be that easy after all. I may have to play the game with professional finesse. The only 100 percent sure way is to develop a sudden and unremitting attack of incompetence. Thus is mediocrity rewarded and reliability punished. Only if they're dissatisfied with your performance will they pay a bonus to hook you offstage. I've entrusted my objective to Seamon. Also, I must place my future in the hands of one Lucy Werner from the accounting department. But Dick says that she can keep a secret—and that "adjustments" can be and have been made in cases like mine. It's not called severance pay but a "settlement," which amounts to the same thing. But I *will* get it one way or other. I have also definitely made up my mind. I'm going to Pago Pago—within three months, sooner if possible.

Frank is now sales manager at Thilmany Pulp & Paper—an impressive promotion. He probably makes more money than any of us. Mother is failing and not happy. She is aware of her declining strength. I just hope I get the hell out of here before she goes. But I wouldn't attend her funeral anyway. Well, we're all dying. Seamon, by the way, and by happenstance, fielded a job offer today in public relations for the College of the Virgin Islands in St. Thomas and passed it along to me. He doesn't understand that that's not what I'm after. I have lost all interest in being useful to others. I want now and forevermore to be useful to me. There's no substantive difference between the Virgin Islands and Des Moines, between *Time* and a p.r. job in academia. He also said, "Did you throw the bottle through the window at the pour Friday in Demarest's office?" No, I said, I wasn't even there, and heard about it only Monday (though I do know the culprit). Too bad, he said, because if you'd done it, and confessed, that's a firing offense—and would have guaranteed your severance pay. Maybe I should own up to a misdemeanor I didn't commit. Well, it's all very suspenseful. I called Fooey Strange last night late, to burden him with my ethical dilemma: that I was seriously contemplating screwing up to get fired on the basis of what my last night dinner companion, who stands close to HAG, told me. Fooey only stated the obvious: that it wasn't in me to screw up deliberately (true, though you can't imagine how tempting) and that Pago Pago would be no solution at all. But I'm not looking for a solution. And anything is better than here and now. Had I been forced to make them fire me, I knew just what I would do. The opening gambit would have been Friday. I would have told Ed Jamieson, who is sitting in again for HAG, that I just haven't had time in a week to corner the human potential movement cover and so, though it's on for next week, it would have to be postponed. In reality, all that's true, but who wants to hear the truth? But the system would have been compelled to go along. Who else would have written the cover? Then I'd have killed a week and pulled a funk: performance block, writer's cramp. But that would have affected too many innocent people. Even so, I'm going to try not to kill myself writing this cover. It will be my last. What's left now to prove? Liquor consumption today: three martinis and a red wine at dinner, three beers since, two in the cab. I have lunch with Norm Ritter and Dick Barkle tomorrow, but I'll let them do the drinking. You probably don't believe that, but you don't know me. My gums are sore and that's one sign I've had enough for awhile. Well, as that ugly girl reporter told Julian

English on the night he died, my back teeth are floating (isn't that an inelegant vision?). It's past one, and I'm going to bed.

I have seen the accounting department person, who has now set in motion a clandestine plan to get my severance pay for me without my having to strain the Protestant ethic. I have since hinted to one or two colleagues that I am likely to get this stake without soldiering on the job. Now, according to Seamon, I must clam up entirely. Not another word because it involves circumventing the guild. So I will, of course, and wait impatiently and nervously for the next maneuver, which won't be mine. HAG must of course ratify any arrangement made. If I get the money, and I do expect to, I'll sweeten *your* pot even more than I've already promised. You'll also get everything I have in my checking account, presently about $1,700. I've also decided to sell the wolf parka, which I'll hardly need in Samoa, and which should produce $150 anyway. Or should I give it to one of the boys? It should fit Bob.

There's a move afoot to postpone the human potential movement cover one week and stuff in one on Allende, the first Marxist ever to become a head of state except at gunpoint. Leon Jaroff informed me of this today (Friday), as I was sifting the notes on my notes. Instantly all the pressure scaled off. I'd planned to work tonight late and take the train in on Saturday to start building the cover structure. But I felt sprung, so instead went to the Steak & Brew, which won't let you empty your beer pitcher, and emptied a good many with three other *Time* writers and ate a brochette of beef and drove to White Plains. As usual, it's late, but I'm in no mood for sleeping and will stay up awhile. I have cigarets and beer and feel released. I may have to write the cover anyway, next week, but presently I'm in one of my manic moods so why not enjoy it? There are few enough of them these days. I've had something to drink four days in a row, which is unusual for me, but on only one of those days was the consumption what I consider excessive. Besides, if I go to bed late I'll sleep late and kill half a day.

More people leaving *Time,* most of them under their own steam. No one trusts the climate there anymore and everyone predicts ruin. It's probably a good time to get out. Some of the departures are for personal reasons, as mine will be. A researcher, for instance, whose apartment has been broken into six times, who has witnessed two street killings (so she says) and who tonight, in a booth across from us at the Steak & Brew with four other researchers, had her purse snatched from beneath her chair. Seventeen-fifty in cash and all those cards that establish a person's existence, together with her apartment key and address. She leaves next Saturday for Colorado, where she was born and grew up. I would never do that. Life consists of steps and I don't believe in dropping back. I may not wear out all my remaining years in Pago Pago, but I'll never return to the old haunts or the old life: New York, *Time,* the rat race, domesticity with you. Nor will my body come back, though I can't say that I much care about that. The dead, to belabor the obvious, don't care where they lie. *Time* is running very scared now. *Newsweek* is consistently beating us on the newsstands, and the orientation of the editorial operation is now more commercial than dedicated to insubornable bold journalism. Examples abound. I was asked this week to submit prospective slogans for the human potential movement cover slash—that yellow diagonal succinctly identifying the subject. I concocted ten or so, and added the injunction that it was imperative to include the term "human potential movement" rather than something more parochial and narrow. But the slash is now considered an act of salesmanship, and so I lost. Unless second and better thoughts take over, it will read: "Group Psychology: Growth Through Encounter." Not only isn't that very sexy. It's plain wrong. Psychology is only one of a dozen scientific disciplines embraced by the movement; "encounter" is only one of several hundred techniques used, and it's being used less and less as the eclectic attempt to redefine man and his nature improvises better tools. One of my offerings was much better and certainly more accurate: The Human Potential Movement: Joy (or Fulfillment, or Growth) through Being. The cover art itself is off the mark, though appealing: a photograph of a youngish and attractive woman, beatifically smiling, framed and touched all over by disembodied hands. Her breasts don't quite show, but one senses they're being touched too. I've just fired up a cigaret without even being aware that I did it. I do have the habit bad. I don't want to pop pills tonight so I've got to drink enough beer to assure sleep. Maybe I won't go in tomorrow after all. It's been after one every night this week before I snapped the lights.

This tepid Schaefer I'm drinking is making me, not ill, not even queasy, but something like either, or both. So my manic state is slipping. Nevertheless here goes another. It's at times like this that I crave companionship—there were seldom times like that in our marriage. I am friendly and harmless with a snootful (I haven't had anywhere near a snootful tonight), except perhaps to you. I won't ever forget that summer's night at the Omaha Country Club when *you* got loaded and very affectionate, sat in my lap at the table, hugged me and kissed me, and then threw up all the way home. I loved that demonstrativeness, and you know I always felt warm toward you when you were sick to your stomach and I held your forehead as you leaned over the bowl. The worst is sometimes the best. People do, after all, vomit, shit, piss, smell bad, have bad breath and sprout pimples on their behinds. In such circumstances, do we stop loving them if we loved them on Sunday? Come to think of it, we had quite a lot of nice sex before whatever interfered with it began interfering with it. No world's record for frequency, but who was trying to set a record? And do you realize that when I married you I was already past the male sexual prime? Just past, but past. And that you were at the female peak, which then endures for nearly ten more years? I don't believe we ever screwed twice the same night, did we? And how long ago was it that you kissed Grosser? At a guess, I'd say 1956 or 1958. You never really wanted to do it. Some women don't. And some women—more women than men—don't enjoy screwing even in the traditional way. Gorillas, by the way, hardly ever do it that way, though they can. In fact, they hardly ever do it. Very under-sexed. According to Desmond Morris, whom I don't always trust, the gorilla penis is two inches long. And, according to Ardrey, whom I do not always trust either, the female hyena is sexually indistinguishable, except at very close range, from the male. Her vulva—or maybe it's the clitoris—hangs out and down just like the male dingus, and she has a rear sac, or hair tuft (I forget which), that closely resembles the scrotum. Ardrey explains (substitute "guesses") why this is so, but my attention strays when he embarks on hypotheses. His favorite game, as a self-taught anthropologist, is to add up two and two in original ways.

I begin to wonder. When you're finally convinced that I'm hauling out, will you try to stop me? I doubt it, because it wouldn't do any good. No one says I have to work for *Time* or earn $30,000 a year. (Actually $29,500, but I always round it off. Ten dollars sounds like a lot more than $9.95. Ten to twelve sounds much later than 11:50.) It's

2 A.M. now, which is quite as late as it sounds. To lull any suspicions of the super here, I'll have to smuggle out gradually such valuables as I have that you may want. In my suitcase, which will hide all my tableware. I'll keep one knife, fork and spoon. Pots and pans on another occasion. You won't want, and don't need, the bed. Or maybe I underestimate your frugality. I may be taking the same chance here as with the severance pay. It might be wiser simply to leave everything behind that I'm not going to take. I do have the feeling that you don't believe I'm serious about going, and that the dawning of realization will come as a shock. Not because you mind where I go or what I do, but because when I leave, the money flow declines to an insignificant seep. I'll find work in Samoa, but it won't pay much. And unless I should hit big with a book, which is not likely, times are going to get lean, and you think they're too lean now. But consider. (You always used to hate it when I itemize, but I love to.) It's a mistake to sell the house on a depressed market (there are hundreds of homes up for sale in Westchester), but you seem determined to do so on the advice of your accountant, who says you can't afford to live there. Let's say you realize $80,000 for the house. That may be high, but say you get it. Your net take on that should be more than $30,000, perhaps $35,000. Plus $5,000 (maybe more) for the Farmers Underwriter shares. Maybe $35,000 net (possibly less) from the profit sharing, which will come in three months after I leave. Plus $40,000 next year from my estate. What have I overlooked? About $1,500 from my checking account. Hold an auction: you won't need all that furniture in a smaller establishment. Realize $5,000 from that—more if you sell the Calders and the Christian Rolf. In a real pinch, peddle your mother's diamond ring or the brooch. Now add it all up: $121,500 to $124,500.

Future—or immediate—prospect: half the value of your mother's portfolio, or $100,000 or more—gross. She's seventy-nine or eighty now. Give her another four years. Plus whatever income you produce plus $50 a week or more from me ($2,500 a year). My God, gal, if I'm not painting too rosy a picture, you're practically in clover. Of course, you'll have to shell out rent, but with one child in college and another about to go, do you really need a house? A roomy apartment will do. As word of my unforgivable defection gets about, sympathetic friends—of which you have, or will have, an oversupply—will spring to your aid. And to all this add your unarguable capacity to meet a challenge. I will keep my life-insurance policies until I go. Then you can either let them lapse (they have some cash-surrender value) or pay the premiums yourself. The same for medical insurance. I'm not going to be covered, and neither are you unless you finance the coverage yourself. You won't need two cars. Sell your car and drive mine. I owe about $1,200 on it, which is a bargain for a faultless little car with 13,000 miles on the odometer. And only a year old.

I'm going to feel tacky tomorrow but my resilience and recuperative powers are amazing, and I've dealt myself punishments worse than this without any ill effects. I snap back fast. Most of my symptomatology is phony anyway. I'm not chronically puny but chronically hale. Now it's three o'clock, and I think I'd better lay some Valium on top of the beer. No harm in that, says the candler, except a head like a cloud chamber the next day. But I'm still not ready for bed. Working on my third can of suds. But if I take pills tonight, what'll I do tomorrow night? Tomorrow's a no-sauce day. So is Sunday, though I'm going to a cocktail party in New York. I've been smoking since my arrival here at the rate of three cigarettes an hour, which is not bad considering that I always smoke more when drinking and writing. I've puffed a lot today though. Now I'm going to turn on the *Late Late Show* and listen through the earphone until those four little yellow tablets take hold.

Martha Wainwright called around 10:30, sooner than I'd wanted to get up, and proposed an amble through the Westmoreland Sanctuary on the road to Bedford—the Frick nature retreat. I didn't want to go, but I did and it turned into a most pleasant rustic afternoon. Loudon is away on a story in Idaho. We had lunch first at her home and came back after the hike—three miles, I'd say—for iced tea. Martha told me the Kunhardts have gone to Groton again for the weekend. Peter's recovered enough to sit in the stands and watch a game that was dedicated to him. Martha is not opposed to my dropout, but she wonders why I'm being so "generous" with you: is it out of guilt? I don't think I'm being generous, so maybe it *is* guilt. She thinks I should keep more than I'm keeping—maybe I will. If I am guilty, it's mostly about the children, but I can't see how I'm letting them down. Frank at an early age had to tap his own strength, and it was the making of him. The children automatically go with the mother anyway, unless she's a hophead or a whore. I'm not going to see them anymore anyway once you leave. Why should I consider staying on in New York when you're the one who first thought of moving, not I? I won't be a prisoner in Samoa. The planes fly both ways. Though the move may be permanent, I won't be stuck there. Even Gauguin, unless I'm mistaken, came back for visits. Moreover, he totally abandoned his wife and kids, and I'm going to give you all I possibly can. Mme. Gauguin never saw a centime whenever he sold a painting. He didn't have much fun in the South Seas though: bad health, syphilitic, chronically broke. And he remained a stranger in a strange land, like the American tourist abroad. I guess I do feel the victimized one, but today I'm not depressed, or if I am don't feel it. Not down, not up. Had an appetite for dinner. Not anxious a bit about the cover, which will have to be written anyway as a backstop to the Allende cover. I brought all my notes out to review and may read them over tomorrow and plot the cover outline. Then again I may not. There's laundry to do and I've simply got to change these malodorous sheets.

A sudden downpour just as I left Martha's, with a strong wind that blew down power lines. Took me nearly an hour to get from Bedford to White Plains. Mail today too: a bill from Texaco and an invitation to join the Christian Science church. The envelope was hand-addressed, so I thought it was personal mail, and when I found that it wasn't I tore up the enclosure in a rage. I'm getting very impatient to go, get the thing started, over and done with. I'm like a prisoner sweating out the time before parole.

Down today, in contrast to yesterday. Except to go out for the Sunday *Times* I haven't left the apartment. Thinking of rolling a joint from that gift lid, before going to the cocktail party, which is my people event of the day. Predictably, I ignored the cover. I didn't read over any notes, didn't draw an outline. Which means I'll have to do it tomorrow, start a day late, and get panicky. Not greatly interested in going to the party. It's a long round trip for a drink or two and munchies, on a dreary overcast day. I saw *Marty* on TV—I'd never seen it before—and bawled all through it, though it isn't that good.

Time has developed new dimensions and values since I took up the solitary life. I don't remember things I've done or when I did them, not through any memory lapse, but because time has ceased to flow processionally. It stops, backs up, recedes, surges—a Doppler effect. Weekends are forever, but the time it takes to smoke a cigaret, which is about five minutes, is five seconds. A TV commercial break often goes by unseen and unheard. I did the Sunday crossword today and don't remember doing it. I dropped a stale cake down the incinerator chute, but when? Today or yesterday? I can smell the trout boiling on the Door County peninsula last summer; but what does my Lilac Vegetal smell like? I don't remember. After 1,001 nights at Franzl's, I can remember well what the place looks like and what he looks like, but not what it's like to be there. I've forgotten where I stored the VW snow tires, in your attic or in your garage? The divorce hasn't happened. I'm still living in the house, not this apartment. I walk down the hall, carpeted in electric blue, and think, what am I doing here? Pago Pago has more reality. I can produce faithful images of you and the children in the camera of my mind, but my face is off the frame. That person in the mirror, examining a skin blemish or shaving. . . . I know it's me but it isn't me. This, I suppose, is what is meant by schizoid—but being schizoid isn't being schizophrenic. I know I'm going to get up soon, shower, shave, dress, tank up the car and drive to New York, dropping first a quarter and then a dime at toll booths along the way. I know where and why I'm going and how to get there. It will all happen, quite ordinarily, and yet it won't happen at all because time is in one of its stalls; motionless. The procession is in a state of arrest. And yet time has a greater immediacy factor than ever before. A week is much too large a piece of it to handle, either in anticipation or retrospect. A day is too much and some hours are. I don't quite know what it is I'm trying to say, and yet I know perfectly well—if I didn't have to say it. Martha Wainwright seemed to understand. We talked about none of this, but except when we were just making talk—most of the time—we rapped. I'll arrive late tonight at the party, with three beers and maybe a little grass in me, and then play things by ear. I mean with post-party dinner possibilities. This is not a pursuit evening, because there will be more men than women there, and there won't be *any* women for me. Prediction: I'll be the oldest guest. How do *you* feel about being on the edge of fifty? If I weren't going to Pago Pago, which might just regenerate me, I'd feel pretty awful about being half a month past fifty-three.

The cocktail party was just another, but I made something of a hit by arriving late by mistake. I'd got into my head that the hours were seven to nine, not five to seven, and didn't show up till 8:20. The evening ended in a crazy way. Leon Jaroff, when I got there, was talking to a twenty-three-year-old Texan with kinky off-blond hair, a shiny unblemished complexion and a smile that would thaw a rent-collector. I hadn't eaten, and proposed a foraging expedition in my bug. Everybody else but Leon and the Texan had other plans, so the three of us landed in a place called Hudson's Bay, on the East side, for steaks and beer. Then at 11:45 she wanted to drive somewhere. I suggested Franzl's, but that was too far for Leon. We dropped him at his apartment and drove out together. The door was locked. The chairs were stacked on the tables, but Franzl and Mac the operatic waiter were there and let us in. I had a Michelob, she a glass of water, and we all had breakfast prepared by Franzl: a tasty potpourri of eggs, ham, onion, hamburger, olives, shrimp, brandy and God knows what else. My companion was an instant hit. Franzl and Mac fell madly in love with her; Franzl serenaded her on the saw, and Mac sang in his bullfrog bass. I spent the night—what was left of it—on the couch of her apartment.

Texas slept on the floor of her bedroom because her sixty-one-year-old mother was just back from Mexico. Texas wants to go to Pago Pago with me—not to be with me but because she's restless and footloose and wants to cut out, it doesn't matter where. She doesn't believe in marriage. Well, who does? I had to get up at eight. I'd left my car on the street, and they tow them away after that hour. I'd had very little to drink and I was tired but not hungover. Worked diligently all day on the cover—delaying action mostly, I still haven't done the outline because I just know it's not going to run this week. At four I met a girl I know at the Roundtable on East Fiftieth to have our palms read by a fast-talking old woman. She was mostly wrong about me. She said that I ran women rather than vice versa, that I would be married three times, that I was forty-four and got married at twenty-two, that I should have been a photographer or a portrait artist. But she made a few scores too: twins ran in my family, she saw an island in my future. And I should "think prosperity"— if I did, in the next twenty years I would make a lot of money. She also said I didn't know what love is and never would. Not a particularly convincing performance. My friend's having her nose bobbed in November—it's more Russian than Jewish, and prominent only in profile, head on it's patrician—and after that is going to Ecuador with friends. I feel a bit guilty about the cover but not much. Anyway, what does it matter?

A letter from a friend urging me to give you nothing, after my split-out, but the 50 percent of my income that you have coming, and putting all the rest of it, the big hunks, into escrow for the kids. I've had much the same advice from several other people, by the way. But I don't think I can or will accept it. I have no ambition, really, to leave you high and dry, though I admit there's some resentment there.

You don't know that you're a ball-breaker. The very idea makes you bristle. In my turn, however, I can see that a part of me wants, or wanted, my balls broken. I can admit that I did, after all, marry one, but if I ever get married again it won't be to another. First I have to get my balls back. Jocelyn Bannon was no ball crusher, and I fell in love with her, or thought I did. I might have got my balls back, too, if I hadn't interrupted what could have been an extended and successful affair by pressing for marriage. But she was applying a lot of pressure too. In Pago Pago it won't matter or show. I'm not likely to get into any woman situations over there, but neither will I recoil if any come my way. I think of Pago Pago as a positive thing to do. It's a last and belated attempt to find out who I am and what I am. I'll take along all the sleeping pills I can stock in advance and then run out and never use them again. It's a move meant to be permanent and irreversible, but that doesn't mean that I'm saying good-bye forever to the past. I'm not going to drop out of sight. Today, Samoa is no farther away in time than New York was from Wisconsin when I was the children's age. I can still remember vividly the first dawn-to-dusk transcontinental flight, and that was no scheduled flight either. In 1927, it took Lindbergh thirty-three hours to fly from Long Island to Orly. Now the trip is seven hours. I don't even care any more if the severance-pay plot fails. I just hope that if it does, it does before I've written this cover. But if I don't get the bread, it'll come out of you. I know I've told you that. But repetition is emphasis. And I may not get it; I've blabbed so tirelessly and lovingly about Pago Pago that anyone at *Time* who hasn't heard it either doesn't know me or is deaf. If I leave *Time* in good odor, I might even get some reportorial commissions over there. If you've read the *Times* lately, you've noticed that the U.S. Trust Territories are making news of late—ripples of independence movement, the thoughts of shifting the American military presence on Guam, which is sick of the sight of it, to some other insular Pacific possession. Before I go, I'm going to read everything *Time*'s morgue has on Samoa. I scarcely know where Samoa is. Pills again tonight.

Last night I went swimming with a girl from *Newsweek* in the health club of the Henry Hudson Hotel, over on the West Side. Swimming was all that was involved. I've known her for ten years. She's a pleasant Italian girl thoroughly indoctrinated in the code of proper behavior. Over the years I've been a minor liberating force in her life. I've been after her for years to drop that forbidding neckline and let the cleavage show. Now she does and I claim part credit. We have had what is best described as a one-way symbiotic relation. She looks to me for support. Recently she sought help and advice from me on some family trouble and got it. I'm very good in such circumstances. I take people's needs seriously if I'm called on; and I'm sure I did her some good. So of course she was grateful, and the result was an invitation to swim. You plunge three floors to the health club, separate by gender, and reunite pool-side. It was all very innocent and quite fun. She looked lush in her bathing suit, which was freckled with holes beneath which lay not body stocking but woman, and which laced very loosely up the front. The pool was at least womb temperature and supersaturated with chlorine, so that when we climbed out for the last time our eyes looked as if we'd both just come from the funeral of an irreplaceable friend. I showed off like mad on the diving board—front and back flips, full and half gainers, bumped my nose on the bottom (a beautiful strawberry), swam twenty-two lengths with her, believe it or not, and felt virtuously healthy despite three martinis at lunch with Matt Mestrovic, back from three and one-half months in Europe and Africa, and two more before the swim, while she gorged on a pannikin of pea soup. Then *I* was ravenous, and tucked down some Coq au Vin at the Mont St. Michel and a cafe royale after, while she ate anchovies on toast. Not in the least drunk, you'll be disappointed to hear. Indeed, she was overwhelmed at the shape I'm in, and said so. I took her back to her apartment and made a ritual pitch to spend the night, knowing that I would be turned down, and I was. She believes in the rules, as much as a Catholic believes in God. I wasn't disappointed—what would I have done if she'd accepted?—took a cab to White Plains and spent today completing my cover outline and fleshing it out with details. I've now been through the raw material so many times, and made so many notes on notes on notes, that I have it as much to heart as any man can with a memory as porous as mine. The cover will probably be up for next week, unless *Time* decides to do something major about Nixon's new "cease-fire in place" maneuver in Indochina. Anyway, I'm *not* going to write the cover this week, though I could. The old guilt feelings have lost a lot of zap. During the last two days of this week I'll review all the old material, polish and compress, take it out with me over the weekend and begin writing Monday—if the cover's still on. I don't much want to write it, but I can and I will. The silly part is that by nearly everyone's standards but my own I haven't goofed off a bit. I know *Time* men who, similarly reprieved, would vanish into thin air.

I ordered all the literature from the morgue on American Samoa and have begun reading. Can't vouch for the accuracy of any of it. Year-around humidity: 80 percent. It rains furiously but briefly five times a day, but no one takes refuge unless the raindrops are almond-sized. Then the sun comes out and dries everything, including you, within five minutes. You'll be delighted to learn that bottled goods just aren't sold in Pago Pago and that there are only two places in town where liquor is available by the drink. The hotel where Maugham stayed and was inspired to write *Rain* is now a grocery store, which dispenses, among other comestibles, *pisupo*—the Samoan term for canned corned beef (I know why, but the explanation would bore you). For no good reason, the Samoans insist on nasalizing the letter "g"; hence "Pango Pango" for Pago Pago. The local women are in physical proportion to the knees and from there down disappoint Western tastes: they have the skinny calves of male sprinters. They are also said to be entirely free of emotional hang-ups, but I don't believe that. Finding myself a job should be no trouble at all. Of the town's two hotels, the one run by Pan Am has 101 rooms and must need waiters, busboys, bellhops, or even an assistant manager. The island has TV and an airport that can take jets. No restaurants, except at the two hotels. Everything molds overnight, and in all that tropical humidity bacteria thrive, so one must treat at once the most minor cut. Lava-lavas are the customary garb for native men, but I think I'll stick to shorts. On a clear day, you can see three other islands, sixty miles away. The biggest, Tutuila, is eighteen miles long and six miles wide—twice the area of Manhattan—and very craggy, so that Pago Pago by necessity hugs the littoral. I'm dying to get there now. If our marriage had been more propitious, and you more receptive, we could have gone there as a family years ago. There are American schools, run by Americans. I look back with sadness on all those squandered years. The hour is late, but better late than never (I have a knack, don't I, for the felicitous phrase?). You might still want to come, but your style is East Hampton.

Here's how derelict to duty I've become: it's 1:30 A.M., and I'm not going to set the clock for any hour. I'll just wake up whenever, take the VW to town, and apologize and explain to no one (except of course to myself—one can't change a river's course overnight). In fact, I'm kind of half hoping that the plot to spring my severance pay honorably aborts before I am committed to write this last cover. Then I'm free to thumb my nose at *Time*, refuse to cut another lick, and beat it to Samoa in jig time with the tiniest of pokes. I'd like the $17,000 in severance but I don't have to have it. Honest to God, Ann, I have never in all my life felt less beholden to anyone and more my own man.

I've learned more about American Samoa, nearly all enticing, much of it probably unreliable. Pago Pago is no city but neither is it a village. The population is 15,000, with a movie theater, a book store, six television channels, a chamber of commerce, Avis and Hertz, and air conditioning. The Inter-Continental Hotel charges $25 for its better rooms, overlooks the town's magnificent harbor and was designed after the Samoan *fale,* or dwelling, by a Honolulu architect. None of what I've read so far tells me how many Americans live in American Samoa, but it's clear that almost everybody, whatever his ethnicity, lives in Pago Pago. One of the islands is uninhabited. The temperature almost never falls below seventy or rises above ninety, but it is wet, with 200 inches of rain a year. There are two fish canneries, where I can almost certainly find work. If not there, then at the Coca-Cola Bottling Company. I'm afraid the hotel is out: it has an all-native staff. Macadam roads trace the shore. Western Samoa, which is independent and much bigger (population 120,000), lies under $30 or so away, round trip by air. I must get permission—from whom, I forget —to stay in Pago Pago longer than the tourists, who in the jet age are beginning to visit in appreciable numbers: 15,000 or 20,000 a year. It was in Western Samoa, in Apia, that the consumptive Robert Louis Stevenson made his home. The house still stands, verandahed and colonial. There isn't much to do in Pago Pago but eat taro, drink beer and watch it rain, but all this I find appealing. I don't want to do anything. I want to live. Until ten years or so ago, this American South Pacific possession was a tropical slum, but an improvement program is slowly, and in many ways markedly, ushering it into the technological age. A pity. But, on the other hand, I'm not dropping out, am I? I'm dropping in. I could ship the VW there and sell it at a tidy profit, but what would I do with it? I'll leave it for you. And I won't sell the parka; I don't need $150 that desperately. I'll give it to Bob for his birthday.

The cover will not run next week—that's definite—but I am to write it anyway. I'm sorely tempted not to, not because I can't but because my whole center of gravity has already shifted to the South Seas and I want to cut all the ropes that bind me here. Also, I miss the pressure of the deadline. You'd think it would be easier to write a cover that's not going to run that week, but I've done it before and it isn't. I'm over-prepared to write it, and have toted all my copious notes home to reread, if I feel like it, over the weekend. There's some comfort in knowing that it'll be the last cover ever. Oddly enough, I can't sentimentalize about leaving *Time*. The thing is done. I've already gone really. I don't and can't imagine how it will be without that daily commute behind *The New York Times*, those long late nights after extended and gin-drenched dinners at La Grillade, the Friday night pours with hollow ice cubes and drinks in paper cups, the diurnal calisthenics in room 2457, the familiar faces down the hall in both directions, the cab rides, some favorite researcher popping in half a dozen times every day, the elevators, the back stairs, the overloaded ashtray, and that awful, late-at-night lung-cancerous feeling as I embark on my third "Behavior" story and third pack of cigarets. I'll miss the scene, I suppose, but I can't imagine missing it now.

It's been a bad week for the drys and for my good intentions. Three farewell parties for defecting staffers, plus three late nights in town, not under pressure of duty but only because I put off the trip back to White Plains as long as possible. Events conspire as well against sobriety. Like last night. I had the car in town and so stayed late enough to miss the rush-hour traffic and, taking a down elevator just after seven, ran into Fred Golden, who suggested one drink. We turned in to Ho Ho's, just next door, for our one drink and found a full table of convivial *Time* people. So the one drink multiplied into three. Then they all left, and as Fred and I drained the last of our glasses another *Time* contingent came in and the evening began all over. I forget how many martinis I had; five or six anyway, the last a bounce—at my insistence—from the Ho Ho house. Then I did go north (I resist, as usual, saying home) but it was long after nine, the hour at which my parking lot closes for the night and so I had to take another Dial-a-Cab. Stopped off first at a deli on Sixth Avenue for potato salad and a roast beef on rye, which was all the dinner I had and eaten en route. Today I virtuously drank nothing at a big drinking lunch. But this afternoon I had first to lift a glass to Margaret Bach, the dropout nun, who tomorrow marries a dropout priest, and later a good many more for the "Books" section's senior editor's secretary, who has been declared redundant. I know one can go to these do's and (1) drink nothing; (2) drink water; or (3) pretend to drink, but my choice is invariably (4). And in the apartment were three cans of Rheingold, which I chilled in the freezer and which helped dilute, or maybe enhance, the flatulence-provoking effect of a TV Mexican dinner. Obviously, my temperance campaign won't begin until I reach the tropics. There really was a Sadie Thompson you know. Maugham went to his grave denying this, but in the stuff I've read voices can still be heard claiming they knew her, or of her anyway. I'll check it all out after I get there. Without my apartment key, which is at the opposite end of the keyholder from the VW's ignition key, I had to ring the super to be let in. About 12:30, I'd say. After some delay I roused not him but his wife who is built and walks like a duck, who accepted in stony silence my Uriah Heepish and semi-coherent apologies, in the same stony silence escorted me to the second floor and let me in and took the two dollars I gave her as conscience money.

Here's a letter to the shrink that I really did send, along with a check for $40—half of what I owe him. The other half is for your visit, and, as I've already told you, I'm just mean enough now to make you pay for that. You could have told me what you told him—that the fire is out, the ashes are cold—without going through the motions of going and spending a part of that fifty-minute hour bolting doors against me and telling him all about that chronicle of hypochondria, the diary I kept in college and a few years beyond up to 1942, after I'd been drafted into and tasted the dubious rewards of conscript life in the U.S. Army. I should never have let you see it.

Progress report—the first and probably the last. I have been drinking, but not much, and as a victim of circumstances rather than from addiction or even thirst: two parties on the premises this afternoon, one for a dropout nun who tomorrow is marrying a dropout priest, the other for a secretary who has been washed away by *Time*'s present economy campaign. What prompted me to write was receipt of your last bill, but for reasons of my own I'm going to make you wait for half of it—the $40 representing my wife's session. (I know she's not my wife and it's not anything distantly resembling a Freudian slip; I just find the designation ex-wife offensive, a jarring and unattractive hyphenation.) By my lights, she went to you under false colors. I told her, before she went, that I saw no point in her going unless some corner of her heart was fractionally—just fractionally—receptive to a reconciliation. She didn't declare one way or the taw that I meant business about going to Pago Pago, but that scratched the last hesitation. I have now set other on this. But she went. And, as you told me two days later, not a single door in her is open to me. She doesn't want to remarry, she most emphatically doesn't want to try again with me, and divorce was inevitable anyway, even though I happened to make the first definitive move. So I'm going to tell her she can pay that particular freight bill. But you'll get it from me if you don't get it from her—and you won't get it from her.

That was the clincher anyway. I guess I knew from in tidal motion the steps necessary to get me there, within two months at the outside, within three weeks if it can be done that fast. I am trying to get severance pay, which in my case is enough to support me in Samoa for three or four years, without making the company can me for incompetence—the only totally reliable way to get it. It would run against my grain, I think (but am not sure) to do it that way—force them to fire me. But I would do it, and might still, just to try something new to my life style; at really fucking up, I've been a failure all my life, and—who knows?—it could invigorate my spirit to violate the Protestant ethic deliberately. But I've been so God-damned reliable and competent for fifteen years that they could conceivably let me get away with murder for months on end, and such a delay would not fit my timetable. I'm very anxious to go. Like everybody, I'm not getting any younger. I don't think I ever quite convinced you that Pago Pago is not a cop-out but a cop-*in*. But *I* know it is. Part of my luggage includes work in my line, which is writing for money, that will keep me busy, and possibly pacified, well past the foreseeable future; and I also intend to get a job over there—it doesn't much matter what. To me the values I now confront are all positive: a fresh start, a situation in which only my own resources will count, a new and unfamiliar scene full of total strangers in which I must make a place for myself. I regret, of course, delaying all this so long, but better late than never. I'm not dead yet.

As for my children—they live their own lives now. I'm not completely sure on this point, but I don't think I'm letting them down. Anyway, as you know, my wife is also beginning a new life herself, two-thirds of the way across the continent. My unlimited visitation rights then—first of next year—become academic. In what some of my lay therapists say is an act of guilt, I intend to leave her all I can: my *Time* profit sharing (which she couldn't possibly get unless I gave it to her), all of my share (about $56,000 gross) of an estate I'll come into next year, my car, and everything in my checking account. In sum, before taxes, something like $125,000. My poke will be the severance pay. If I don't get that, then I'll have to extract my stake from the profit sharing. She'll also continue to get half—off the top, before deductions— of everything I earn, which would be peanuts (after all, what would they pay a middle-aged beach boy for running the umbrella concession?) or real money, if

I get lucky and hit big on a book. If you ever find the will to do it, write and tell me some time if this generosity on my part—if it *is* generosity—is motivated by guilt—if it *is* guilt. I'm going to leave a trail. Any letter sent to me care of Time Inc., Rockefeller Center, N.Y., N.Y. will be forwarded to Sadie Thompson's old beat.

I never felt, in the times I saw you, that we ever established a relation. I felt it was strictly professional. Maybe that's just me, and maybe that's all there ever can be in therapy; maybe I looked for too much. Maybe I do that all the time, with anybody who counts. But I don't think so. I think, really, that in fifty-three years I simply haven't found just where I am, and who I am, in the human scene. Pago Pago would be a good new place to look.

You don't know it yet, but that load of hand tools that I dropped off today is the first consignment of my earthly goods that will be making the return trip to the old house before I go. At the other end of this year of living alone I took them because I missed my tool chest and its contents. That was where my self lived—in that tool chest. A man has got to be king in some little corner, which is a statement I read as a boy in one of Ernest Thompson Seton's books. The house does look a lot neater than when I lived there too; I suppose you have to keep it clean because it's on the market and open to the inspection of critical strangers. It's going to be a full week with the cover, but since it's not running next week the weekend should be free. All my weekends are free. You have no reason to envy my social life, which compares unfavorably with Simeon Stylites'. At least he was out in the open and saw people. After I left you I did stop in at the Kunhardts to say hello to Peter. He showed me his scar, which looks like a ladder. What hurt most, he said, was when they tapped his stomach with a needle as big around as a soda straw, to draw a tissue sample from the spleen. He would know when they reached it, they told him, by a moment of unendurable pain. The whole family was pool-side, including my godson Michael; I'll send him something from Pago Pago. Kathy gave me a hamburger lunch. Phil is not eager to go to the Ritters tonight; he was out last night too. Jesus, this is a drinking culture, isn't it? I'd hate to know the condition of my liver. I've been drinking every other night now for months, and you know my consumption. I can't remember the last time I went two whole days without a drop. Yesterday's intake was about average, maybe a little below: one glass of white wine at lunch (and didn't want that), five or six half scotches at the two *Time* pours (you can't put much in paper cups), three cans of beer in the apartment. Yet I know I rank low in the magazine's fraternity of drinkers. Most of the serious ones drink at every lunch and every dinner, on the town or at home. I'm not even considered a drinking problem; I'm sure the brass are unaware of my imbibing habits, because I do my work. Alcohol stains none of my copy. You can be sure I'll drink my way through the cover, in a familiar pattern: write all day, with sandwiches at the desk for lunch; two-and-a-half-hour dinner break with three martinis and maybe cognac with coffee; then write till midnight or so and repeat the following day. I can knock out a cover in two such long work days, but because there's no pressure to do this one it is certain to take longer. All week maybe. Cover-writing is just one hell of a lot of hard work, and no fun. I'll be glad when it's over. So much nearer the point of departure. What would they say if I simply refused to do it? But I can't. I'm chicken. Well, like Scarlett O'Hara, I'll think about it tomorrow.

We have a new art writer who thinks—really thinks—

writing for *Time* is a piece of cake. He is an Australian in his late thirties, thin and tall and seamed but not rugged, who wears hippie gear and knows his subject inside out. *Time* found him in London; he's done several books on art and is presently under contract for two more, one a biography of da Vinci. This is the first salaried job he's ever had. He took it because he was curious about the disciplines of journalism and because he wanted to live awhile in the States. Don't know why I bring him up except that I envy anyone who can write for *Time* without stress. Maybe there are more such than I think. I find it very hard going, and I know a lot of others who do too. The loneliness is a part of it. One reason I hate to do covers is that I begin writing them on Mondays. Monday is not usually—indeed, scarcely ever—a writing day, so I already feel uneasy and out of phase. Things aren't as they should be. They're out of pattern. And then I must eat dinner alone. Everyone else has gone home, which makes me uneasy, too. Ahead stretch four or five more hours behind the typewriter, and more of the same tomorrow. Five thousand words, the length of a typical *Time* cover, may not seem like much, but it's a very meticulous job that must flow smoothly from the lead paragraph to the last, must leave nothing important out, must capture and reflect the sense of a subject that could easily fill a fat book—a terrific job of condensation and compression.

No appetite at all tonight. The choice lies between a frozen shish kebab (very expensive, two skewers for $3.29) and a beans and frankfurters TV dinner (49 cents). I'm usually hungry, though, and eat well when I've been invited out to dinner. Why is that ? The same is not true of eating at restaurants during the week with *Time* people. But if it's an occasion it's different. I have a lower belly-ache today besides. Cancer of the bowel, no doubt. Entertainment prospect for the evening: *Mission Impossible* at 7:30 and *Beast with Five*

Fingers at 8:30, a horror movie of which the *Times'* TV list-ings says: "May help your dandruff. It cured ours."

Settled for the kebab and the five-fingered beast which was about as scary as a church choir. These interminable evenings, the wasted evenings and the squandered years. The only Westchester summer with any definition in my mind was the first, twelve years ago. Very hot—remember? The cat dragging in its prey, a little wild rabbit, half skinned but half alive. The mosquitoes at night, singing in our bed-room. I remember a few I flattened against the ceiling. And the late night when I forgot my way home from the station and got there mainly by process of elimination, trying one turn after another until that way didn't seem right, then going back to a familiar reference point and starting over. The first mantis I'd ever seen menacing me with its saw-toothed raptors under the lovely birches. The handsome young couple on the turn-around. No sidewalks. I'd never lived before where there were no sidewalks. We had them even at Lochhyrst Beach on Lake Winnebago, poured con-crete squares laid on the sand. Each fall, Charley Wilz, the caretaker, took them up and stacked them in neat piles between our cottage and the Rosebushes'. Each spring he laid them down again. Suddenly another of my chest pains, which probably has nothing to do with cigarettes. But they have been more frequent in recent months. This clinical observation will remind you of my youthful diary, which should have been written with an oral thermometer (or would anal be better?). That first Westchester summer has taken on a sepia tint now; it seems as long ago as my youth. I keep forgetting that I'm fifty-three—not forgetting really, ignoring. Just seven years from sixty, which is old, old; and already I'm on my way to fifty-four. Twelve years ago I was only forty-one, if forty-one can be called "only"; seven years ago I posed for the passport picture, a print of which is still on my office wall. A girl noticed it once on a visit and asked how old I'd been when the picture was taken and then guessed thirty-six before I told her. I was ten years past that birthday—and a year past the deadline I'd set before I got out of the Army: by forty-five, I promised myself, I would have accomplished all that I wanted to do—but what I wanted to do I didn't know then, no more than now. Too many of us define and live life by negatives. Happiness is the absence of pain; success, whatever success is, doesn't matter as long as nothing gets too far out of kilter. The best approach to old age and to death is not to think about it. It's enough to have friends, though their parties are dull and homogeneous, each one the same as the next; it's enough to have a job with a little status to it, though it is not fulfilling any more; it's enough to be married even though the love and the meaning have gone; it's enough to be in reasonably good health, to smoke cigarettes, to drink—though not too much or too often—to catch the trains and eat the meals and get the tartar scraped off your teeth and keep two cars and one dog and the insurance premiums paid, to send the children to college and reach retirement age and retire and look back down the procession of undistinguished and indistinguishable years and say, "Well, it wasn't great, but it wasn't too bad, it could have been worse." All this is a pep talk. The lily-livered rebel in me tells me not to wait while secret machinery grinds out my severance pay but to take whatever I can pull together and go now, leaving a bad taste in *Time's* mouth. We are so conventional. When you told me today what your accountant said—that you can't afford to keep the house or even to rent it—guilt hit me at once for what I am about to do to you: drop your income from just about enough to nowhere near enough. But, still, Ann, you live at the same scale as before. You haven't economized, except perhaps on food, and we've all had to do that. The

)146(

man still comes, I see, to wax the floors; not an extravagance, but not a necessity either. Lights burn all over the house, as before. You've acquired a lot more *objets,* and sold none of the old ones. Has your wardrobe shrunk? You go to the hairdresser just as often. You should have married a rich man as your sister did. You don't want much from the man in your marriage anyway, or don't expect much of him. Your life is far more active than mine and more expensive too. No one owes anyone a college education. If our children want one as earnestly as our middle son wants a bike, they can work for it. Frank put himself through college. It's just as easy to do now as it was then. We were always an extravagant family, considering my income, and my income was and is well above the average. We wasted money and food and lights and everything. Considering my upbringing, and my atrociously bad schooling, and despite myself I got pretty far. Furthermore, it was in a chosen direction. No one helped me into journalism. I did it unassisted, and I rose, not to dizzying heights, but to $30,000 a year, which is good pay for a writer. You can work for a year on a book that has a respectable sale and not make half that. But now I'm sounding as if my objective were to be rich. Maybe it was once, but not now. HAG couldn't keep me with an offer of a senior editorship and $10,000 more a year. You'd skim half of that off anyway. I don't think you quite yet realize what a fair shake you got. A guy I know with five children and an ex-wife to support pays her less than I pay you—and makes appreciably more. Even if I were back in the sex business I don't see how I could finance a bed or a marriage campaign. It doesn't interest me much anyway. I go for the wrong ones, and the right ones don't attract me. Who are the right ones? I have no idea. It may be true that I want a mother and a caretaker and a companion first and then, after those needs are satisfied, a bedfellow. I'm certainly not interested in men.

They're just not built right. Women can probably smell my psychic impotence, as they say a dog can smell fear. At any rate, they must sense that I'm no threat. The other night, when I got so loaded with Fred, I called Barbara Smith and asked to stay the night. I put it on a need basis, but not piteously so. I said I just didn't want to be alone, and I confessed that I'd had a bit too much to drink. She declined, as I'd known she would do, but she gave a curious reason. She said she was "afraid" to let me come over. It was probably meant as a sop to my pride. She knows all about my hang-up, but it would have been honest, too. We all think too much. It's the movers who get places (to score another of my brilliantly original points). Well, guess who's moving at last.

To Franzl's as usual to kill a Sunday. If you're wondering who dropped off all those goodies at your door—the boxful of drill attachments, extension cord, roasting pan, deck lounge chair—it was me: the second transfer installment. You were there—at least your car was, and behind it, a white Mustang I didn't recognize. At the time, I assumed you were upstairs with a man, either forming the beast with two backs or taking a midafternoon nap. No concern of mine anyway, is it? But to avoid interfering with your enterprise, whatever it was, I was as quiet as I could be. Then to Franzl's quite fit and thirsty for beer. Tony Lo Massimo, one of the regulars, a potbellied northern Italian with a basset hound's mournful eyes, came in dressed all in black, but it was an odd mourning costume: black twill work pants, black cotton jacket, black tie against a white shirt. He had just buried his elder brother, whose death he blames on medical science. One moment a hale sixty-seven eating a pear before going to bed; the next moment a sudden attack of acute indigestion; rushed to the hospital and given two injections of morphine. Dead within the hour. It was the morphine that killed him, Tony suspects. The waiters, Franzl, and Jack, the helicopter pilot, reextended their sympathy; they'd all already sent him condolence messages and wanted to know if Tony had got them. He had. So the neighborhood tavern *is* really a club, isn't it? And its members show a tribal loyalty. Tony bought everyone a drink—me too—and set out to reduce the level of a bottle of Chivas Regal himself. I left about nine, after six Michelobs and a duck dinner, impulsively called the Clintons in Idaho (old friends you don't know) and sought George's advice on an ethical dilemma that has nagged at me all weekend: should I write the cover (the old me?) or just tell HAG I don't feel like it (the new me, with one foot and all of my spirit in Samoa)? George thinks I should flush the cover, which made me feel so good that I decided to make a night of it. I first called Gretchen (who couldn't go), then the Ritters (Norm begged off—he was leaving for Europe early in the morning) and then the Matzes, who met me at Franzl's at 10:30. We had drinks and talked until after midnight, when they left. There was little I didn't confide to them, which was probably a mistake. I stayed on. Franzl was joyously bellowing in a *Heldentenor* arias composed on the spot ("I am pouring three dark beers, yes, I am pouring three dark beers, and I will put them on a tray for the party in the corner") and laughing loudly at everything. Slim, the square-dance caller, arrived in his Gene Autry outfit, and was served a dark beer with the handsomest lobster sandwich platter I've ever seen ($1.50), personally wrought by Franzl. Then Franzl made us all his eggs-and-everything breakfast—Mac the operatic waiter, Franzl's sister-in-law Helen, and me—this time with no cognac and too much salt. Franzl acknowledged its salinity: "I salt it once and I forget and I salt it again. But I tell *you*, you don't tell me." The words don't communicate the pride in his voice at having recognized his own mistake. All the same, I gobbled every bite. Home and in bed by 2:30 and up in time for the 10:46 train, a disgraceful hour to be going to work. Now, I don't know whether I'll write the cover. I probably will. I told Leon all about my indecision; as my senior editor, Leon would be the only victim, and I'm afraid I just can't do it to him. But just in case, I sent him a memo which will certainly reach HAG's attention. I reproduce it because the recent history of this project is such a classic example of how *Time* sometimes does business. And the cover still has no schedule. It is sure to run, but at the moment no one knows when.

For the record, may I state with all the graciousness I can muster my low opinion of the way the encounter cover has been procedurally handled?

1. Arriving at my desk on Friday, September 4, after having been away all week at a convention of sociologists in Washington, I was told to send out cover queries that day. I balked at this. There simply wasn't time to dig deeply enough into the subject to send sensible queries. The cover was then assigned to the issue dated October 5. I rustled up everything we had on the subject, took it home, and spent a large share of my weekend wading through it.

2. I was informed that great haste was necessary because some *Time* editorial authorities (unnamed) were fearful that *Newsweek* would get wind of our marvelous color act and would rush into print ahead of *Time* to spoil it. This anxiety was chimeral. *Newsweek* did an inside cover on the human potential movement (a lousy job, by the way) in the fall of 1969.

3. The cover queries went out the following week.

In the meantime, the cover was reassigned to the issue of October 12, then reassigned to the issue of October 5.

4. At one time, I had one week in which to master the considerable material the subject involves, including a dozen books (half of which I've read). I have *never* had a researcher with me on this project.

5. Since then, the cover has been further postponed, many times. It missed the issue dated October 19, it missed this week's issue (dated October 26), it will miss next week's (November 2), and it has stern competition (the prisons cover) for the issue dated November 9—which, in calendar terms, is week after next. Nevertheless, I have been asked to write the cover *this* week. I know, and you know, what happens to covers written in advance—long in advance. They wait around, gathering criticism and dust, for a schedule.

6. My motivation has begun to sag like all get out. As I have said before, it is not easy to sustain an erection forever.

Accomplished very little today, beyond rereading a portion of my notes. Tomorrow I'll reread them all, a four-hour job, and Wednesday if I'm in the mood, I'll begin writing. Mike Demarest is in town to assign Arthur Schlesinger a new version on an article commissioned for *Playboy*. Mike has lost weight and doesn't look well. His complexion is blotchy, and his lips were ringed with what could have been dried toothpaste or Bisodol. I'm to have lunch with him tomorrow. I deserve a hangover today but I don't have one. Isn't that a shame?

Going to bed early tonight and getting up at 6:30 in the hope that it will make me feel virtuous. I'll see a new platform crowd too, waiting for the 7:20. Four Valiums in my stomach. Didn't have to take any last night, naturally. HAG gets back tomorrow. Presumably I'll get some action, not necessarily instant, on the maneuver to get my severance. If this God-damned cover had held to schedule, it would be behind me now. Like an actor before the curtain, I get anxious before a cover. Never have I so delayed starting one —and never before has the system given me so many opportunities to postpone the moment of truth. The plain fact may be that I'm lazy. Since the Pago Pago decision was made for real, I've looked upon it as a *fait accompli,* and don't think about the reality much, the things that have to be done before I go. Telling you, so that at last you believe it. Telling the children, and trying to convince them that it's not an act of abandonment, that I love them still. It is abandonment, of course, but that's not the motive. I know I love my children, and need them. It was an act of abandonment to pull out of the marriage, but life requires many compromises. I'll be back some time; I'm not leaving with my fingers crossed, but neither do I overrule a return trip if things work out right financially. I'm sorry you haven't sold the house, but that you haven't is academic. You want to sell it, intend to sell it, and sooner or later will sell it, and that's an act of abandonment too. Mine is no more malicious than yours. It's mostly the strong desire, put off too many years, to add flavor to my life. As for adding point to my life—I'm largely indifferent to that. There's no point to it now. I have little idea how you're going to take the news, once you accept it. You were disbelieving when I broke the news about Jocelyn Bannon, then laughed nervously about it—I did too—then insisted that the kids would have to know, as if that hadn't occurred to me, then said I'd have to move out at once, that you couldn't stay under the same roof with me. And then, after I *had* moved out, you did a lot of crying about it. All normal enough, I guess. Someone told me today about a guy, someone from *Time* but no longer with the magazine, who is on either his fifth or sixth wife. Surely the anesthesia of habit must have reduced the traumatic content of divorce in his case. What kind of man does it take to marry five times? Not my kind, that's all I can say for sure. I'm not likely to find the second Mrs. Koffend in Samoa; the pickings have got to be slim. And anyway Grosser will wait his chance to spoil any ripening alliance. One of Samoa's American governors, who are appointed by the Department of the Interior (isn't that silly?), with presidential approval I would guess, married a native Samoan woman—quite beautiful they say. Aspinall was his name. But he was recalled after several years. On my limited stake, I won't be able to drink many of the Inter-Continental Hotel's martinis. That fact, and the torrid sub-equatorial climate, may rekindle my banked fire. Perhaps just the act of will required by this step will have a positive effect. I know exactly what I'm missing; my memory has not dimmed to those carnal pleasures that I have denied myself, and in a way you, for so long. If I were secure in that department, I could have had plenty of women in the year we've been apart. Of all ages, too, from twenty-three to my own. I have the feeling that a sexual advance from me, even under suitable conditions (I confess I can't think of any) would repel you. I had that feeling before we split. But I recognize that I may be projecting, that it would be me who, if not exactly repelled by women—and I am not— am fearful of them now because they spell failure. My roomie and I, last spring, barred no holds, and I did manage to get it in a time or two, but the results were without exception on the disappointing side. For her and for me. In a phone talk to her the other night I sensed what was not said: that her feelings about me, at a lesser level, corresponded to your feelings about me. How often you told me, with consummate kindness, that my failure at coitus constituted solid grounds for divorce. You were absolutely right. But what an effective way to guarantee further failure. It reminds me of the way *Time* sacked the last contingent of writers. They were summoned to the "Presence." HAG informed them that their work (like mine in bed) was inadequate, and each was given three months to improve (produce regular erections) or else. It takes the strongest of wills to perform under that sort of jeopardy. Moreover, the law of the self-fulfilling prophesy defeated them before they began. Even if they did improve, those who invoked the law would not have noticed. The analogy's not perfect; after all, a hard-on is unmistakably that, but the principle applies. It relates to the advice your mother dispensed to you when you were in high school and which enrages you whenever I bring it up: if a boy tries to kiss you, laugh at him. Whether or not you realize it, your mother despises men, and she passed the sentiment along to her daughters. It's hardly by chance that both of you married men—in each case two of them—who weren't quite secure enough in their masculinity—maleness, whatever you want to call it—to assert it in alliances that count, to assert it without some understanding and support from their partners. A little patience, gently applied in the early months or years of our marriage, might have made all the difference. I don't absolve myself. I didn't meet your standards. And to repeat, I did find what I was unconsciously looking for. If I had it to do over again, I would have acted first and told you of my decision after the fact. I'm not talking about just sex now. I would, for instance, either have decided to go or not to go to *Time* without consulting you, and only then have informed you of my decision. I would have bought the land on Eleuthera and then told you, at the risk of losing you, that we were moving there. And as for sex, when in the early months you bitterly complained because I came too soon, I would have said, "Well, then, hurry and catch up." But all of that would have been out of character, and I could have brought none of it off. Why did you ever marry me at all, when you cherished for a year such doubts? Why did you go gunning for me, and then, having bagged me, turn and run? You may have been playing a game with yourself, but we both lost, didn't we? Or maybe at last you won. You have your independent life and enough to get along on. Though that won't be for long. I'd be out of here in three weeks if I could swing it. But I'd like to have a day with the children, and a long dinner talk with you, before I go. Maybe we can do it *en famille*; maybe it would be better that way. The children have been prepared; they've known since summer that I was thinking seriously about it.

I've taken the irrevocable step. Today I told HAG that, for personal reasons, which I would detail to him if he were interested or curious, I was leaving *Time*. With that, I passed the point of no return. Fantasy became fact. The encounter and the announcement were both disappointingly undramatic. To begin with, you don't see HAG when you want to see him; you see him when he condescends to see you. I bid yesterday for an appointment. He did not condescend. This morning I urged upon his secretary my impatience to see him, but she was protective, as secretaries so frequently are. She reminded me, with some acerbity, that my request for an audience lay in his *In* basket along with all the other levies on this important man's time and that there was little purpose in repeating it. But I did anyway, in a note to him, and just after noon I was called up. He has no sense of people. HAG does these things through his secretary. A man more sensitive to the human nuances would have called me himself, or, better yet, have dropped down a floor and materialized in room 2457. But I was summoned by her, not by him. Henry would see me now. I came straight to the point, which was that I was leaving, and I made it quite clear that the reasons were personal rather than professional. Then I pitched for severance. I said that I hoped that in this instance the company would depart from custom, which is to reward incompetence (fuck-ups get severance without asking) and punish competence (the competent employee, departing on his own initiative, doesn't). HAG expressed doubts about that. He extended no hope that I would get my severance, though he said he would do what he could —which means, I suspect, that he will do nothing at all. I know Henry that well. His reaction to my news was impassive. He said the predictable things—"Of course we will be sorry to see you go," etc.—but tonelessly. The situation called for such a response, and he met the minimal requirements. But what really seized his interest was the cover, which, he told me, is not on for next week but the week after that. How, he wanted to know, would my decision to leave affect the cover? "I don't suppose you have any interest in doing it now," he said. I agreed, and it was left there. And that was about all there was to it. He did ask for my personal reasons and I told him, as succinctly and unemotionally as possible. And then the interview was over, and I left with my stomach somewhere down around my knees, saturated with anxiety and guilt, and went out to a semi-bibulous lunch with Marcia Gauger, a researcher who worked with me in "Press" a century ago, who listened patiently to my narrative of this radical direction-changing decision in my life. I wanted support and didn't get it. Announcing to HAG cut the last connecting thread, and I wanted to hear her say that doing it took a lot of guts. But she wouldn't say it, either from perversity or because it didn't take a lot of guts. I still think it did. Anyway, for reasons I myself don't understand, I have decided to do the cover anyway. I told this to Leon, and I also warned him to betray no gratitude at all because, if and when he did, I'd stop writing it then and there. I'm not doing it because I'm a good guy. You know better than that. I don't know why I'm doing it. I'm just doing it. It means four rough long days next week and it's not reverse blackmail. Henry made it clear enough that I'm not going to get my severance, and I'm not writing the cover in the hope of changing his mind. To hell with severance. What it means, practically, is that my stake will be my checking account balance plus whatever I need of the profit sharing, which will come along in three months or so after I go. So in a literal sense *you* are helping to finance my life's reprogramming. It was guilt money anyway, wasn't it? By throwing at you all the bread I could, I was letting myself off the hook. Some day, maybe, you'll understand that my going to Pago Pago is not negative—to do something vengeful, something against you—but positive, to do something *for* me.

I had the car in town today and drove Phil home and talked over all this. Later on—not now, because it's late and I'm tired and slightly pickled—I'll reprise that evening, which had its illuminating moments. Phil asked me in for a drink, which quickly multiplied into many, and long-suffering Kathy threw together a dinner. I'm sure I bored them both by going on forever about you, and us, and Samoa and all that. But I don't want to talk about it now.

Somewhat disquieting news from Hugh Sidey in the Washington bureau, whom I'd asked to investigate the residence requirements in Samoa. One does need the governor's permission to stay longer than thirty days—Samoa for the Samoans and all that. And as a guy at Interior told me when I called for more information, though he could see no reason why the governor—John M. Haydon—would refuse me, still he might. It's no cinch. I sent a letter of request this afternoon presenting the best possible case for myself, not all of it strictly true: I was leaving *Time* on my own initiative to do some writing of my own (true); from such sources as the profit-sharing program, a modest stock portfolio (false) and advances on two books I have contracted to write (true and false), I had ample means to support myself in Pago Pago for years without stealing breadfruit from a Samoan mouth (partly false); that I was fifty-three, divorced (true), and that our children are grown (false). He will be in Washington within the next ten days, for hearings on the Samoan budget; I said I'd be happy to call on him there if there's anything else he wants to know about me. Well, I'm not going to worry about it until I have to. But it is to Pago Pago that I want to go. Don't ask me why. It just seems right. If not Pago Pago, then some other South Seas American possession, the Marianas perhaps. Possibly one of the more remote islands in the Hawaiians; and, if nothing else, Curacao in the Caribbean, though the Caribbean just doesn't satisfy the sense of distance—and I don't mean simply map distance—that for unexplainable reasons is so important to me.

After having told Leon I would do the cover I'm now sorry I did. I don't want to at all. I don't want to do anything. I'm cross at the magazine—HAG—for denying me the $17,000 or so in severance, and am in no mood to do him or it any further favors. If I'd taken the dishonorable course and just not come in to work, pleading any reason, the more implausible the better, I could have got fired in short order —*and* with full severance rights. That's twice in a year that being honorable has cost me plenty. Had Jocelyn and I deceived Guy—had I remained invisible—we would have been married, though God knows, and I do too, we'd never have stayed married.

Last night Phil joined the company of counselors who don't think I should give you *everything*. And maybe I won't. He suggests I give you half the profit sharing, peel off what I need, and sock the rest in, say, Mexican banks, which pay 10 percent, and send you that income. The same for the trust, when and if it comes through. It would be mine, but you'd get what it earns and I'd dip into the principal, as necessary, for expenses like the children's education. And who knows? Maybe if you became a hardship case that sister of yours would let you have her house for the taxes and utilities. Phil also said you had our house on the market for $79,500 and that you're putting it back on the market for $89,500. Even in today's bearish real estate market, that first figure was low. You should get at least $80,000 and I'd advise you to hold out for it even if it means waiting. Meanwhile, rent it; surely you can get enough to clear expenses and a bit more. It's an old house and needs cosmetic surgery, but you've decorated it inside in very good taste and it's roomy and comfortable. It has a good feel to it. The pool's no strong selling point this time of year, but it is after all there.

I *am* indecisive. Should I or shouldn't I do the cover? I may have to. I can't leave *Time* before I'm ready to take off for Samoa; that's the day the money stops. And I can't possibly leave before the end of November, if then. If I can swing it, I'll buy that medical-insurance policy and pay it up for a year. After that it's your baby, unless I get rich. Don't entirely discount that possibility; stranger things have happened, and I'm way overdue for one of fortune's smiles. The break with *Time* should have exalted me. Instead it has depressed me.

The word has swept through *Time* that I'm leaving. It's too soon to distill the response; I haven't heard feedback from that many people yet. Anyway, as I've said, the hole seals fast. Now that it's known that I'm going, most of my colleagues will accept the fact even before I'm physically gone. We are simply not missed. HAG already doesn't miss me. I didn't expect him to get down on his knees—a difficult feat for him, given his rotundity—and beg me to stay, but it would have been nice all the same. I have a good idea now of my rating, after fifteen years of conscientious potato peeling and a steady obbligato of discontent: not low, not high. I won't miss them either. Some of them, yes, on and off the premises of *Time*. Barbara Smith has been away for a week and I already miss her. She's a true human connection. I warm myself at her fire, though it doesn't burn for me. Just for the hell of it, I'm going to try to go through the weekend without drinking. Nothing today, nothing tomorrow, despite a lunch date at The Sign of The Dove with Warren Avis, who got out of the car-rental business into the human potential movement. Nothing Saturday, but maybe a keg of beer at Franzl's Sunday. I will really miss him and his German tavern, most of it hand-hewn; so many evenings spent there in the last year, at only a few of which did beer and the cameraderie of the bar fail to buoy my spirits. I think I'm a totally accepted club member by now; at least by its president.

My sex life is less active than a monk's. I don't even have dirty thoughts. A tour through the latest *Playboy*, which bristles with pubic hair, was no more titillating than a tour of the Cloisters. Less. It's 8:20. I'm going to overdose myself with sleeping potion, turn on the boob tube, watch until I'm groggy and go to bed.

Now it appears I'm likely to get my severance pay, under some other designation, after all. Late last night after a drinking dinner with Dick Burgheim, I dropped in on the "Business" section, which, even under Marshall Loeb, has *Time*'s gayest Friday night pour. Ed Jamieson of all people was there. They say of Ed that he takes a shower in his vest, but there is a streak of *bonhomie* in him that liquor brings out. He knew all about my resignation of course, and periodically during the time I was there kept telling me, with elaborate overemphasis, that I was not entitled to severance pay and would not get it. All said with a Cheshire-cat grin. It took me a long time to catch on; too long for Ed, who at last broke the truth. "You don't think we'd let you go away empty-handed after fifteen years? But, Koffend, you talk too much." I agreed I was a blabbermouth. "Not any more," Ed said. "Just one more word, and that cuts it." So I'm to have my Pago Pago stake. Which means I've got to do the cover next week, so once more I've brought the notes and cover outline home, will go through everything once more tomorrow and begin writing Monday. But however hard, it's worth $17,000.

I've wondered occasionally whether you'd try to thwart my skip-out, but I don't think you're the sort. I hope not, because even if you are I don't see how you could stop me. Certainly no divorce decree in the world can command a man to make a certain income. Or work at all, for that matter. And what would it benefit you to restrain me from leaving New York? The word last night from Ed Jamieson is good news to you too. You'll get your half of the profit sharing and *all* the income from the other half if I can find work in Samoa.

It's bitter cold today, down around freezing with a stinging wind and flurries of corn snow. Yesterday, I wore a sweater and my canvas parka to watch my son the football player in action and was still chilly. I won't miss the New York winters. I don't yet feel any sadness at leaving all the familiar scenes. I took a cab through Central Park on the way to my lunch date, and tried to feel regret at glimpsing, for one of the last times, the handsome spires that look down upon that sylvan setting from its south end and along its east flank. It is a beautiful landscape, one forever reproduced in *New Yorker* ads. But I felt nothing, nothing at all. The same for the familiar faces and corridors at *Time.* All that will soon enough be 8,000 miles behind me, but I feel nothing, no sadness, no regrets. Kind of like after Dad died. The event didn't touch me emotionally. No sense of loss. Several years passed before I missed the little guy, and I miss him still. Not actively, I don't think about him much, but when I do, the memories are tender ones. I feel sorry for him—what a drab and pointless life, with no mountain tops. I find it difficult to feel sorry for mother, whose life has been as level and monotonous as a prairie.

I am drawn back to our house as the salmon upstream. Today I took all my cover notes over, knowing you wouldn't be there, and not expecting to see the children. Our trees are shedding my leaves—but this is the second fall, isn't it, that I haven't had to rake them? I wandered through the rooms, upstairs and down, inspecting them with the trespasser's eye. But I'm not an outsider yet—perhaps never will be. The pool pump was running, past the swimming season. I turned it off. It was an act that in other years officially marked the death of summer. I removed an enormous burr from Grundy's neck while she patiently, trustingly, waited for the operation to end, as she has done so often in the past.

When it was over, she wagged her behind off in gratitude. I looked again at the hole I sank for no good reason two inches into the rock that juts from the front lawn—our lawn —when I first acquired a star drill, while the kids, then forgotten years younger, squatting on their little haunches watching, lent inexpert help. You can still see it there if you look. It will be there after you sell the house and strangers move in. It will be there as long as the stone. Why does this thought bring tears? They're running down my cheeks, as they did yesterday during *Stella Dallas* on TV, an outrageous travesty on maternal unselfishness. I stayed at the house maybe an hour. Now I'm back in the apartment pretending to watch a ridiculous early Victor Mature movie, *1,000,000 B.C.* I've an unattractive agenda before me: read through my detailed cover outline, exercise, go early to Franzl's for a sleep-inducing load of beer or stay in and buy sleep with pills. It takes a great many pills now. I went to bed last night at 8:30 without taking anything and slept till nine; even so, I waked groggy, and still am. But if I am to begin the cover tomorrow I must be rested. Why? For Christ's sake, you'd think the job ahead of me was to draft the U.S. Constitution. Reading the cover outline is an hour's work, and I don't have to memorize the God-damned thing. Carole Landis and Victor Mature have just encountered a garden lizard, blown up to brontosaurian size; it flicked its reptilian tongue at them, then turned its reptilian tail.

Eight beers, one delicious fresh roast pork and dumplings dinner later. It would have been so easy to have stayed at Franzl's, but discipline interceded and I left. Enormous discipline, really. I've done today everything I set out to do, and am fully on schedule. I feel the eight beers, but only slightly. It's early—short of eight—so that in an hour or so, with some

Valium in me, blending with all the malt, I can sleep more than I need and begin writing. All, all today done as planned. A costly evening: $3.50 for dinner, $4 worth of beer, 90 cents for a cherry cordial for Helen, the wife of Franzl's brother, and a dollar tip—overtip—for Tony the waiter, who no doubt has more spending money than I. A letter off today to brother Joe, informing him of my decision and warning him to say nothing yet to mother, who, like you, will be told at the last moment, on the outside chance that the whole thing will come to naught. I have trouble sometimes believing it myself. And I suppose that even at this eleventh hour I could be persuaded to turn back. But by whom? And for what? You could conceivably do it, but only by discovering, unprompted, and granting the concessions that you have never discovered and that in any case you cannot make. *Time* could say or do nothing. Ditto New York. Ditto any friend. (What friends?) The hour comes, soon or late, when a man must put himself on the line, and while I recognize the theater in that remark, it's truer than it is phony.

Maybe it is, as the head candler said, a form of suicide. I had a reason to make that observation, and something to say beyond it, but in the course of two sentences it has entirely escaped my mind. It seems typical of me that I've done this, as I do so much, precipitately: moving first and considering the consequences later. Resigning from *Time* before guaranteeing the severance. Choosing Pago Pago and then applying at the last minute for permission to live there. Taking terrible chances all along the way. But something inside me rejects the cautious planning that assures everything will work, or that takes every imaginable contingency into account. I'm going, and that's that. The little boy (of fifty-three) proving to all the nonbelievers that he really had it in him. The leaper declining to look. It's a part of our times, isn't it? Widespread dissatisfaction, alienation, the feeling that nothing you do counts. *Time*'s mortality is undeniable now. You can smell death in the air, but still it's likely to last a lot longer than I. I will die first, and if I hung around, I would die the way everybody else does, in the same old uniform, the same old habits, and the same old place. The ultimate move—laying it out to HAG—reawakened all the old suicidal thoughts, but only at half strength and in an abstract way. Driving somewhere in the Beetle, I think suddenly: why not rack it up? Then I won't have to make another decision ever. The thought passes as swiftly as it comes. It will return often, no doubt, in Pago Pago, as reality swamps what is probably still a dream. But I'm going anyway; I'm going; I'm going. My last years weren't going to be good anyway here; that's given. They might just as well be bad somewhere else. And they don't *have* to be bad.

My curiosity is boundless to know what you're doing for sexual kicks. My guess is, no more than I am, but I have little faith now in my guesses about you. I would have guessed, for instance, that there was something left of the marriage. (That has a familiar ring; have I said just that before, in just the same way? But then, there are only so many themes in life, and the ones that enlist my attention are down to a precious few.)

Monday and drunk again, and at the Algonquin, because I've decided to stay in the city. Spending bread like water. One dollar for the cab, one for smokes, one for the hop, and now embarking on my first stinger on the rocks. The table bells in the lobby are bolted down. Unless I'm mistaken, Aline Saarinen is sitting at the adjoining table, looking younger and blonder than she does on television. She is showing her knees, between the hemline and the boots. There may be other celebrities at other tables, but I don't recognize them and they of course don't recognize me. Will I be able to read this tomorrow? Should I go up to my room and call people? We once sojourned here, you and I—remember? Years past. So there are ghosts around—of Bernard Hollowood, then the editor of *Punch,* for one, taking dinner with us. I have begun the cover and am well into it. I feel that at my age dignity demands that the evening move towards me. The last time I sat in this hotel lobby on business was to interview Lillian Hellman. We didn't click, but neither did we collide. I retain very little impression of her because she's no self-advertiser. I don't remember the "Press" story I wrote about her, except that it was not complimentary. One cool customer, but I'll bet she hasn't forgotten me, because I charged. I forced her to talk, although she didn't give much. At all the other tables here people are relaxing with drinks and making the small inconsequential talk that people make on their social guard. As part of the reading I had to do for this cover, I waded through a reprise of the human potential movement by one Donald Clark, a CUNY professor of education, who confesses that eighteen months spent surveying the movement have spoiled forever for him the social occasions of ordinary life. He sees now the yawning chasm between the disciplined and controlled deportment of conscripts to a cocktail party and what these same people really want to do: reach, grab, feel, break the rules. I feel much the same way tonight, but at fifty-three and semiloaded, I could no more penetrate another of these social spheres all around me, all dutifully subscribing to the rules, than could a graduate of the Tombs make out in Gracie Mansion. I've just cased the population of this room and it looks pretty paltry. That's defensive; if any of the other tables were to open to me I'd jump at the chance. Maybe in Pago Pago I can do it; maybe I'll have to. I shot the evening, but not by design. Since I've elected to stay in the city I can sleep late and still get in early. It's only Tuesday. I'm past the lead, into the justification part—this is why *Time* is doing this cover now—and into the central hard stuff. The week will end. I'll finish the cover, and anyway I am in a strong strategic position to revolt. If the system doesn't like my contribution it can redesign it, without help, to the system's taste. I'm writing on a tiny note pad provided by the Algonquin, while the pleasure-bound scurry in, sit, and scurry out. No one takes any notice of me; I'm a part of the scenery. Or if they do, they don't say. Why should they? A couple just paused outside the elevator, both my age, past their sexual prime. "You going to ask me up?" the man wanted to know. His companion did not respond. He repeated the question. More silence. At that point I lost interest, and they moved away somewhere beyond my ken. I would bet he's going to get what I'm going to get tonight, which is a fair night's sleep and no more. But what do I know about it? For all I know, there's fellatio, cunnilingus and everything in between going on all over this hotel. Well, enough. I'm reducing my second stinger, and when it's drained, I'm going to bed. It's 11:30—early—and I'll make real tracks in the cover tomorrow, or try.

Why in Christ's name do they make tear-open beer cans open at the seam? Gives one the hiccoughs. I'm within sighting distance of the end of the cover and could have completed it tonight, but instead drank two pitchers of beer with Fred Golden at the Steak & Brew on Seventh Avenue, wrote a letter to a friend holidaying in Paris and at ten hired a cab north. Called this afternoon to the presence of HAG, who advised me that I can't get my severance but that I won't have to leave destitute; I am to be appointed *Time's* Pago Pago stringer—South Pacific correspondent—and get eighteen months' pay for that honorary title: $12,500, less deductions, I imagine. Naturally I accepted. I also called Pan Am and made reservations, so now it's in motion and definite. And I served notice—warning—on Leon Jaroff that while he'll get his cover from me and this week to boot, he had better reconcile himself to the possibility that if they want to fuss with it, they'd better be prepared to do all the fussing. In short, the writer's version is my last will and testament to *Time*. I may take next week off. I want to get a passport just in case it becomes necessary to knock about the Pacific a bit—Australia, New Zealand, Hawaii, Fiji, Tahiti, Japan. More readily procured here than there. I also want to make contact with *Asia Magazine*, which is published in Hong Kong but has a Manhattan office, and which is in the market for writers. Pays $12,000 to $15,000. I'm not terribly interested, but it could be a useful escape hatch if things go sour in Samoa—if, for instance, I can't work there. So you see this isn't really Gauguinesque, nor am I motivated in the least to make you suffer financially. You'll get half my profit sharing, plus rights to all of it if you need it, as you may. I still feel guilty, for no good reason, and because of the guilt, you're going to get everything I can give you without qualifying myself for welfare. Governor Haydon hasn't had time to reply, but I don't anticipate any real trouble there. Incidentally, for the record (my defensiveness is showing), I drank nothing Tuesday, and will drink nothing tomorrow. I'll finish the cover (maybe), polish it Friday and Xerox one copy for Leon, who will be gone all next week. Yesterday I was depressive; today, semimanic. The cover's back is broken, I have charted its terminal portion, I can do it featly, and—in an obvious analogy—I can see at last the end of my life here. You will scoff, but I'd gladly take you and the children with me if you'd go. They'd go, you wouldn't. Maybe one day you'll join me, but I wouldn't bet a nickel on that either. I'm guessing that American cigarettes are $1.50 a pack in Pago Pago, so it isn't unlikely that I can do there what I haven't succeeded in doing here in thirty-seven years: stop smoking. What a frightening statistic: thirty-seven years of cigarettes. Here's a more upbeat one: in a relaxed moment during this week's cover writing, I totalled on my Addiator the push-ups I've done so far this year: nearly 21,000. How many men my age, excepting William Scranton, can say the same? If Tutuila has a sandy littoral, I'll get my exercise jogging up and down the shore for so many miles each day. The same guy I am now is going to live in Pago Pago. A sudden unsolicited thought: Ann, isn't it unbelievable that we're divorced, and have been for nearly a year? I still don't quite accept that reality, as I refuse to accept the reality of Nixon in the White House. Well, as the cab driver said who drove me out tonight, "There are only two things I *have* to do. One is to pay taxes and the other is to die." I added a third, which is not compulsory but should be: to be happy, whatever that means, to extract, being careful not to hurt anyone (and that's not as easy as it sounds), all that there is for you in life. In a mechanistic way I have at last begun to try. The driver wholeheartedly agreed with my proposition, which, like all my propositions, is about as original as sin. These are queer times for me: everything out of phase and askew. Unreality has superseded reality. The building rising outside my office window has simply disappeared; it isn't there. I called Jess Birnbaum in San Francisco from my room in the Algonquin and talked to him $12.40 worth and then completely forgot the call. Getting up in the morning, I noticed four cigarette stubs in an ashtray in the sitting room (I had a suite) and was dumfounded. When and why did I smoke them? Then I remembered. I'm on my third pack tonight; writing and smoking, as you know, go together for me. Once I climb out the far end of this cover, my consumption will recede to a pack a day. Too much—one cigarette is too much—but moderation for me. I'm sitting here in my apartment, writing to you on a clipboard, drinking a can of Rheingold and igniting one Camel after another. It's midnight. I'll go to bed when I feel ready and get up when I wake up. Drive the VW to town. It will cost me $2.50 for parking but who cares? I just planted a $343 expense-account refund in the bank. No profit though; I owe all of that and more to American Express. I also owe a life-insurance premium, your medical policy, Mobil and Texaco, and Brooks Brothers for underwear and shirts. You'll get the bill. I know I can depend on you to pass it along to me (no meanness intended; I'm just surprised it hasn't come along yet, since I made the purchases in July). I've already lost one of the shirts, in a disappearance as mysterious as the vanishing act of a new paring knife from my berry-box kitchen. Maybe that bill—just short of $50—is one I can beat; are they likely to chase me all the way to Samoa for half a century note? I'll find out. In such modest ways I have become conscienceless and unscrupulous. I need the bread more than my creditors do. But that lid of gift grass in the closet preys on my consciousness if not my conscience. I don't want it and I don't want to risk transporting it to the city. So I think I'll flush it down the john. Seems a pity, but I've just done it.

I do feel somewhat liberated, I guess, or like a good soldier I would have done my duty tonight and finished the cover. But I didn't. It's raining. The tires of passing cars hiss beyond my window. Where are they all going at this hour? At any hour, where do they all go, and why? No mail for three days, not even bills. Each time I open and peer into that empty compartment I now say, good; this clinches it; nobody knows or cares where I am; all the more reason for cutting out. I see the dentist Monday morning at seven; my bite is naturally as old as I am, but there's no reason to worry that it will give

) 170 (

me any serious trouble over the next seven years. After that, when I'm sixty, life becomes another game entirely. Sixty isn't the end, but it sure as hell is the beginning of the end. Looking forward to sixty—the debut of one's seventh decade —is not unlike anticipating in May, as a grammar school student sprung from classes, the end of summer: it's too far away, unimaginable, it just won't happen. I don't believe it still. John Koffend sixty? Out of the question. I have a beer to finish, a Camel to smoke and my teeth to brush. Then to bed. It's 12:45—why do I keep referring to the hour? Sleep well. I will. Jesus, what prisoners all of us are.

What a totally disorganized life I live now. It's just past seven Sunday morning and I've been in bed since 5:30 yesterday afternoon, having gone to bed without any dinner. The night before, an impromptu, wine-sodden dinner at Patty and Mayo Mohs' apartment uptown, with several others, after a wine-sodden pour in Leon Jaroff's office. Haven't done my exercises all week, but finished the cover. It's on for this week, then my duties with *Time*, as far as I'm concerned, are over. I must hang around for a while, but I'm counting on their not making me work. I have other things to do: get my passport, set up loose reportorial connections with *The New York Times*, *Asia Magazine*, *East Magazine* (Tokyo) and Cranston Jones's *Travel & Leisure,* among others. If I'm not allowed to work in Samoa, occasional free-lance commissions will—or may—keep me alive.

Going through my desk Friday—a sad business—I came upon a copy of our separation agreement and find that I've been overpaying you all these months. Nothing in it—if I have the final draft—stipulates that I must pay you more as I earn more, much less half off the top of everything I make. I owe you $6,000 a year alimony, $6,000 a year child support, plus 50 percent of each year's college education expenses for children. There's also a complicated paragraph that gears what I pay you to the rising cost of living but that I can now, if I choose, ignore. If the cost of living goes up 3 percent, so must my payments to you—*if* my income has gone up. My income is going down. Presently, you should be getting $12,750 from me a year. Nothing binds me to give you a dime more, nothing except the cost of living. But I am bound by the figures cited in the agreement. This departure is going to test us both: your charity and my mettle. You'll get all I can possibly give you, which may be a good deal less and could be appreciably more than you're getting now. In the long run. A lawyer here told me that you could indeed have me clapped into civil jail here for default, but not in Samoa; he also said you couldn't legally restrain me from going. I'm still hoping that the profit sharing and the family trust will pacify you—and that I won't need either. *Plus* the VW. *Plus* the $1,500 in my checking account, if I can spare it. Enough of this high finance. I'm driving over in a minute with the rug. You won't be up but I'll be quiet. Maybe I'll go to church this morning—the First Baptist Church in White Plains—to hear Mac, the operatic waiter at Franzl's, sing.

You *were* asleep. I left the rug in the front hall. It may dawn on you, as these gift deposits accumulate, that they're being left for a reason. I don't like to think about going now because it makes me anxious. I prefer to look upon it as an inevitable part of the near future that the mere passage of time will bring: an event as unpreventable as Thanksgiving. Where did I spend last Thanksgiving? I don't remember. Not with you. I think alone.

It is chastening to discover how many people at *Time* don't yet know that I'm leaving, after I told HAG. Reminds me of the time Jack Leonard, back on his job as "Science" writer after a month's vacation, bumped into a fellow writer just returned from a year's leave. "The reason you haven't seen me around," Jack said after they'd exchanged greetings, "is that I've been on vacation." Martha Duffy didn't know I was going until I told her; neither did Georgia Harbison, who was my "People" writer last June. The accumulation in my desk was mainly trash: unused and now useless check pads for our joint account; paid-up repair bills on the VW; notes written in wrath to HAG and sensibly never sent; letters and a birthday card from Jocelyn; misbegotten starts, running anywhere from five pages to fifty, on misbegotten novels; keys to unlock God knows what doors; a copy of my birth certificate; notes to myself as, on some late night at the Winslow Hotel, I launched self-improvement campaigns. All this heavily seasoned with tobacco shreds. Nothing of any value, except for a few things that I may save for sentiment's sake. Nothing, sadly, that spells you: no picture, no letters or notes, nothing. Like Scobie in Graham Greene's *The Heart of the Matter,* I don't establish or assert my existence with objects. My office is more cluttered than was his, but with papers and books and things that define my work, not me. I wish now I hadn't risen so early, it's still only ten-ish; what am I to do with all the hours stretching between now and bedtime? Thank heaven I've got to sack out early: tomorrow morning at seven is my dental appointment with Burt Stark. I've done the Sunday crossword puzzle; anyway, crossword puzzles now bore me, I've done so many of them to fill empty moments in these vacant months. I think that's one reason I've smoked and drunk more lately (more but not more often). It's something to do. I say now that I won't go to Franzl's today, but I'll probably end up there, and blow Burt over tomorrow with my breath. Maybe I'll ask Dick Burgheim to take an afternoon train out and have dinner with me here, if I can find him by telephone. Warren Avis, a recent lunch companion, said in the course of our long talk about car-renting and the human potential movement that the working stiff should recruit at least half his friends from outside his work place. This, he says, is one key, among other things, to a successful retirement. One reason why cops don't understand noncops, and vice versa, is that they spend 90 percent of their time on and off duty in the company of other cops (Avis's percentage). Avis would be a useful connection. He's rich, and liked me; has called twice since the lunch. Except that I've never been able to do things like that. Cultivate useful connections.

The weatherman, who forecast a fine day, is wrong. You've just introduced a ray of sunshine (what clichés!) by inviting me over for supper. I think you caught on about the rug, but shied from approaching too near the truth; perhaps I'll tell you tonight. But on second thought, no: it would be too soon, give you too much time to think and possibly to act. Pray God you'll be reasonable when the time comes, have a little faith in me and in a now entirely unpredictable tomorrow. I'll go to the Meadows Farm first and bring you all some apples; the new harvest must be in. Wow, what a difference a natural night's sleep can make. Why do I ever drink? Now if only I could stop smoking, like you. But believe it or not, I can still pass the match test.

Well, now you know it's for real—I'm going. It's Monday night and I'm in my apartment, but spiritually I'm in the living room with you after the dinner at Franzl's, and you're crying as we discuss what you called "the ultimate rejection." You should see me now. I'm as shattered as you were last night. I've been fighting back tears all day at the office and barely made it to my apartment door. I simply don't know

Ann, the answers to the questions you asked last night: "We can't go back, can we? We can't start again, can we? It wouldn't work, would it?" I don't even know if they were questions or a plea. But you're right; this step is in many ways more traumatic than the divorce. I *will* be lonely in Samoa, as you predicted. I know that. But I'm lonely here. I know very few things for sure, but I do know that things with us never again can be what they were, and that, for complicated reasons many of which you've heard, I am *driven* to do what I'm doing, perhaps even against my own desires. I think I wish that things *could* be the same again between us, and they nearly are. But not quite. Undressing in the old house, after you said I could stay the night, in the same tiny bathroom together—it was like a page from the common book of our past, suddenly materializing in the present. It's difficult for me to imagine life without you, as it has been all this year; more difficult than ever since last night. But I've got to try this, sink or swim. The only alternative is despair, and I've had too rich a taste of that. What do I want? I want you, and the children, but not in the old scene. All of us together somewhere else—not necessarily Pago Pago—some far-off place not in this country, squeezing out of each other what there is to life, together trying something new. *Everything* new. You remember, after my shock at the hasty divorce, your saying, with an embarrassed laugh, "Well, we can always get remarried"? The same is true still. I can always come back. And, after the children are grown, you and I can always get together again, can't we? But is *that* a question or a plea? Thank God for *Laugh-In* in half an hour.

Leon is visibly nervous about the cover, which he read over the weekend. I've already done some patchwork on it for him, with more coming up tomorrow, and I'm beginning to feel rebellious to the point of defiance. I anticipate more trouble from HAG—it could be deadly. I'm in no mood at all to play their silly perfectionist games. I've written what I've written; if they want to change it, let them do it themselves. Such an insurrection would cost me more than Brownie points. It could cost me the $12,500 I've been promised as *Time*'s South Pacific correspondent. But I just can't care. My head and heart reel with thoughts of you and last night, of Samoa, of terminations and good-byes. Against all this the cover weighs no more than a cloud, but a dark one.

A lonely letter from Bob, who has been told I'm leaving. He begs me to come by Spokane as if it were just around a corner; even if it costs me more, he writes, "I think it's worth it, don't you? I really wish you would." And then: "I would really dig to see you a lot. I really would. It would be far out to show you around . . . Please do it for me . . . Really do it. We could have good raps." Quite a moving compliment from an eighteen-year-old son. I'll have to go, won't I? No matter what it costs. The nearest I get to Spokane is Los Angeles, first stop after New York. Then to Pago Pago via Honolulu. If I can possibly swing it I will.

Somewhat cheering news for you: my profit sharing is back up to $38,000 in round numbers. Only capital gains comes out of that. *You* can have all of it, no matter what some of my counselors say. Get Jim Lebenthal to put some of it into tax-free municipals. As to my pension rights: they're secure and I'll have $300 a month from my sixty-fifth year. I can continue to give me and the children—not you—medical coverage for about $56 a month, a bargain I hope I can afford. This is not going to be easy on any of us, Ann. You must know I nourish no illusions of a South Seas idyll. Someone who knows me well—I'd rather not say who—said to me today, "The sad part is, you don't really want to go, do you?" And it's half true. I'd like to turn the clock back to Los Angeles, when we were happiest together, to the best years of our marriage, and stop it there. They *were* good times. I should never have left and come to New York. Today, besides futzing with the cover, I had a martini lunch with Larry Barrett and Ruth Brine from *Time*, applied for my passport and sent a letter to the publisher of *Asia Magazine* in Hong Kong. I'm available for assignments if he wants to use me. I can't help thinking it's time something broke right for me for a change. I know good luck is earned, it doesn't happen—and have I earned any? You *do* miss me, don't you? You made it clear last night, but you wouldn't say so. What is it in you, what hereditary adamantine or lousy maternal tuition, that keeps you off your knees? I know you understand that the move *must* come from you. I'm glad you can't make it, I guess. I despise *Time* now and all it represents; New York; the foolish patterns of life out here, the senseless coming and going, the competition, the final exam that the *Time* writer must pass every week.

In any event, I'm out of the "unmanly" weepy stage. Now and then, out of curiosity, I walk into the bathroom and look at myself crying. It's not becoming; I look silly; the sight would extract sympathy from no one. Then I can laugh.

No word from the governor of Samoa, who is in Washington now. Well, I don't have to think about going yet; it's at least a month off. I'll see you and the children as often as I can in the interval. I want one fancy, a to-hell-with-the-cost, tête-à-tête dinner with you, preferably at Nino's, and I want to drink at least three martinis, and I want you not to mind. I'll charge it to American Express and let them hound me for it—they'll be our host.

Another Dial-a-Cab ride home, with a driver named Johnson, a six-pack and his stammering conversation to shorten the trip. He grew unafraid of me and as he relaxed the stammer disappeared. We got along fine. He's a month older than

I and prey to the same ambitions to chuck all this and try something new. In his case the impetus comes from his wife —he's the reluctant one. Her fantasy-land is Miami, which is not all that different from mine. But they won't go. I can tell. A call today from Samoa's Governor Haydon in Washington. We are to lunch Friday at Le Bibliotheque near the Ford Foundation's handsome headquarters, where he has appointments. The call is cheering. I take it as preliminary evidence that he's going to grant my request and let me live there. Otherwise, why call at all? I make a good first impression, and he will lend official weight to my scheme. Progress report on the cover: my tailored version runs 1,078 lines, which is far too long but it reads satisfactorily enough. Now it's up to Leon to edit it to size and smuggle it past HAG. If he fails we're all in for bad days and nights the rest of the week, but I still may insurrect. Is HAG shitty enough to deny me $12,500 just because I refuse to overhaul the story? I have no idea. It's almost worth that to find out. The worm that turns becomes a new worm. It's after one and I'm not going to set the alarm. How I've changed. In an earlier incarnation I would have bled from a dozen self-inflicted wounds awaiting this Jupiterian judgment from the managing editor, then sighed in helpless resignation and done what was asked. Now I think: let HAG dare to differ. Just let him dare. The beer is getting to me, together with a battalion of cigarettes. I shall sleep. My toes itch again; is that an omen? It's 1:15. But I slept nine hours last night on thirty milligrams of Valium, and raced recklessly, carelessly, through the alterations Leon suggested in the cover. I'm finishing a beer. The bed sheets are clean. Underwear and towels, all laundered but tumbled together, are perched precariously like a snow cap on the promontory of my typewriter. I will not brush my teeth tonight. Why should I? Burt Stark scraped and polished them day before yesterday. I'll have to drive into town tomorrow; I hate those midday, biddy trains, especially on matinee day. Why go in at all? Leon will be hermetically sealed in his office, reducing the cover length.

The cover week is over, though it's not a cover. On Wednesday HAG changed his mind in favor of another subject, the blue-collar worker, so my text had to be cut from 1,078 to 650 lines, a major piece of surgery that calls for a cleaver rather than a scalpel. Now it's running as a text block wrapped around the color act. I did most of the work, but it wasn't finished Friday, so Leon is in today, not I. All very unrewarding and unsatisfactory. There was a time when I'd have blown my stack at this decision, so typical of HAG, who has been known to juggle as many as five cover stories in the same week. When my cover on human aggression and violence was killed last year (it still hasn't run, and now never will), I felt as if I'd lost a baby. I guess it's a measure of the distance that I've already put between myself and *Time* that I accepted with almost careless calm the fate of my last major enterprise for the magazine. I just got out the old cleaver and chopped away, with all the emotion of a butcher trimming a pork loin.

The lunch with Governor Haydon got me permission, renewable, to stay a year. He's a personable sort of man, originally from Seattle. We didn't empathize, but he seemed delighted to have someone like me coming over there. I take it that the American colony, such as it is, is on the dull side. Housing may be a problem, but not insurmountable. There are rental properties owned by Samoans and modernized (kitchens, etc.), but they're not cheap—about $150 a month, although the governor wasn't sure. The American administration owns housing that it lets to contract employees. If I can wangle one of these, I could get a one-bedroom concrete bungalow for $30 a month. Haydon recommended I stay the first two weeks at the Inter-Continental Hotel, reconnoitering, and I may have to. He also suggested I buy a motor scooter which is sold over there and not expensive. Several other writers live there, he told me, one a New Zealander who lives or lived in a *fale* with a Samoan family. If I can stand the togetherness and the casual Samoan attitude towards hygiene I may do it too. The drinking water is far from pure, with a dangerously high coliform count. Haydon, who's been there fifteen months, contracted amoebic dysentery on arrival and lost forty-six pounds. Now his system has apparently adjusted, but his lieutenant governor, a sixty-eight-year-old man, is hospitalized and may have to be sent home. The beautiful main bay, around which Pago Pago sprawls, is polluted: much of the town's sewage empties into it. There is a filtration plant but the necessary pipes haven't been laid so it's not much use. The U.S. Government, which has owned Samoa since 1900, has never shown interest in investing the money necessary to improve life on the islands. The annual budget, if I remember correctly, is something like $20 million. I'm not going to perish from idleness. There's quite a wide range of activity, among it the community college that Haydon has started. It's not a college, nor does it have a campus or buildings. Maybe I can get into that as an instructor in English, and I'm sure I can find work at one of the two weekly newspapers. I'll be busy. I may even like it. Dress is quite informal; since there's no dry-cleaning facility it scarcely pays to have suits. No fresh milk but plenty of eggs, taro, breadfruit, coconuts and fish. Meat is imported frozen from New Zealand. This much I've learned from the governor and from a brochure he sent me, *Sojourn in Samoa,* the same provided to all contract employees before their departure for the islands. It could use a rewrite and maybe that's what I'll do.

Back in my digs after dinner with you in the old quarters, and mulling over the evening. We're married still, aren't we? There was that feel to the evening, except for the trend of the talk. Husbands and wives don't discuss the disposition of the second car, one spouse's imminent departure for the South Seas and the finances of separation. But it was all amiable, as most of our years were. I'm sure we could make it work again after a fashion, but there are better goals to life than that. You're a pleasant partner. If I regret anything about our marriage it's that neither of us had the sense to see its dissolution in the shadows and to do something about it in time. But then that would have condemned me to a life sentence at *Time*, on the eastern seaboard, and in Westchester County. And it's all that, more than the marriage, that I'm trying to leave behind. I'm glad you've recovered from your black mood of last Sunday. It wouldn't have done you any good to try to stop me, but I like it that you're not going to try to do something else silly. That's not very honest; it's not even what I'm trying to say. You say friends have said that you should be furious at me for leaving, for jeopardizing your future, for forcing you to shoulder the risk of short stakes. You say that you're not furious, that you half understand why I have to do this. Your attitude pleases and comforts me. Something like *that* is what I'm trying to say. I won't leave with a clear conscience or with peace of mind. But after tonight I won't feel so much like a heel about it. And that isn't honest either. I don't feel like a heel at all. But I'm not mad at you, and the vengeance quotient in me, which I don't think was ever very high, has now dropped to near zero.

I'm curious to know whom you've gone to bed with in the

last year and how rewarding or otherwise those dalliances were, and even where they were. It is amusing, as you said, that you've had affairs but no real dates. And I confess it was gratifying to hear what you said not today but last Sunday: that none of them (meaning of course the experiences and not the companions) compared to me. I understand exactly what you mean. That's what comes of living years together. Husbands and wives develop a sort of shorthand communication in which a certain arch of the neck, a barely perceptible gesture, the most trivial change of expression, all speak volumes. That takes years of practice; no matter how satisfactory in other departments, affairs never reach that level of communication however long they last. I can still tell your mood at a glance; I can premonitorily anticipate a change of mood in you. I can almost read your mind—still. Now I wish I'd stopped off at Franzl's because I'm lonely without you, the house, the children. And I'm also running out of cigarettes. I'm having a beer—the same beer I refused from you—and have taken Valium as usual. I'll be loaded with it before leaving for Samoa—a prescription for one hundred ten-milligram capsules. But in Pago Pago I won't have to sleep. I don't think I've idealized about life there, but I'll have to go there and be there to determine whether I'm right or wrong. Barbara Smith called me Saturday morning from the city and talked for an hour. Very flattering and cheering. She does love me in her way, but then she gets nothing but my good side. She doesn't have to live with me, make love to me, meet my needs; and I unselfishly and patiently meet many of hers. She's like Jocelyn Bannon in some respects, but smarter and warier. The Jocelyn thing began when she decided to fish for me to see if she could catch me. She did that all right, but in the process she got more than she expected; she got half "hung up"—her way of falling in love—herself. Only half; I never had her, and when the weather turned stormy she came in out of the rain. Good night, Ann. I can really see you when I talk to you with this *Time* pencil stub; you're emphatically and almost palpably here.

If this passage strikes you as incoherent, ascribe it not to the effects of drink, of which I have had far less than an ordinary dose, but to the psychedelic mood generated by a period of great change. I'm not mixed up, but I *am* undeniably affected by the disintegration of old patterns and the beginning of many new ones. Nearly everything I do now, every move made, every letter written, lies beyond the boundary of familiar experience. Giant emotional jolts follow one upon the other. I can give you a commonplace and yet dramatic example. On the way out to White Plains tonight by cab, I asked the driver to pull into a gas station so that I could buy cigarettes. The attendant refused, pleasantly enough, to change my dollar, claiming he hadn't the coins. I boiled over at once; it was so patently a lie. "You're open for business," I said. "What would you do about a driver who bought $3.40 worth of gas and gave you a $5 bill?" "I'd make it come out to the nearest dollar," he said blandly. No answer at all. I was more amazed—amused?—than angry. Why this inexplicable bit of churlishness from a total stranger? I solved the problem by getting the change from my driver, explaining the contretemps, who got far more outraged than I. But I got my smokes anyway. The incident, like much of the human traffic now passing me, seems curiously in harmony with the new vistas about to open on my horizons. I could go on. Everything that happens now happens six degrees askew. It's as if this individual decision to take a new tack had kicked the world I know six degrees off its axis. I am dramatizing, of course. Eight million New Yorkers have never heard of me, and their lives will scarcely be affected

) 183 (

by the change in mine. And, yet, there it is. I'm not who I was; I'm someone else; me, but not the same me. It's the same old world, and yet it's a brand new one. Another eccentric shift in the patterns. Still another: I called Pan Am and am committed to a ticket to Pago Pago on or about November 30, a Monday. Not everything is in an alien warp. HAG, for instance, is running true to form. He will shortly lose a hand who has performed at a consistently high degree of competence. One would think—or hope anyway—that that sub-surcingular chest of his (forgive the neologism) would house some shred of desire to see me occasionally in these last weeks. But he has a magazine to edit and the idea does not occur to him. Still another strange change. It's been so pleasant coming to work every day without having anything to do for *Time*—I'm officially on vacation—that I've decided to do the same until I leave. I've decided I need this feeling of liberty in a sweatshop more than I need the money. I've done little this week but call people, write people, rid my office of part of its accumulated rubbish and have lunch every day with someone new. I've lost weight, but I'm down to fighting trim. Camels, beer, martinis, late hours, Valium overdoses and all. Tomorrow I'm going to lunch with Phil. It's very late, thus I will get into town late, with a tobacco hangover (my only kind) and maybe let the lunch fall through. God knows I'll need no Valium tonight. The Matzes have asked me to dinner this coming Saturday, but I suspect it will be just the three of us, and may beg off. I take typhus shots Friday, which are supposed to give you the miseries, so I have an excuse ready to hand. I am likely to arrive in Pago Pago as a skin drum-taut with party beverages, but so be it. They have amoebic dysentery over there, and maybe a load of booze will protect my alimentary canal from hostile invaders. Once you get the bug you never lose it. I have the sixth beer of a six-pack to drink and then I'll go to bed. This weekend I'll start moving my few valuables. I haven't paid the rent, the phone bill is unopened and will stay so, and even on vacation I'm building an expense account and ordering cabs home. I figure the system will tolerate these petty larcenies. I have also dropped sledge-hammer hints that I want an Olympia portable as a going-away present. If not, it means shipping thirty or forty pounds of Royal Standard, crated, at $2 a pound air freight. I've just reread Bill Cabell's financial agreement, which we both signed, and I must say it makes of me a piranha lunch: stripped to the bone. That God-damned agreement condemns me to financial servitude for the rest of my life, unless you happen to be human. As I think you are. I want to do as right by you as I can, but all you have to do to blight my remaining years is insist on the letter of the law, in which event we'll both lose: you the money and me my long-postponed start at life.

From Jack Dowd, *Time*'s legal eagle, I now have a realistic—and horrifying—idea of what you can do to me, if you choose to, under the conditions of our financial agreement. Indeed, the only sustainable hope I can cherish is that you're not a vindictive woman and that, under the lash of necessity, you won't become one. Under that agreement I am legally bound to pay you a minimum of $12,000 a year no matter what my income, *plus* insurance premiums, *plus* medicalization for you and the children, *plus* half the college expenses of each. I must also give you 50 percent of whatever I earn, over and above those obligations: half my profit sharing; half my share of Uncle George's trust; half, even, of my pension. If I default on any of that you can (1) attach everything I own, which isn't much; (2) have me extradited from Samoa, which is American soil; (3) clap me into civil jail and keep me there. In short, literally interpreted, that contract would force me to continue earning money at my present rate of income until the last child leaves college—

say, 1978, when I will be sixty-two. Jack's suggestion was that I get you to agree to cancel that contract and draw a new one more in line with present realities. But I can't expect you to do that. In a sense, you've imprisoned me in *Time*. I tried to explain to Jack that you're not a vindictive woman. To which he replied that in all his years of practice and his experience in these matters, he's never run into any other kind. She may feel reasonable now, he said, but how about when the money runs out? When those checks stop coming with such soothing regularity? I'll talk over all this with you when we have our last dinner together. I think I'm going to ignore Jack's advice anyway, and take a chance on the woman I loved enough to marry, whom I still love and who, I think, still loves me too. I just can't believe that you would ever destroy what's left of my life out of malice, particularly if revenge will be all you'll get out of it. I can't make a dime from debtor's prison. Moreover, to get a job paying an equivalent salary at my age after I leave *Time* will be rough. I'm almost sure I couldn't.

Without going into detail, I can tell you that other parts of my life are turning a bit sour. I'm not going to fulfill the Putnam contract, which means that I'll owe them $2,000-plus, Steve will be furious, and I'll never get another advance on an unwritten book. Things are likely to get messy here. My agent is communicating my decision to Putnam's today; I'll hear back this afternoon. I'm also having lunch with Steve and the young sociologist he wants to be my replacement. I doubt that Putnam will go for that. What tangles we make of our lives. Pago Pago beckons even more imperiously now. Turn my back on everything. Maybe I *am* copping out. Notice I've paid toward your medical policy; I'll pay the other half from Samoa. Incidentally, I have no such protection. I'd better stay healthy. I have to stay healthy.

Now that departure is so near I don't like to think about it. I deliberately put it out of my mind. I can't believe that I'm really going. I've been with *Time* almost as long as I've been with you; another full set of patterns to break of nearly equal duration. I feel very much at loose ends, just as Gretch-en feels now that she's committed to going to Malta. But she's going with money; I'm going broke, and, broke, must somehow continue to persuade the governor that I'm solvent. The $12,500 will keep me at least a year, possibly two years, in some style. For tax purposes, I'm taking $1,500 of that with me and will get the rest after the turn of the year.

I've asked Barbara to let me spend a night with her before I go and she has agreed. I'm terrified, of course, as I was before marrying you, before that Christmas Eve. Like you, she's a Neenah girl, and you don't screw Neenah girls. You screw Menasha girls. I don't screw anybody. We both agree that in our next incarnation, if we're born nearer together in years, we'd marry. I marvel at these feelings in her. I'm not an old man yet, but I'm getting there. Curiously enough, my feelings toward her are not particularly sexual, though they are, of course. Maybe that's fear of non-performance, in part. It'll probably culminate in a dinner in her apartment, some good grass afterwards, some harmless love-making short of sex, and then I'll either leave or spend the night sleeping—and I mean sleeping—beside her. One reason I value her so much is vanity. Another is that she *is* an attractive woman. And another is that I have so few connections with women —or with men, for that matter—that have meaning to me that I overinvest in each one. She's the only woman I've ever loved whom I haven't mooned over—you know, the way young lovers do. Everything about it is up, nothing is down, unless you count the psychic impotence. I just tore open my smallpox scar. I've been shot full of everything you can think of, with two more injections to go. One is gamma globulin, for hepatitis; the other I forget. But there's no immunization against amoebic dysentery, though I do have a prescription for something, Lomotil, that is supposed to counter its effects. It's 11:30; I'm going to watch *To Kill a Mockingbird* for a while, until I'm sleepy, and then go to bed and be waked by your call in the morning. I can't get over the fact, Ann, that we still love each other. It's sad, but at the same time it isn't sad either. The marriage isn't over; it's just shelved. How nice, really, to survive divorce and separation with warm, affectionate feelings. I feel not the slightest hostility to you; I'm sure there's some there, but it's down deep, out of sight.

The waiting is beginning to pall. I slept late this morning after that gay dinner with you and Gretchen at Dedi's (which I won't be able to smuggle onto the expense account), feeling none the worse for wear after all those martinis. I didn't reach my desk until after twelve and have since done nothing more useful than wade through some sexy German magazines I swiped from Peter Bird Martin's office. I feel quite out of things. Across the corridor, in her doorless cubicle, sits Virginia Adams, doing my work, writing the "Behavior" section —and writing it very competently—while I sweat out the last few interminable weeks on *Time*. It's a wet and gloomy day. I could go to a movie but I hate to go alone. Being with you in town last night set me to thinking about what once was, rather than what is to be. It was one of our better nights together—no fighting, no bitter words, no quarreling. Not the least of my pleasures was to see you take three martinis and part of a fourth. So unlike you in the old days. We haven't lost the knack of communicating. Remember, before we were married, how you worried that we'd run out of things to say? I think we could make it work again, but I agree with you that we shouldn't try. Too much else is involved. Moreover, as you, more so than I, have discovered, there are advantages to being single. Not many on my side, but as long as the money holds out you can live much more actively and independently. I'd like to come for Thanksgiving but not if your mother is going to be there. If I don't go to you that day, I have nowhere to go. Which makes me realize that, for all your protestation, you've made more new connections this last year than I have. I have no women, really, and no dates, with the single exception of a middle-aged divorcee who now won't let me come over any more. I called her last night after you and Gretchen left and tried to talk her into giving me a night's lodging, but no dice. All I wanted was company. She knew that too. So the hell with her. I'm not going to call her again before I go.

What a down today. Most likely the guilties from all that gin last night, second thoughts about leaving—I'll have a hundred second thoughts before I go—the fact that things aren't going too smoothly in the "Books" department, the new sense of isolation at *Time*, fears that my Samoan grubstake is going to exhaust too soon, guilt feelings too over leaving you in a financial lurch, and on top of it all the inherent anxieties of a thoroughly conditioned rut-dweller who is about to climb out and take a shaky look around. My agent tells me that Putnam is a mite cross about my defection; I'm to meet with the editor this week if I can get hold of Steve in Princeton, which is no cinch. Other problems too, undiscussable. But I've always looked on the dark side of things. Smallest problem of all: I shouldn't have any Valium before my physical (Thursday), but I know I'll never get to sleep tonight, or tomorrow either, without help.

You should see this apartment. A cyclone victim. I'm to take my physical tomorrow but I've decided against it. I'm either healthy or I'm not; if not, there goes Pago Pago. I don't want to know. We're all dying of something, we're mortal; if some killing instrument or agency has taken up residence in my system, why borrow trouble by letting the doctors detect it? I feel fine at this moment, after enough drink to decompose stone. I feel great. If the apartment weren't so cluttered with dirty laundry and other slum effects I'd get down on this parquet floor right now and do fifty-three push-ups and 150 sit-ups or more. If lethal germs are breeding in my body, so be it. The truth is I'm scared of physical exams. They're a form of test which you can fail. So why take one? Besides, there are medical facilities on Samoa. One can't and shouldn't live life too sensibly. To cross any street one must dare traffic. Naturally, I feel more positive when I'm awash in gin and beer. Right now, I'm convinced that Pago Pago makes all the sense there is. To-morrow I'll change, no doubt. Guilt will rearrange my interior decor and refit it with remorse or something. I'm sitting here naked writing at 12:30 with a beer beside me, separated by tissue-paper walls from the sleeping strangers who occupy the apartments to either side. I don't know them, they don't know me. In the next few minutes I will don a minimum of clothing and drop down to the first floor to play the cigarette machine. I'll probably have another beer, smoke some more, and pay later, in the afterlife, for all my excesses. If there is an afterlife. Once again, my "good intentions"—quotes deliberate and very corny—have been defeated by circumstance. My objective was to leave the city early, eat here in the apartment, gulp some Valium, get up at a decent hour, take my physical tests and squander the rest of the day. Now, instead, I'll sleep late, miss my appointment in medical, drink nothing all day, go home (home!)

late and suffer insomnia for the first time in a long time. I'm
overloaded with ten-milligram Valium tablets, the strongest
kind, and need three blues—the equal of six yellows—to
assure sleep. Or is it four? No matter. I take them—none
tonight. Then I rise stuporously, reach the office, do all my
exercises, go back to my den, and knock myself out for another day. It is beginning to occur to me that we *don't* have
to catch the bus. I once prided myself on the fact that I've
never lost a reportorial note or missed a train. What a dismal
record. God: "State your entrance credentials." Me: "I've
never lost a note or missed a train." God: "Welcome. This
place is crawling with your sort. Come on in and be wretched
for eternity."

Well, I don't believe in an afterlife. I'm just superstitious
enough to copper the bet. If it's possible in Samoa or wherever I wind up, I'll donate my old body to a medical school.
I don't want to be planted, incinerated, mummified or
mourned. Life without death as the last chapter is as incon-
ceivable, and incomprehensible, as death without life as the
first. There are nine billion dead; I haven't manufactured
that figure. And there are something like 6.7 billion quick.
You've read the literature; one day soon this species will
outnumber the mustard seed. Then what? Who kills whom,
simply because there are too many of us? When the annihilat-
ing rain falls, it won't fall on Tutuila. It's not only not a tar-
get, it's too tiny to hit. Jerome Frank has written that mass
slaughter, now within human capability, is inevitable; the
passage of years only improves the odds. It won't happen in
our time, perhaps, but it will happen in some generation's
time. And even if human reason somehow cancels that prospect, the end of everything we know and feel on this small
and insignificant planet is already cosmically inscribed. The
sun is as mortal as we are. It will balloon into a giant, turn
all its satellites into Melba toast, cool, and leave this particu-

lar corner of one out of billions of galaxies as lifeless as those billions upon billions of other corners of the universe that haven't yet ripened into life. The process may go on forever—who knows?—but wherever it has begun and has produced sentience the end has begun too. Levi-Strauss wrote that one life can have a little meaning, one generation a little less, one world a lot less, but that on the cosmic scale there can be no meaning at all. If there are, as has been estimated, 100,000 planets similar to earth in this galaxy alone, consider how many of them are cinders today. Whatever they were, they are nothing now. No mark, no impression, no trace. Almost makes you believe in a deity, except that if there were one, I can think of 10,000 better ways to handle the show. What's He out to prove? And if He's out to prove nothing, what's the point? I say fuck all that metaphysical shit; live and feel, since we can do both and nothing else adds up. So many dead. For what? Why did they live? A Remington oil has haunted me ever since I first saw it: *The Scout.* It's the nineteenth-century American West, and Indians (the artist knew the tribe but I don't) have caught an Army NCO in his blues, have roped him to a horse and are taking him away to unimaginable tortures before they let him die. The sun smiles neutrally on this scene, of which he is the commanding figure. One sees only his back. His shoulders are squared. He stands straight and strong. He knows what he's in for, but Remington has not limned him with fear. The impact is powerful. You know this happened, more than once. And somewhere beneath the grass this man's bones lie, one of the world's nine billion dead. He has no name, no identity; he died for no reason. I identify with him completely. His world, like that of his captors, had already ended. It was the last day of his life and the last chapter of theirs. Read Erikson on the Indian tribes he studied after coming to this country. They weren't savages. We're the savages. We killed them off and felt guilty about it and then devastated the survivors with reparations. Why is cruelty in charge? The meek shall inherit the earth—what a crock of shit. The sad part is that it's probably true. Bullshit, but true. We spend our days contending—for what? Nature is neutral. She doesn't care who loses or wins; the terms have no meaning. It's all too much for me, and at the same time not enough. Why do we have to contend? Whom do we want to defeat? The Scout? Flayed alive, no doubt, eighty years ago, by strangers, other men. You can justify his death if you were an Indian then, but there's no way in the world to justify it really. He was just a traffic victim of his day. That was all the point there was to his death, and it simply doesn't do to say that he would have died anyway because all of us have to die. Any of this make any sense? God knows. And to say that is a cop-out; nobody knows.

No letter as yet from the governor. There's been bad news from Pago Pago. Someone put an AP dispatch dated November 13 on my desk: the two-story building housing the Samoan legislature has been destroyed by fire, at a loss of $410,000. I don't think the U.S. administration occupied that building, but I don't really know; if it did, it wiped out the governor's wife's museum and his records too. But now I'm in the process of establishing contacts even more influential than Governor Haydon: Harrison Loesch, Assistant U.S. Secretary of the Interior, and Orme Lewis Jr., Loesch's deputy—both directly responsible in Washington for administering Samoan affairs and both good friends of John Frank, whom you may have heard me speak of. I grew up with him in Appleton. He followed the law, first in Washington and then in Phoenix (for his health—asthma), where I saw him many times on Arizona assignments out of *Time*'s

Los Angeles bureau. I don't think you ever met him. John is going to send these men a letter of introduction and suggests that, if I can, I visit them in Washington before I leave. Which, if I can afford to, I'll do. It also developed that both John and his wife know the U.S. Consul General in Malta, so I got Gretchen a letter of introduction to him. She seemed delighted when I dropped by yesterday afternoon to give it to her; it'll be good for a cocktail invitation at least, as well as entrée into Malta's top diplomatic circle. Also looked in on you and to pick up my glasses, but no one around.

A dinner honoring my departure at Mary Cronin's apartment Saturday night, co-hosted by Dick Burgheim. I "took" some gal you don't know, someone half my age. For her own reasons, she was embarrassed to arrive with me (I picked her up), but I made her, and we went in together. There was a sign on the door welcoming me in Samoan; also, lava-lavas for everyone to wear. Present: eleven friends, nearly all from *Time*, including Bobby and Priscilla Baker, the Mohs and Mary's date, a man who works for American Standard (plumbing fixtures). The drinks were standard American, but I was made to drink my martinis from a coconut shell. I was pretty temperate, considering me. Taking my date home I was seized with the sudden desire to drive her to Franzl's, but as soon as I'd made the first wrong turn she demanded to know what I was up to, guessed the answer and asked to be taken home. "Would you get out of the car at the first stop light?" I asked. "Yes I would," she said. So I took her home. We were very self-conscious with each other all evening. I went to Franzl's anyway, where I was hailed as the prodigal son, had two beers and sat down with the help, Franzl, and Franzl's wife, Eda, for one of his potpourri breakfasts. Didn't leave till 4:30. The tap, of course, turned off at three; it's the law.

The days have begun to drag. I feel no excitement about

going, no impending sense of loss about putting so much behind me; emotional stasis, I guess, until the actual move begins and I'm on the first of three planes.

Tomorrow's my official farewell party, at which, as you'll see, I'm only one of many being feted with drink and music. The others are twenty- and twenty-five-year masthead veterans, and I suppose there will be speeches about us all and gifts for us all. You know what I want and am expecting. I thought of writing and memorizing a short and gem-like farewell speech but have just about decided against it. Many of my dearest friends here can't stay, and some of them can't even go. So I'll just work up a few polished lines, a yock or two, and let it go at that. They'll laugh at anything anyway. Or not listen. Now this self-imposed idleness is beginning to bore me. There are more good-bye parties coming up, but they sort of bore me too. I didn't enjoy myself Saturday night. Incidentally, a friend thinks we should give the old lady her 10 percent of Uncle George's estate; she's got us by the nuts anyway and the rest of the estate can more than recover her slice within two years. The money would be most welcome to mother. And, of course, to you.

Add statistical trivia: as of today, November 16, I have run in place 149,300 times (298,600 footfalls) and done 16,475 foot-free sit-ups so far this year.

I'm sorry you wouldn't come down to Ho Ho's with Loudon and me for a drink night before last, before our dinner with the children. I can't imagine why it upset you so, unless it was because you're hurt that the Wainwrights haven't had you over since we split. Neither the Wainwrights nor the Kunhardts are having a farewell party for me, and now it's too late. I leave week after next, and I may have to go to Washington next week to talk to those people at Interior. I want very much, for many reasons, to get work within the U.S. Samoan administration. I'm sorry, too, that you changed your mind about coming to my *Time* farewell party. You would have had fun: lots of goodies like stuffed mushrooms, meatballs, shrimp, canapés of all kinds, tiny quiches Lorraine and a cold buffet of turkey, ham and rare roast beef. I got what I wanted as a going-away present: an Olympia portable typewriter, De Luxe model, the next best thing to a standard. So I'll bring my standard over—maybe tonight—and you can keep it until and unless *Time* asks for it back, which is not likely. HAG's remarks about me fixed on my eccentricities, like padding about the corridors in socks and exercising in my office and laving myself afterwards with Old Spice out of consideration for visitors. He also recounted a few of the enterprises that have made me something of a legend: when, for instance, years ago, I was forced to write a gossip story for "Press" linking Nelson Rockefeller and Happy Murphy (this was before anyone could name her) and I called Jack Dowd, *Time's* attorney, and Jim Keogh, who was then still assistant managing editor under Otto Fuerbringer, represented myself as Mrs. Murphy's counsel and threatened to sue. The story *was* killed, but then I confessed to Otto, and it was reinstated. And also the time, at some big office bash during the Christmas season, that Bernie Auer, then *Time* publisher I think, approached me and said, "I'm Bernie Auer. I don't believe we've met." To which, so the story goes, I replied, "In that case, why did you send me a Christmas card?" But the story is apocryphal; I never said it. HAG also reported that I called him one afternoon and asked to borrow a towel. Yes, a towel. I don't remember that at all; if it happened, I must have been drunk. I knew I'd be expected to say a few words and came prepared. First

I pulled a huge collection of typewritten notes—old story notes—from a coat pocket, an old sight gag that drew a reliable laugh, and began, "Ladies and gentlemen, senior editors (prolonged laughter) and friends (more laughter) . . ." Whereupon I launched directly into that old political oration, I think from the 1912 presidential campaign, that I had to memorize for a speech course in college and still remember after all the years—my God, thirty-three years. You've heard it a hundred times: "Public duty in this country is not discharged, as is so often supposed, by voting. A man may vote regularly and still fail essentially of his political duty, as the Pharisee, who gave tithes of all that he possessed and fasted three times in a week, yet lacked the very heart of religion," etc. All delivered dead pan and letter-perfect. Believe it or not, I was a smash success; got a tremendous hand.

I have my letter from Governor Haydon, which lets me stay in Samoa a year, but is somewhat ambiguous about an extension: "Upon the expiration of your one-year's residence permit, should you still be engaged in these projects (writing a book, being *Time*'s South Pacific correspondent), *fair consideration* will be given to an extension of the time of your stay here." (Emphasis mine.) I also have my ticket. So it is for real.

I spent last night with Barbara. There was no chance of sex; but even if there had been, it would have been no dice with me. We lay together, performing (I hate that word) gentle intimacies; but nothing stirred in me, nothing at all. It was as if I were dead down there, a Jake Barnes phantom-castrated. It is just too much. I can't succeed. All the vibes are wrong there, and everywhere else all the vibes are right. I've thought of dropping all the depressant factors and forces mitigating against the assertion of manhood: the Valium (up to 40 milligrams a night now), the sauce, the cigarettes. But what good would it do? It would still leave me a chronic depressive, and nothing I can think of would chase that critical spectator and spoilsport from the room. I've even thought of asking Gil Gordon for a surefire aphrodisiac, because I am to see Barbara again before I go. But there is no such thing, and I'm too clever to be duped by powdered rhinoceros horn. Besides, even if there were such a magic potion, he wouldn't give it to me. It was a tender and very natural and easy night all the same. I slept fitfully, and had explicit dreams. In a fragment of one, I was lying between her legs, fully erected, and though her nightgown kept getting in the way, I did succeed in penetrating her. Then, abruptly, though I was going through the motions of intercourse, I was no longer within her; her back was to me, we had separated. Anyway, it wasn't she in the dream; it was Jocelyn Bannon. In another fragment, she was chiding me for saying "fuck you" too much; the meaning of that is nakedly obvious. It will come to nothing in this life, so I nourish myself with the Buddhist belief that I've spoken of before: that this is not my seventh and last incarnation and that in the next I will meet someone just like her, and we will marry and love in all the ways there are. It's part calf-love; something out of Greene again (read *The Confidential Agent*). She is so honest and natural in so many ways. The experience made her purr; she purred all day, and smiled that all-over impish smile that would melt an ogre. Now I think I understand a little why love must at last lose its voice and unite a man and a woman so they are truly one. Sex, and I don't mean balling, is all the things that can't be put into words because there aren't any words. Her attitude is healthy and normal; she doesn't invariably have orgasms, but it doesn't upset her when she doesn't.

Now the days are really numbered. And I am numb. I have my ticket and leave at three Tuesday afternoon, just around the corner of the week from now. Have I told you, by the way, that I have glaucoma? But nothing serious; mine is not the sort that requires surgery. The eye is filled with a fluid, called aqueous humor, which is constantly pumped in and out through what the ophthalmologist described as a sieve arrangement. The pressure is constant, and should fall within a certain range. But sometimes the sieve coarsens, letting less liquid through. So the pressure rises, past normal or acceptable limits. That's my form of glaucoma. If nothing were done about it, the pressure would gradually mount and my vision would gradually become impaired, as the rising pressure deprived my eyes of the necessary blood supply. And eventually, if I lived long enough, the sun would stop shining for me. But all I must do to arrest this process is take eye drops twice a day for the rest of my life. Then I keep all the vision I have now, which is plenty for a man my age: 20-20 for distance, reading glasses for the fine print. I'm already on the drops, which sting a bit, throw things slightly and momentarily out of focus and turn everything a little darker than usual (the pupils don't dilate). I go back to this guy once more Monday to see if my prescription is the right strength. Then I'll take a three-month supply and reorder through friends at *Time*; it may not be available in Samoa.

Thanksgiving at the Kunhardts. Dinner was bounteous. Present: all the kids of course, Sandra looking darling in a short dress; Michael looking just like a girl in his long hair; Shana Alexander and her mother, a Mrs. Ager, in what appeared to me to be a crocheted yarmulke; Phil's brother Ken, Mrs. Kunhardt Sr., Shana's Irish bard Harry, and Shana's daughter in braces and a bratty mood. Drank more after the K's at Franzl's, where I have become something of a celebrity because I'm going to Pago Pago. I'm totally accepted there now, I'm one of them. Called Fooey Strange to say good-bye and took forty milligrams of Valium (for shame!) and the 10:05 train next morning. This is my last day at *Time*, but it doesn't have that feel to it. Martha Duffy took me to lunch— at La Grillade, for auld lang syne. I paid my respects to the brass and am now waiting to take my favorite human connection to dinner and maybe spend the night. Nothing will happen. How much I wish something would. But I know old Grosser, that dirty flabby traitor of an appendage who gets his kicks denying me mine. There's just no dealing with him. I waked this morning with the kind of proud erection they make dirty jokes about, but that was just Grosser—he knew damned well there was no one around.

I've cleaned out my desk. There wasn't much. I've bought a pocket pencil sharpener and two Olympia typewriter ribbons, which are not likely to be available in Samoa. Everything on schedule. I haven't transferred title to the cars and don't know how but will do that before I go. I have my stake in traveler's checks and a little money in the bank account. My mood, as *the* hour approaches, is best described as resigned. I am merely the creature of momentum, which is bearing me in a certain direction to a certain small island riding our most majestic sea.

Dark, dark depression—which is black rage, of course. It's Saturday afternoon, a suicidally gloomy November day with snow in the sky, and I've come from a night with the woman I'm going to marry in the next life. It will have to be my credo; man must have faith in something, and that must be mine. I have never had anything but warm and good thoughts about Barbara Smith, just as I have never had a sad evening at Franzl's, and we both understand that marriage is quite out of the question in this world for so many reasons I won't begin to list them. Grosser's rebellion is one, maybe the main one. The two nights I spent in her bed were a mistake; they've made our equation lopsided, destroyed its equilibrium. Grosser's performance was very much under par. He just lay there as if anesthetized by Novocaine. My shyness makes her shy; then her shyness makes me shyer. Only once did he stir, and then quite actively. We were lying spoons, and I was touching what I thought was her right breast (she calls it bosom, and she doesn't like Grosser as a synonym for the penis; it is after all ludicrously inappropriate in my case) when abruptly it occurred to me that I had a handful of the left breast. So I went searching for the other one, which lay flattened against the mattress. And as my fingers probed with some persistence for a purchase, a very modest act of sexual aggression but aggression all the same, Grosser began to grow. I was caught totally unawares; as soon as I noticed his turgidity, which was ample enough for penetration, my head took charge and he collapsed at once. That was all. That and a good deal of intimate caressing. She does love me in a curious way, in a way I've never been loved by a woman before. I think she wants me, but she's afraid to want me, too, because wanting, in a loving situation, is a final commitment, and raises the price of involvement to a pitch where it can hurt like anything to lose. Like all the good feelings I had and still have for you, and were *not* transferred to Jocelyn Bannon, though I had and have good feelings for her too, I have another set of them for Barbara that competes with and detracts from nothing else. You would like her, I think. She called just minutes ago from New York. It was a compassionate call; she knew I'd be down after last night's unsuccess, and said all the right things to cheer me up. Maybe the only way I'll get back into the business is to begin all over in Pago Pago with a dusky Menasha girl. You were a Neenah girl and when I was growing up in Appleton I never dreamed of fucking a Neenah girl, or even putting a hand on her in all those soft warm places. They were *decent* girls, probably dying to get laid and doubtless getting laid; but not by me. The Menasha girls—they're a genre, the name is not confined to that little mid-Wisconsin town —got all my business. As you know, I was never the world's champion lover, but I sure as hell fell within the normal range, if only just, and collected a normal raunchy share of what we then called quiff. In the army, too, naturally. But in the years at *Time* I had more than a few satisfactory bed connections until things began to falter (why, I wonder?) and Grosser began hanging his head. He knows just what he's doing.

I feel lousy and without appetite; oversmoked; bloated with air; unhealthy. The prospect of a TV dinner—ham—makes me want to throw up. So I'm going to get some health foods—dates, honey comb, canned almonds, fruit yogurt— and a lot of beer at the A&P. It won't kill me. It's that or TV and four blue caliums and neither appeals to me. Tomorrow I must clean the apartment after a fashion, do some preliminary packing and get ready to move. Then the Last Supper with you and then off to the unknown.

Things didn't work out as planned. I did lay in all those goods, among them two iced G-bottles of Miller's from the deli and two un-iced six-packs from the A&P; polished off the first quart watching *Mission Impossible* and munching barbecue-flavored almonds, opened but never finished the second quart. Next thing I knew, *Mission Impossible* had yielded to *My Three Sons*; after that unscheduled nap in a chair I went to bed. About nine, I'd say, though I didn't look. Up at six—dawn still unbroken, and have since scoured the bathroom and its fixtures and will do the kitchen next. The eye drops have, as usual, cast a pall over the scene, which is just as well; nothing in this room is worth a second glance. I'll bring the six-packs over when I come for dinner Monday, or maybe today; it might be good strategy to stay the last night with you. I feel nothing, except an upset stomach; no doubt nerves. I'll bring the *Time* TV set over too. If they ask about it, tell them you know nothing. It will require a special wall plug, like a telephone jack.

On Wednesday, the real estate people who rented me the apartment will get this letter from me, which I intend to mail from Kennedy:

Please accept this as official notice that, as of Tuesday, December 1, 1970, I have vacated apartment 2-A at 499 N. Broadway, White Plains, N.Y. Your records will disclose that I have not paid the November rent. I would suggest that you consider my deposit, to an equal sum, as payment in full for November— which is just the way I'm going to consider it.

You will also notice, on inspecting the apartment, that I have left a good many things behind, including some kitchen utensils and cutlery, clothing, books, towels, and some rather ratty furniture. I would recommend that you consider this inventory as reimbursement for the cost of cleaning the apartment for its next tenant—which is just what I am going to do. I have cleaned both the kitchen and the bathroom. It should not be necessary to repaint the walls. From experience, I would predict that you should have the apartment reoccupied within two days of receipt of this notice, so nobody loses on the deal, you or I. Should you feel otherwise, it should not be difficult to trace me. But I can assure you that I will be one hell of a long way from White Plains—about 8,000 miles, in fact.

I've got an overweight problem now: the barracks bag of soft stuff, the suitcase, the typewriter and the attaché case must easily scale eighty pounds together.

I'm back at the apartment after delivering the Herman Miller dresser to you. Hide my shirts and my gloves. Watching some pro game and drinking the world's flattest beer, Schmidt's, brewed in Philly, which the A&P specialed for $1.09 a six-pack. I've done my exercises. My spirit is surprisingly tranquil—it's run the gamut these last few weeks, from manic to depressive and back again but in no rhythm. I can guess, though, why I'm momentarily calm: in a sense, I'm waiting for the train, it's down time, no-account time, my time, I have nothing more to do but finish packing, take my last two shots tomorrow, have the last family dinner with all of you and catch United to Los Angeles Tuesday afternoon. Detachment—that's the name for it. The TV station commercials announce "don't-miss" programs that will be transmitted beyond my field of vision. Stores will open soon on mornings when I won't be around; the people at *Time* will work late, in varying states of agitation, on issues that I'll never see; and if you love me at all, as I do you, you'll miss me as soon as I'm gone, as I am certain to miss you. You said this afternoon that I'd hate it in Pago Pago, but my guess is that it was less forecast than hope. God, this is foul beer. Now I believe all the uncomplimentary things they say about Philadelphia.

I simply can't imagine missing *Time*. Some of the people, yes; I learned to know them better in the year I lived alone, and to appreciate more than ever those I learned to know. I needed them, and need forms friendships. But the weekly round, the inevitable late nights, the soul torture of cover stories, the System, the new versions, HAG's pettish marginal notes, his unawareness of the peopleness of people—all that I'll miss about as much as a toothache. The same goes for New York. I endured twelve years of that intolerable city, which grew worse as I watched. I'm glad to be leaving it, and will come back only out of necessity. Virginia Adams bet me $5.00 I'd never go to Pago Pago, and paid off Friday. I took it, too. She's also bet me $5.00 that I'll come back to *Time*—as a staffer, that is—but she's going to lose again. I know I won't. It's said that HAG, too, thinks that I'll be back. But I know myself. Pride wouldn't prevent me; it's just that I don't reverse course, and I can be one stubborn son of a bitch when my mind's made up. Witness our marriage. It took me a year of unremitting effort to get you, but I got you and I knew I would. Witness the end of our marriage. I take no pride in having moved first (pure happenstance), but when I moved I moved, and there was no turning back. Witness Grosser's sit-down strike. I dream and talk about its ending, but in my heart of hearts I know he's going to be a hold-out to the grave. The woman hasn't been born who would dedicate herself to his reclamation, and nothing short of that, I'm afraid, would work. And witness Pago Pago. I really made up my mind last June, though even I didn't know it then. And now I'm going—really honest-to-God going. One stubborn son of a bitch. Which means that Pago Pago will work. I may not be happy—I'm not built to be happy, I guess—but one way or another I'll make a go of it. The beer is now tasting a bit better, which shows what persistence will do. And, for that matter, if I sincerely want to stop smoking, I know I can do that, too. I have a kind of sandpapery, rasping sound in the lungs.

I also cough mornings, from all those Camels the day before; and I'd hate to see a color photograph of the inside of my chest. But somehow I can't believe I'll die of lung cancer, though the twenty-four-cigarettes-a-day smoker, according to some recent medical research from England, stands one chance in ten of getting it. As any horse-bettor will tell you, those are pretty long odds. That smoker also stands a ten-to-one chance of *not* getting it. In Pago Pago I'll be jogging up and down the shoreline in lieu of the RCAF exercises, pedalling my bicycle miles each day, breathing far purer air and—most important of all—succumbing to a life tempo that simply has to be less stressful than the one here. I know we manufacture our own tensions, but circumstances play a vital tributary role—the difference, as one example, between one late vacation night in Nassau and one in room 2457 in the Time & Life building in midtown Manhattan, bent over the typewriter on a cover story.

Barbara called again today. To you it may sound like a queer alliance; she'd spent the night with her guy in her apartment—the night after I was there—and stole the chance to phone when he went out to lay in some breakfast provisions. Called to tell me she knew how much she was going to miss me, that she'd cried last night about it in his presence (assuring him meanwhile, quite accurately, that he and I are not in the same league), and that she'd had a barely disguised dream in which she clung to the tail of a red airplane that was to take me to Pago Pago, refusing to let me go. The symbolism of that is rich and obvious. What's the point in telling you all this? That it's nice to feel loved; for one thing, it frees the scared one to love back. You and I both had trouble in that department. I could have used a lot more demonstrativeness from you, and I know you could have used a lot more of the same from me. Somebody, or something, long ago, taught me to hold back, for fear of losing, of rejection, and I got very good at it with practice; so good that I can now spend a night naked in the same bed with a woman, in what you used to call a loving situation, and deprive us both of the ultimate expression of togetherness.

I wish I had company now. But if I want it I'll have to go out and get it—at Franzl's, where else? I half promised the last time I was there that I'd drop around Sunday, and it's still early enough so that I can grab some of Frankie Mondschein's good cooking (I tasted his turkey dressing Thursday and it was, I regret to say, better than Kathy's) and tank up on Michelob and still get a good night's sleep. There's nothing I really have to do tomorrow but see the eye doctor and finish packing; I can skip the shots.

I am impressed by the tidiness of my bathroom. It looks like an operating theater. I've decided I'll have to go to Franzl's, if only to move some things into the VW—the typewriter and the barracks bag—so that tomorrow it won't be so obvious that I'm pulling out. None of the people here, of course—the doormen, the super—would stop me, but they might report me. I've taken out-of-town trips from here, so to leave with a suitcase and a briefcase shouldn't strike anyone as suspicious. There are still things here that you could use—your mother's lamp, for instance—but it's an ugly thing and you don't need it. The Kunhardts' bookcase. The typewriter stand, which dates back to Omaha. The card table. Some ancient and threadbare summer and winter suits, not one of which would bring a buck on the Bowery. That hallway strip of Persian carpet. And the bed. My God, that bed. I've completely forgotten, Ann; where did we sleep in the first few weeks or months of our marriage, a lifetime ago? In your single bed in your apartment, before we moved to Chicago Street? I can't believe it, and can't remember either. But I do remember that scary dream of yours about the

H-bomb and the world coming to an end; you sobbed half the night in my arms. And whoever it was who picked me up every morning in her Packard and drove me to work in my leg cast. And the headline in the World-Herald after it happened: *Skiing Reporter Breaks Leg on Honeymoon.* And the story I wrote about it for the Sunday magazine section, drawings by you. Those were mostly good years. Then, in Los Angeles, they got better. And then, in New York, they got worse. Not bad; not ever really bad. Have I told you that I still consider our marriage, which ended, better than most marriages of the same duration? I'm sure it was.

It has begun. I still don't quite believe it, and I've got such a bad case of the nerves that my hand trembles as I write. I'm in the United waiting lounge at Kennedy. There are fewer than ninety minutes before takeoff time and naturally I'm scared. This is after all a dramatic step to be taking at my age, with enough money to see me through maybe three years. And then what? I can always give up and go back, tail between legs, but I know I won't. I can't. You were the only person in the world who could have kept me from going; you're the only one who could beckon me back and we both know, don't we, that there's not the slightest chance of that? You just don't want me. What is it about me that makes you so positive I'm beyond redemption? Well, there's little point in discussing it. I doubt that you yourself know. I've felt, all the years with you, that I was on permanent probation: that I could at any time have lost you as a man loses his job; that once I lost you I could never get you back. And it's all come to pass. The affair was nothing; a wife determined and wanting to keep her husband could have busted that up in a week. As it was, her husband did it anyway.

The lounge is nearly empty: a nun in rose-rimmed glasses; a thin, Latin-looking father feeding his bald baby a bottle; a young Marine flanked by his parents; a middle-aged Jewish couple, she showing too much porridge thigh, he reading the *Times*; a solitary Oriental male in Western dress with trousers much too wide at the cuff. And me. A few amblers, but the place has a deserted and frozen feeling. We're all part of the decor, the hands of the big Elgin clock have stopped forever at 2:04, the tiny planes in the brilliant winter sky beyond the windows are stage props; part of the set. Everything about the nun is black: not only her habit but her purse, her carry-on case and her watch strap. Only that one touch of color, of life: the rose rims of her spectacles. Nuns fascinate me. Childless mothers, unmarried brides. True cop-outs; betting their lives against unbeatable odds on a losing proposition.

It's 3:07—by my $10 Timex anyway—and I'm in seat 10B on United Flight 009 to Los Angeles. A delayed takeoff, just like the Penn Central four days out of five from North White Plains station. They're going to show a movie en route— Sophia Loren in *Sunflower*. I haven't made up my mind whether to see it. I have letters to write, among them this one, and many miles to go before I sleep. The film's two bucks, or so I'm told by the sheaf of literature bestowed on me by a stewardess. I hope the advertised meal (tenderloin steak, sliced egg and tomato salad, noodles, mixed vegetables and Mainliner cheesecake) doesn't come down the aisle too soon. I just ate a spinach omelette at the Savarin coffee shop in the terminal. We're still motionless and silent at 3:23; didn't I tell you this was a frieze? Here we'll sit, like those plaster life-size statues and, after 2,000 years, appear as a scene in a movie, the third of a series: *Return to the Planet of the Apes*. With Charlton Heston, John Godspeed and a nun (yes, she boarded the same plane). I asked the stewardess for stationery fifteen minutes ago and am still waiting for it. Now I'm beginning to worry. "Ladies and gentlemen," announced the pilot, "the no smoking light has been turned off. You may smoke if you wish." Ominous: a long wait at the least, possibly something worse. So I'll miss my Los Angeles connection to Honolulu, the Honolulu connection to Pago Pago and arrive dead of exhaustion or not at all. No, I'm wrong as usual. Takeoff imminent.

I'm not going to reset my watch until we make Pago Pago; it's my last contact with the old life. Presently it reads 8:45. A prideful note: because of the fifty-five-minute delay in departure, complimentary drinks were offered to the coach crowd. Guess which confirmed lush declined the invitation? I'm going to be bored silly before getting there. I'll pick up a paperback in L.A., where I must wait two hours for the Pan Am Honolulu flight. I think that an hour before plane time in Honolulu I'll take a couple of tranquilizers; if I don't, I'll be so pooped in Pago Pago that I'll waste most of my first day there flaked out in my $25 room at the Inter-Continental Pago Pago. I want to get into action at once: rent a post office box, send my address to *Time* and a few other places, call on Governor Haydon and set up a lunch date, and begin scouting housing possibilities and maybe call on an American named King who publishes a newspaper there. King should be a useful source. Maybe I'll get him for lunch Wednesday, if I have the energy. You can well imagine my state of mind: a high degree of free floating anxiety, bound to go higher the nearer I approach journey's end. *Am* I out of my gourd? A certifiable lunatic? This is high adventure, and I should be exhilarated, but I'm sure as hell not.

It'll be good to get to L.A. Even the airport scene, however changed, will generate echoes, the clearest of which will be of the night in 1955 when I met the plane—a prop-driven plane then—that reunited me with my family. Deny that our life had more than a fair share of good times and sweet memories, like that one. They flock to mind, but I'd rather not think about them. What's over is over. I think neither one of us has any right to complain or be bitter. We've been damned lucky, all considered: fine children, a comfortable if not splendid income, no serious problems or illnesses, no tragedies, a marriage that, on balance, belongs on the black side of the ledger. Got to stop here; the pilot has announced we're just twenty minutes out of Los Angeles and descending.

I'm in Pan Am's Clipper Room at Los Angeles International Airport. The "special service representative," a statuesque German blonde, Brigitte E. Zimmerman, is catering graciously to my every need, though I have scarcely strained her resources: one scotch and soda, very light, and a cup of black coffee. She also introduced me to another traveler, name forgotten, who makes a living catering specialty dishes to air lines—kosher and dietary foods and so on—on an international scale. I know no one here; none of them looks any more important than I do. The decor reminds me of a Holiday Inn. From the available reading matter, notably *Rendezvous*, a bi-monthly published "for Inter-Continental Hotels in the South Pacific," I have copied the name of the publisher, Gareth Powell, and of some Pago Pago residents whom I should meet: Ed Engledow, director of information, Government of American Samoa; Graham Jeffrey, general manager of the Inter-Continental Pago Pago Hotel, and Homer Davies, managing director, American Samoan Development Corp., which owns the hotel, presumably through Pan Am. It's nearly midnight, New York time; I'm about to take the eye drops that will preserve my sight. Brigitte has announced she's going to send me down at nine o'clock no matter what. The Honolulu plane is late, too, but no strain; the one that will carry me to Pago Pago will wait for us.

The 747 is no big experience but one hell of a big plane; a winged auditorium. It's 4:35 A.M. Wednesday now, New York time (I think); my eyes are sandy from watching a comedy, title forgotten, with Maureen O'Hara and Jackie Gleason; obvious and cornball but funny. Honolulu coming up, but only God and the pilot know when, and neither is telling. Another dinner. Chicken this time and I ate it for health's sake, down to the last cold snap bean. I have a three-seat section all to myself, on the port side of this airborne amphitheater; it's too big to feel like an aircraft. I'm dirty and need a shave and have oversmoked as usual, but then I've been up nearly twenty-one hours straight. This flight goes on to Sydney; I'll be curious to see who peels off with me for Pago Pago. I'm rambling. My mind is tired too, so I'll sign off.

Now I'm on the last leg: in Flight 807, which is jammed with a variety of ethnic types, only some of which I recognize: Maoris, Scots, Samoans, New Zealanders. I've had my first quick look at the sky of the Southern Hemisphere; it's spottily clear in Honolulu and a muggy seventy degrees at what is 1 A.M. here and 7 A.M., or thereabouts, back where you are. Economy class here is a pilchard can: six seats abreast, with so narrow an aisle it's impossible for two persons even to sidle past one another. My ass is beginning to drag, but I've vetoed Valium; I want to be aware of what's going on. I suspect that most of the passengers are bound for Auckland, the next and last stop after Pago Pago. I'm getting confused about the time; my ticket says we're scheduled to take off from Honolulu at two, but we were an hour late coming in and yet, by my computation, we're leaving an hour early. In fifty-five minutes I'll have been up an entire day.

Takeoff! Don't know why I'm so bushed; have done nothing for the last nineteen hours but sit, eat, and write to you. They served us guava juice crossing the Pacific. It was as delicious as it looked: a coral drifting towards pink. I'd love some more right now; my mouth tastes like brass cartridges. Now how in the hell did my fingernails get dirty in three airplanes? Maybe I will sleep despite myself; if I could lie down I would.

There's so much to tell, after just six hours in Pago Pago, that I scarcely know where to begin. Already I have: got a post office box, displacing 200 others on the waiting list; found a place to stay, a kind of bachelors' dorm of government workers, for $45 a month, with a common kitchen and two bathrooms; compelled Pan Am to shell out $25 for emergency gear, since my luggage didn't arrive with me; toured a large part of the island; established some excellent contacts, many Samoan; written a dozen cards with my new address: P.O. Box 23, Pago Pago, American Samoa 96920. It does rain here intermittently all day, with olio bursts of blazing sun. The island is a riot of color, mostly green. The weather is uncomfortably humid, but I've been up for the last thirty-nine hours straight so fatigue is a factor. The water is heavily chlorinated—tastes like our pool—so I'm not likely to get dysentery. American cigarettes, alas, are only 35 cents a pack; less than that in some shops. A three-minute call to New York City costs $12. There *are* sand beaches, but they're narrow and I suspect the sand was trucked in. The governor and his wife leave town tomorrow on a ten-day vacation cruise. Many of the Samoan women are willing and beautiful, but as they age they turn beefy. The handsomest of the men look like Jon Hall but only in profile; splay noses are a common feature. These first impressions are kaleidoscopic and probably not accurate; there's so much to absorb and I'm dazed with fatigue. We arrived at 12:05 P.M. Wednesday New York time, which was 6:05 A.M. Samoan time but don't quote me on that. I'm thoroughly confused. Tutuila needs lots of face lifting, but it has a kind of ingenuous, who-cares charm. Everyone in Samoa drinks quantities of New Zealand beer, which is reported to be 20 percent alcohol by volume. I can't write much more; I'm going to grab five hours of sleep to reorganize my biological time clock—or try anyway. The governor, who was out this morning, may return my call this afternoon and may grant me a short audience tomorrow (Thursday) morning. Now I'm going to draw the blinds, shutting out Pago Pago Harbor, and go to bed—at 12:55 P.M.

Ed Engledow, who produces a daily four-page *News Bulletin for the People of American Samoa, Pago Pago,* took note of my arrival in the December 4 issue:

Time Magazine Writer Will Base Here
John Koffend, writer for *Time* magazine, has arrived here and will use Pago Pago as his base to cover the

South Pacific for the magazine. Koffend has been with the magazine fifteen years and has spent the last twelve years in New York.

I've been here almost two months now. It's been a long day, I'm tired and awash with beer and my thoughts are as unsteady as my hand. Samoa, I've half decided, is not a solution or an escape route from whatever I was fleeing, but it is at the least a quantum change and has churned the components of my life so thoroughly that they will never ever again be the same. You and the old ways have lost definition. I remember everything, the past lives still, but in much the way that you never really forget all of any book you've read, or the melody of an old song. I keep wondering: have I changed or have I only shifted? These are all head thoughts, and I'm sick unto death of my head. I want a woman and have not found one. I want a minimum of structure to the days, a few commitments stacked somewhere in the future, and peace. As in New York, I stubbornly resist and resent facing the mirror. There he is, that middle-aged man, showing his years plainly, pretending that he has somehow evaded their toll. I'm going to die, sooner than you, sooner than nearly everyone younger than I; and still I persist in the self-deception that I don't look fifty-three and am not fifty-three and can slide under that accumulation of years to retrieve the lost time, beat the clock. I dream. With little effort, I can imagine that others are blind too. Here, there's a choice for me of girls underripe or overripe. I'll take the former, and can't get them, and don't want the others. There are no women on this little island for me. There is just beer. Beer and cigarettes and more beer and cigarettes. And the silly business of chasing stories and doing things that seem exciting and different only because, or mostly because, I'm in the

South Pacific and not Westchester County. I feel sure that the Samoan displaced to Westchester would reel, as I reel here, from the new tilt to everything he's used to, and would fire a stream of manic letters to his friends back home, just as I have done. Which really leaves me nowhere. I've made the move, but what have I left behind and what have I gained? I had a busy day, as I said. I won't reprise it, but in terms of productivity as measured by the standards I supposedly left behind, I have industriously done all the useless things that in New York—and here too, I guess—are supposed to make sense. They don't make much sense. I'm not down, but the Big Move hasn't exactly honed any points; not yet anyway. I don't know any more than I did. I'm no wiser. I'm still living to die, though I don't mind so much any more the prospect of living. The years at *Time* have simply fled my memory, as if they never were. The same for our marriage; what happened to those nineteen years? I can't sincerely say I'd mind if I never saw you again. I find it hard at times to realize that I'm the father of my children, even though I keep their images vividly. I've lost, or mislaid, the capacity to invoke the past; I could never live on memories. I want to see the children and get them over this summer, or some time, and yet these feelings are not entirely real; they have a dream quality to them. They are things that *could* happen but haven't happened so they don't count. What does count? I can't supply an answer that makes sense. The last beer, the last moment; the next beer, the next moment. How and what I feel now, which is tired and hazy and full of Kiwi beer, have more meaning than the full fifty-three-year reach of the past. I haven't changed, I've just changed locale. And yet everything *has* changed, though I go on in much the same ways beneath the Southern Cross, a world away from the world I knew and was trained for: compulsively sharpening pencils, keeping notes, sniffing out stories, dropping Valium, doing push-ups, drinking beer. It's as good a note as any, I guess, to end on. What *has* changed, Ann, is that the endless year without you, and the living alone, and all those instant breakfasts and TV dinners —all that and Samoa have conspired to annihilate the past. What began, last June—just the other month, just yesterday —as a letter to you and a *cri de coeur* has become a letter to me. Dialogue into monologue. There was never enough feedback; you dropped out. I think I've ceased to care. I'll never be sure, but I think so. I can visualize you readily, but I keep forgetting how it was to be married to you, how life together was. I have difficulty now feeling that you were my wife. My wife. How it was to be inside you, the weight and the taste and the scent of your body. If we were to come together again it would be as strangers, and we're both too old for that. Aren't we? Aren't we? I know you won't misconstrue when I say that I've lost my need for you. I'm *all* need, more so than ever, but our marriage didn't fulfill it, for which I blame no one and nothing, and now it's past; dead. We're designed to need; we're designed too to have our needs met. And since that didn't happen with us, I can accept calmly now that the end was probably foreordained. Our time together was more good than bad, as I've said so often, but the end was written down before our time began. I miss you still, and I would have you still, and perhaps I love you still, but it's all over, done, finished, and I've got a few good years left. Nothing ever comes out even; we're fools if we expect things to; there are rough edges that can never be burnished smooth. But that's head talk too; I've run out of things to say.

I'm pumping the dregs of a bottle of Falstaff into me— typical, right?—it's well past the witching hour of any old morning, and at eight that God-damned island siren is going to blast me out of bed feeling and looking just the way I deserve. I'd like to say that I regret our separation, but it wouldn't be true. I'd like to say that I don't resent our separation and the part you played in it, but that wouldn't be true either. I'm through. I tried and I failed—*it* failed. I can't and won't try again. You were my one and only wife, all that I ever wanted, and less than enough. I'm trying here not to care, not to think about you at all, and with some success. So I'll live without you till I die, and it just happens to suit me to sign out on what I consider an up note. To borrow inspiration from one of those old barroom songs: I had nineteen beers with the wrong woman. Now I'm going to have nineteen beers by myself.